DEADLY DUST

DEADLY DUST

SILICOSIS AND THE POLITICS OF
OCCUPATIONAL DISEASE
IN TWENTIETH-CENTURY AMERICA

David Rosner and Gerald Markowitz

PRINCETON UNIVERSITY PRESS

PRINCETON, NEW JERSEY

LIBRARY OF CONGRESS CATALOGING-IN-PUBLICATION DATA

ROSNER, DAVID, 1947–

DEADLY DUST : SILICOSIS AND THE POLITICS OF OCCUPATIONAL DISEASE IN TWENTIETH-

CENTURY AMERICA / DAVID ROSNER AND GERALD MARKOWITZ.

P.   CM.

INCLUDES INDEX.

ISBN 0-691-04758-8

1. SILICOSIS—UNITED STATES. 2. OCCUPATIONAL DISEASES—SOCIAL

ASPECTS—UNITED STATES. 3. OCCUPATIONAL DISEASES—POLITICAL

ASPECTS—UNITED STATES. I. MARKOWITZ, GERALD E. II. TITLE.

[DNLM: 1. HISTORY OF MEDICINE, 20TH CENT.—UNITED STATES.

2. OCCUPATIONAL DISEASES—HISTORY—UNITED STATES.

3. POLITICS—UNITED STATES. 4. SILICOSIS—HISTORY—UNITED STATES.

5. SOCIAL ENVIRONMENT—UNITED STATES. WF 11 AA1 R8d]

RC774.R67   1991   616.2'44—dc20   90-9218   CIP

DNLM/DLC

FOR LIBRARY OF CONGRESS

THIS BOOK HAS BEEN COMPOSED IN LINOTRON TIMES ROMAN

PRINCETON UNIVERSITY PRESS BOOKS ARE PRINTED
ON ACID-FREE PAPER, AND MEET THE GUIDELINES FOR
PERMANENCE AND DURABILITY OF THE COMMITTEE ON
PRODUCTION GUIDELINES FOR BOOK LONGEVITY
OF THE COUNCIL ON LIBRARY RESOURCES

PRINTED IN THE UNITED STATES OF AMERICA BY
PRINCETON UNIVERSITY PRESS, PRINCETON, NEW JERSEY

1   3   5   7   9   10   8   6   4   2

To Kathy and Andrea

CONTENTS

ILLUSTRATIONS

Following page 169

PREFACE

IN 1982 we had each completed major projects that led us to the subject of occupational safety and health. One of us had spent his time researching urban health care history, while the other had focused on the cultural and political history of working-class America during the New Deal. As we exchanged ideas and talked, the idea of joining our interests and focusing on the history of workers' health became increasingly intriguing. At that time, there was intense interest in the impact of the Occupational Safety and Health Act of 1970. Especially as the Reagan administration sought to dismantle federal regulation of the workplace and undermine gains that labor had made over the past generation, the topic of labor and health seemed timely and important. As we surveyed the literature and discussed the topic with those involved in labor politics, there was almost universal agreement that there was little to study in the history of occupational safety and health prior to the OSH Act. Except for the history of workers' compensation and momentous tragedies such as the Triangle Shirtwaist Fire, historians virtually ignored the role of health and safety in workers' lives.

It did not take long to uncover a very rich and extremely complex history of safety and health, a history that transcended any simple or obvious definition. In fact, as we began to plan out our research agenda, it became clear to us that health and safety was central to the lives of workers and to their organizing efforts throughout the twentieth century. With the help of small grants from the Professional Staff Congress–City University of New York, we began looking at particular crises between labor and management over workplace control in the early years of this century. In 1982–1983, David received a National Endowment for the Humanities Fellowship, which he spent at the Hastings Center, and the following year Jerry took a sabbatical. In 1985, Sidney Lee, then President of The Milbank Fund, took interest in our work. In the coming years, the Milbank Fund provided us with two grants that gave us the flexibility necessary to pursue our research. This initial support was critical. In 1986 we were awarded an Interpretive Research Grant from the National Endowment for the Humanities, and David was given a Guggenheim Fellowship. This good fortune allowed the two of us to take the academic year off and begin the intensive research for this book. The conjuncture of the awards also allowed us to hire a crackerjack researcher, Mary Rivers, who brought to her job both extraordinary skill and enthusiasm.

We were also extremely fortunate to develop an ongoing friendship with Lorin Kerr, the former director of the United Mine Workers program in safety and health. It was, in fact, some early comments he made regarding the importance of the silicosis issue to the developing debate over black lung that brought our attention to a mass of material we had haphazardly collected in our various journeys through the National Archives and other repositories. It soon struck us that silicosis, a disease that has caused intense debate over the course of the twentieth century, captured the complexity of the issues of occupational safety and health in general.

As we wrote drafts of our early research we had a series of discussions with two people who have had an important impact on our thinking. Dave Kotelchuck, the director of the Occupational Safety and Health Program at Hunter College and Tony Bale, a sociologist currently an NIMH Fellow at Yale, provided us with detailed and extremely comprehensive critiques of our work. They were particularly attentive to the continuing and reemerging theme of the foundry. In fact, they suggested that we visit the International Molders Union in Cincinnati to more thoroughly research the impact of silicosis on workers in this important trade. It was there that we met Jim Wolfe, John Morawetz, and Michael Donahue of the International Molders and Allied Trades Union, who were gracious, helpful and informed guides through the union's archives. Equally important, they organized for us a visit to a local foundry, where we were able to see firsthand the foundry process and its inherent dangers. We would like to thank Kenneth H. Snyder, executive vice president of the H. P. Deuscher Company in Hamilton, Ohio, who was kind enough to accompany us on our visit on March 30, 1988.

Around that time, David Willis, then editor of the *Milbank Quarterly*, and Dan Fox, now the president of the Milbank Foundation, invited us to participate in a Milbank Roundtable. This experience expanded our scope to include the debates about disability in the current book. Their comments on a paper that ultimately appeared in the *Quarterly* were extremely helpful in framing our argument.

In the course of writing this book, we have accumulated many debts to scholars, librarians, and archivists who were interested enough to provide their expertise and skills. Joel Tarr of Carnegie-Mellon University in Pittsburgh kept in touch with us over the years and periodically forwarded to us material he came across through his own research on environmental health. He was particularly helpful in identifying documents at the archives of the Mellon Institute at Carnegie-Mellon University. Daniel Heifetz and Richard Greenwald aided us in developing bibliographies and tracking down references to tuberculosis and miners' phthisis.

The librarians at Cornell University's Industrial and Labor Relations Archives, the Metropolitan Life Insurance Company Library, the National Library of Medicine, and Yale University's Sterling Library gave generously of their time. Cassandra Volpe at the University of Colorado's Western Historical Collections, Bill Creach, Jerry Hess, Aloha South, and David Pfeiffer of the National Archives in Washington, D.C., and Suitland, Maryland, Erica Godfried of the Tamiment Collection at New York University, Judson McLaury at the Department of Labor, Michael Rhode at the Armed Forces Institute of Pathology Otis Historical Archives, and Ray Kondratis at the Smithsonian Institution all were extremely helpful.

Betsy Blackmar, Roy Rosenzweig, and Blanche Cook deserve a special note of thanks for their detailed comments and close reading of one of the final drafts of the manuscript. All scholars depend upon helpful criticism but their detailed commentaries went well beyond the bounds of academic responsibility. Their extraordinary efforts were an uncommon act of friendship. Our colleagues at Baruch College and John Jay College were also supportive of our efforts. Tom Frazier and the faculty of Baruch's History Department have provided a warm and friendly environment, and Norman Fainstein, the dean of the School of Liberal Arts, provided release time necessary for the book's completion. John Cammett, the faculty of John Jay's History Department, Carol Groneman, Billie Kotlowitz, Dennis Sherman, and the faculty of Thematic Studies have provided a supportive and intellectually invigorating atmosphere. Kathy Conway gave the manuscript an expert reading, and Andrea Vasquez gave the illustrations an expert's touch.

In the final months before this manuscript went to press we sent it to one of the leading experts on occupational lung disease, Irving Selikoff. He was both gracious and supportive and we want to acknowledge his close attention and detailed comments. Dorothy Nelkin, Josh Brown, Barbara Rosenkrantz, Evelyn Ackerman, David Rothman, and the participants in the History of Health and Society Seminar in New York all provided helpful suggestions. Gail Ullman, our editor at Princeton, has been an enthusiastic supporter of this project and has expertly guided us through the various stages of production.

Finally, we want to express our love for our families who, for better or worse, now know more about silicosis than they wish to. Zachary and Molly Rosner, Billy, Toby, and Elena Markowitz, and Isa and Anton Vasquez have forced us to abandon our ever-narrowing focus and to remember that smiles and hugs are great antidotes to long days in dusty archives.

DEADLY DUST

INTRODUCTION

O N JUNE 21, 1933, George Silinski was admitted to the Ray Brook State Sanitarium in upstate New York. He had developed a chest cold six months before that he had been unable to shake. A low-grade fever, hoarseness, a severe cough, and nearly constant pain in his chest had led him to fear he had contracted tuberculosis. For the next six months, Silinski's symptoms worsened. In December his coughing became so severe that during one fit he fractured a rib. He died the next month at the age of forty-eight.

Silinski, a Polish immigrant who spoke very little English, had been a farmer in the Buffalo area for fourteen years before his admission to Ray Brook. At the time of his admission, newspapers, magazines, and professional journals were filled with stories about the threat of a new scourge—silicosis—that was crippling workers in a wide variety of industries. Silicosis is a lung disease caused when workers inhale fine particles of silica dust—a mineral that is the primary component of sand, quartz, and granite. Doctors at the sanitarium were suspicious that Silinski might have been exposed to silica sometime in his past. Their suspicion was correct. After questioning Silinski, they discovered that between 1901 and 1918 he had worked in a Buffalo area foundry as a sandblaster. He had quit because so many of his fellow-workers became sick and died on the job, where "the dust at times was so thick that he could not see." Leroy U. Gardner, a noted pulmonary specialist, performed the autopsy on Silinski, confirming the diagnosis of silicosis: The ash of his lung tissue was 16.5 percent silica.[1] Other autopsies uncovered even larger amounts of silica in workers' lungs—sometimes as much as a third of the weight consisted of silica dust.[2]

Today the general public is increasingly aware of the suffering experienced by coal miners, asbestos workers and textile workers stricken by black lung, white lung, and brown lung because of the popular movements and medical studies that have developed around each. However, silicosis, another occupational lung disease, remains virtually unknown. The small cadre of specialists in occupational medicine and industrial hygiene who are aware of the condition differ dramatically in their assessment of the threat that it poses today. Some argue that silicosis as a workplace epidemic is over and done with, while others see this disease as still potentially disastrous to a large number of Amer-

---

[1] The name of the patient has been changed in accord with the requirements for anonymity. See P-34-93, A. J. Vorwald Collection, Saranac Lab. 1931–54, Box 122, in Otis Historical Archives, Armed Forces Medical Museum, Institute of Pathology.

[2] Reprint of M. Kummel, "Medicolegal Aspects of Silicosis," *Medical Record*, May 16, 1934, 3. Armed Forces Medical Museum, Otis Historical Archives, Vorwald Collection, Box 62.

ican workers. A recent National Institute of Occupational Safety and Health (NIOSH) report estimates that silica dust produced in over 238,000 industrial settings exposes 3.2 million Americans to the threat of difficulties in breathing and lung cancer.

If today there is virtually no public controversy about the hazards of silica dust, this has not always been true. In fact, for most of this century, the dissension about the threat of silicosis has been part of an extended public discourse among physicians, public health officials, government administrators, labor leaders, business executives, and insurance representatives. During one decade, the Depression years of the 1930s, silicosis became an issue of national import. This book examines how we, as a culture, proceed to define disease and how disease itself is understood at different moments in American history. It is our contention that popular and professional awareness of disease is not necessarily due to medical advances or epidemiological changes. Rather, it is shaped by social, political, and economic forces as well as technical and scientific innovation. Further, we maintain that it is impossible to understand the history of disease without understanding its social context, including the social constraints that allow for its emergence or disappearance as a problem. As Irving Selikoff has pointed out, "Silicosis is a social disease with medical aspects."[3]

Silica is a ubiquitous mineral in our environment, the chief component of sand. The earth's crust is approximately 90% silica. Every time we go to the beach or climb through the mountains, we tread on silica in combination with other minerals. The material is so common that it is difficult for us to see it as a threat to our health and well-being, but in crystalline form, as quartz crystals, it most assuredly is. Although silica dust has been perceived as a health risk for workers in a few trades since ancient times, it was only in the twentieth century that this material was defined as a widespread hazard. The emergence of silicosis as a major threat to the American work force can be traced to the technological innovations that accompanied the country's rise to world power at the turn of the century. The enormous movements of people from the open air of the nation's farms and into the confined spaces of factories, mines, and mills was the precondition for popular sensitivity to the relationship between work and disease. The introduction of all the power equipment that drove those mines, mills, and factories created vast quantities of dust that greatly altered the health experience of the millions of industrial workers.

During the Depression, with millions of workers unemployed, this medical problem was transformed into a national social crisis. Throughout the 1930s, books and films, popular articles in magazines, scores of reports in medical journals, and news articles in such weeklies as *Business Week* and *Newsweek* proclaimed that the health of millions of Americans was threatened by this

---

[3] Irving Selikoff to authors, May 24, 1990.

ever-present substance. Even Hollywood produced a major motion picture on the subject in 1938. Adapted from the best-selling English novel *The Citadel*, by A. J. Cronin, and starring Robert Donat, Rosalind Russell, Ralph Richardson, and Rex Harrison, the movie brought home to millions of Americans the story of a young doctor's crusading efforts to eliminate health problems, including silicosis, among his patients in a mining community and the personal and professional crisis that the disease's identification precipitated. Congressional investigations and federal conferences addressed the problem.

Silicosis assumed such importance because professionals and the public alike recognized that it represented a new kind of disease, unlike those, such as lead or phosphorous poisoning, that had posed major threats in earlier times. Here was a disease that was chronic and irreversible in nature, that developed years or even decades after first exposure, whose symptoms were often ambiguous, that was rooted in work and factory production, and that had enormous social and economic implications for industries at the heart of American industrial might.

The story of silicosis is more than the story of a particular crisis in American medicine and public health. Rather, it is the story of the discovery of chronic industrial disease and its relationship to industrial society. At different moments, the crises around workers and their health have transcended narrow professional bounds and become part of a broader discussion of the relationship of illness to dependence and social welfare. In the early part of this century, the extraordinary number of industrial accidents were in part responsible for reformers' interest in compulsory health and social insurance and for the enactment of workers' compensation laws in various states. During the economic crisis of the 1930s, silicosis would also lead workers to use the issue of industrial illness as a means of achieving social welfare objectives. During this time, the social conditions of the Depression would force a blurring of the line between health and welfare, disease and dependence.

Ironically, despite the controversy and conflict over the nature of the silicosis hazard, by the 1950s, silicosis was virtually forgotten. The same symptoms that had forced physicians in the 1930s to look for an occupational history of work in the dusty trades now led to diagnoses of asthma, emphysema, or other nonoccupational lung conditions. The popular and professional press no longer published the large number of articles that had made silicosis a national issue. Silicosis was no longer integrated into plots of books and movies, and workers no longer saw it as a major threat to their health. Doctors, when forced to confront an undeniable case of silicosis, now saw the patient as a mere curiosity, someone who was a reminder of an earlier era.

The debate over the scope, importance, and threat of silicosis, begun at the turn of the century, is reemerging today as a new generation of medical and public health workers question the role of silica in the creation of cancer and heart disease. As we will show in this book, the changing nature of the silicosis debate tells us as much about our social environment as about medicine or scientific method.

The second half of the twentieth century has been marked by a growing awareness of the centrality of chronic disease to the health of Americans. This period has also been marked by the growing perception that many chronic conditions, such as various types of cancers and heart disease, are shaped by environmental factors, which are in turn influenced by societal decisions about the way we live. Air pollution, chemical waste, food additives, smoking, and drug and alcohol abuse have all been linked to chronic disease. It was around silicosis that many of our most basic ideas regarding the relationship between the human environment and chronic disease were formulated. Thus silicosis was to twentieth-century chronic and environmental disease what cholera was to nineteenth-century infectious illness. Neither cholera nor silicosis was the leading cause of death in its era. Yet both reflected the social and scientific assumptions of their time and, in turn, both framed the professional and public understanding of disease. The historical specificity of time, place, and circumstance makes each disease emblematic of its century.

Throughout the late nineteenth and twentieth centuries, the history of silicosis has been intimately intertwined with that of tuberculosis. Today, most historians see tuberculosis almost solely as a contagious disease born of debilitating urban and industrial life. Almost without exception, they have mapped onto the history of this condition modern perceptions about its relationship to the bacillus discovered by Robert Koch in the 1880s, which fundamentally altered contemporary and modern notions of disease. Historians of medicine have assumed that the history of consumption is synonymous with the history of the germ and its transmission among populations. The most recent literature accepts without question the idea that the industrial revolution, for example, promoted tuberculosis mainly by forcing large populations to work and live together in close, unsanitary, and physically debilitating circumstances, where the tuberculosis bacillus could propagate and spread among a weakened, malnourished work force. While this model may account for the vast majority of tuberculosis cases in the broader society, it delayed the recognition of silicosis as a distinct condition in the United States, and it clouded the role of silica and metallic dust in the creation of tuberculosis among the industrial population.

The century-long controversy over silica dust and its threat to workers' health has involved most of the major forces that have shaped American life. The history of silicosis reveals a federal government that at various moments has been forced to play an important role in the regulation of a disease that was neither infectious nor a threat to the general public. Following the crisis over silicosis, the federal government began to accept a role in the identification and control of chronic disease in general and specific diseases linked to heavy industry.

The federal government in the nineteenth century limited its involvement with disease to protecting the ports and commercial centers from the threat of infectious disease. But federal involvement in the silicosis issue illustrates how critical industry was to the nation's survival. Silicosis was an industrial disease whose roots were in the changing production methods—automation, assembly lines, and modern notions of efficiency—that had produced the affluence that twentieth-century Americans had come to believe was their birthright. Labor involvement in the silicosis issues reflects its changing role in American culture. During the Progressive Era, labor had formed a united front with social reformers, settlement workers, consumer groups, and state officials to address the growing scandal over the rising tide of industrial accidents. In the 1920s, organized labor was in retreat and largely abandoned agitation over conditions on the shop floor. By the 1930s, however, the labor movement had reemerged as an important force in American life, and some of the new industrial unions added safety and health issues to more traditional demands for shorter hours and better wages. These unions saw their interests more broadly, venturing into aspects of American life that had heretofore been the preserve of professionals.

Even the language used in the public debates among these different groups tell us much about American culture and society in the twentieth century. For much of the century, in fact until after World War II, the arguments over the nature of disease, its origins, and its effect on human beings were written and spoken about in terms understandable by and accessible to a wider public. The language was often the language of class, rather than the language of the technician or specialist. To speak of disease was to speak of human suffering, and of exploitation. But after World War II, a new rhetoric was introduced and dominated the discourse. This language was remarkable in the dramatic difference in tone, argument, and terminology and for its inaccessibility to laypeople, its lack of a clear class base, its abstraction from the human suffering it generally described, and its impersonality. There was a message in this new language, and the message was that few other than technical elites had a right or ability to discuss disease. This reliance on expertise and impersonal analysis reflects the growing prestige of the scientific and medical communities in postwar American life.

The tragedy of silicosis was also rooted in fundamental changes in popular and professional perceptions of the health experience of Americans. While cardiovascular disease and cancers have been major causes of death throughout the twentieth century, the emergence of silicosis corresponded to a growing awareness of chronic disease. For much of the first half of the century, the infectious diseases, such as tuberculosis, diphtheria, and influenza, dominated public awareness of the threats faced by those in the prime of life. Silicosis brought to national consciousness a new form of occupational illness, which caused progressive deterioration into old age. It also merged with a growing awareness that chronic disease had been largely ignored as a health threat. As

Ernst Boas pointed out in the 1930s, until very recently, there was "little awareness of the social implications of chronic illness or of its pressing importance in all matters of public health and welfare."[4] However, by the 1930s, Americans of all classes were living longer, and workers began to consider the meaning of living into retirement. The passage of social security in the midst of the Depression was a legislative acknowledgement of the fact that a larger number of workers could contemplate living into old age. In this context, silicosis was a denial of retirement, the reward of a lifetime's work. Silicosis therefore played a part in raising fundamental issues about society's obligation to its work force and industry's responsibility to ensure a decent quality of life after retirement. This set the stage for a broader societal discussion of the issues surrounding chronic disease in the 1960s and 1970s.

The silicosis crisis of the 1930s brought into question one of the central beliefs of the twentieth century—that technological innovation and the growth of industry would produce general improvements in the quality of people's lives. This disease was understood to be produced by the very machines and technical innovations that were at the root of America's industrial might. Coming as it did, in the midst of the Depression, the silicosis crisis became a powerful symbol of the potential threat that America's industry posed to the quality of life. It is only in the last generation that large cross-sections of Americans have begun to question the link between industrialism and progress. But the very questions raised by environmentalists and social critics today were first raised in the context of the silicosis crisis. During the Depression, technology still appeared to hold the key to answering the problem of industrial disease, but in the postwar era, the complexity of chronic illness, and its relationship to the environment we have created, would undermine our faith that technology can solve all problems.

The silicosis crisis also brought into question the ideology of science and medicine. For much of the twentieth century, an important part of the constellation of belief in science resided in a public faith in its neutrality and objectivity. But because silicosis was of industrial origin, and because every issue faced by public health, medical, and engineering professionals had legal and financial implications, many people began to see that the questions posed by scientists and technicians were framed by the larger social and political context. The developing specialties of occupational medicine and industrial hygiene were shaped by their relationship to industry and the financial community.

Chapter I examines the recognition of silicosis in the United States in the early years of the twentieth century. This identification did not take place in the laboratory or clinic but rather in the social discourse among labor, man-

[4] Ernst P. Boas, "The Unseen Plague of Chronic Sickness," *Survey Midmonthly* 74 (December 1938): 376.

agement, the insurance industry, and professionals over the nature and causes of workers' ill-health. For the most part, the medical and public health professions played a peripheral role in the unmasking of industrial lung disease and particularly silicosis. For these professions, dominated as they were by the revolutions in bacteriology and laboratory science, the great plague of bacterial disease, tuberculosis, camouflaged industrial dust as a source of disease. By the 1920s, medical and public health professionals were finally beginning to grasp the significance of silica dust as a source of disease, not simply as an aggravator of preexisting tuberculosis among a wide variety of workers. They were also beginning to address its importance in triggering tuberculosis itself.

Chapter II is a case study of the role of labor, social reformers, and industry in the evolving definition of industrial lung disease. At the turn of the century, American foundries underwent major changes in both labor practices and production methods that set the stage for the emergence of widespread disease among their workers. As sandblasting and power tools replaced hand-held hammers and hand polishing and were joined to more basic production reforms that undermined the autonomy and control of the labor force, working conditions deteriorated, and labor-management conflicts increased. The foundry industry was central to the metallugical and metalworking industries and critical to America's emergence as the leading industrial power. Therefore, the growing health crisis in the foundry industry attracted the attention of social and political reformers. They, in turn, brought to the analysis of workers' health a perspective that emphasized the relationship between workers' disease and working conditions. This joining of labor and reform perspectives once again forced a redefinition of this industrial lung disease and a rethinking of the role of doctors and public health workers.

Chapter III outlines the broader social conditions that contributed to the emergence of silicosis as a national crisis. By the late 1920s, silicosis was accepted as a disease entity by professionals and workers alike. In the early years of the Depression, as large numbers of workers, especially in the foundry industry, were forced out of their jobs, many who had worked in the dusty trades sought redress for their dependence and/or disability through lawsuits for damages against their former employers. In the absence of a social welfare system, disease emerged as a legitimate means by which workers could provide support for themselves and their families. These lawsuits forced tottering industries and their insurance carriers to pay close attention to the economic implications of silicosis and to seek means by which to shape and control the silicosis issue.

Chapter IV describes the attempts by government, industry, and insurance to resolve the silicosis crisis. Under the New Deal, the Department of Labor sought to address the crisis first through negotiation and compromise among the various contending parties: organized labor, industry, insurance, and public health professionals. It was thwarted by the various parties' distinctly different perceptions of the nature of the silicosis crisis as well as by the business community's desire to define who was and who was not an expert on the subject. Business promoted the development of an elite scientific corps whose expertise and technological sophistication could redefine silicosis along lines it favored. It sought to channel through this definition what was then a problem of broad social and political significance into a more narrowly conceived medical, public health, and engineering issue. Ultimately, insurance and industry tried to move silicosis from the arena of public discourse into the confines of relatively conservative expert panels in workers' compensation boards. In the late 1930s, silicosis became the first chronic disease incorporated into workers' compensation legislation in the various states.

Chapter V returns to the region of the country where silicosis was first identified as a public health problem. The Tri-State region of Kansas, Oklahoma, and Missouri had been the site of a massive investigation in the second decade of the twentieth century, after labor unrest over working conditions had forced the federal government to investigate. Despite the intervention of state, federal, and private agencies to alleviate the hardships created by silicosis, the issue remained a major point of conflict for thirty years. By the later years of the Depression, the federal Department of Labor was once again forced to intervene in the area through conferences, National Labor Relations Board (NLRB) hearings, and even the establishment of alternative wartime employment for the local population. In contrast to the activities of management and the insurance industry, the Tri-State represents an attempt by labor and its New Deal allies to recapture silicosis as a labor and political issue in the last years of the Depression and at the beginning of World War II.

After World War II, the waning power of the labor movement, the growing status of the scientific and technical communities, and the changing social epidemiology of silicosis and tuberculosis combined to redefine silicosis once again. A disease that only ten years earlier had been considered a major social and public health crisis was exiled to the recesses of specialized medical and technical journals. Chapter VI reviews the waning interest in this condition on the part of business, health professionals, and even most labor unions and the unsuccessful attempts by some radical elements of the labor movement to resuscitate the issue. It also reviews the growing attention among labor and activist groups to a variety of other industrial lung conditions that previously had been slighted by the attention to silicosis. In the wake of the silicosis crisis, health workers and union activists turned their attention to the dust diseases afflicting coal miners, asbestos workers, and insulation workers, as well as textile workers. Out of this labor activism emerged a series of major struggles during the 1960s and 1970s around coal workers' pneumoconiosis, byssinosis, and asbestosis. These, in turn, helped set the stage for the new round of health and safety activity that emerged in the wake of the landmark federal Mine

Safety and Health Act of 1969 and the Occupational Safety and Health Act of 1970.

The story we relate in this book might too easily be seen as the preserve of medical or public health professionals and historians concerned with questions of technological change and disease recognition. Yet an understanding of the political, economic, and social dimensions of occupational disease provides us with a window into the complex relationships that determine modern understanding of the environment we create and the costs for human health. As we will describe, the study of occupational disease reveals the interlocking relationships among labor, business, government, and public health. Over the course of the twentieth century, workers, management, government officials, and professional groups have negotiated over fundamentally different approaches to the problem of occupational disease. In doing so, they have not only reached compromises on specific legislative issues, but have also engaged in an ongoing discourse that has raised fundamental questions regarding health risks in an advanced industrial society: What are the responsibilities of government, management, and the worker for the risks of work? What role should government play in regulating the workplace? Can occupational disease be distinguished from diseases of nonindustrial origin? Is industrial disease an acceptable and normal condition of modern industrial society? What are the maximum levels of toxic substances to which workers should be exposed, and who should set those levels?[5]

For much of this century, workers, management, health professionals, government officials, insurance executives and others have engaged in a prolonged, often contentious, negotiation over these issues and even over the very definition of disease itself. Unions sometimes responded to the new conditions

---

[5] Historians for the most part have ignored the extent to which working-class life was shaped by long-term disease, disability and death. Labor historians have addressed the problem of accidents, especially in relation to the development of workers' compensation systems during the Progressive Era. But the impact of chronic disease on workers and the importance of health as a cause of labor strife have been ignored. In recent years, there has been a growing literature on labor and health. See, for example, Martin Cherniack, *The Hawk's Nest Incident, America's Worst Industrial Disaster* (New Haven: Yale University Press, 1986); Barbara Ellen Smith, *Digging Our Own Graves: Coal Miners and the Struggle over Black Lung Disease* (Philadelphia: Temple University Press, 1987); Barbara Sicherman, *Alice Hamilton, A Life in Letters* (Cambridge: Harvard University Press, 1984); William Graebner, *Coal Mining Safety in the Progressive Period: The Political Economy of Reform* (Lexington, Mass: D. C. Heath, 1976); Carl Gersuny, *Work Hazards and Industrial Conflict* (Hanover, N.H.: University Press of New England, 1981); Edward Beardsley, *A History of Neglect: Health Care for Blacks and Mill Workers in the Twentieth Century South* (Knoxville: University of Tennessee Press, 1987); David Rosner and Gerald Markowitz, eds., *Dying for Work: Workers' Safety and Health in Twentieth-Century America* (Bloomington: Indiana University Press, 1987); Alan Derickson, *Workers' Health, Workers' Democracy: The Western Miners' Struggle for Health and Safety, 1891–1925* (Ithaca: Cornell University Press, 1988); Gerald Markowitz and David Rosner, eds., *"Slaves of the Depression," Workers' Letters about Life on the Job* (Ithaca: Cornell University Press, 1987).

of work by making safety and health central issues in organizing drives. Workers often saw disease as rooted in long hours, poor ventilation, exposure to dusts and other toxins, and low wages that eliminated the possibility of proper housing, clothing, and food. Management and the insurance industry often downplayed the significance of working conditions as a source of illness. Instead, they often placed the major responsibility for illness on the life-style and living conditions of the workers and their families. Government officials, physicians, and other professionals assumed differing positions, depending upon economic and social conditions as well as the pressures that were placed upon them by labor and management. Together, collective bargaining over working conditions, strikes, attempts at government regulation, and professional movements to set standards for exposure to toxic materials constituted an ongoing negotiation over occupational disease. Each group's changing perspective gained ascendancy and legitimacy at different historical moments and under particular social and economic circumstances.

I

THE "CABINET OF CURIOSITIES": SILICOSIS AND THE

RECOGNITION OF INDUSTRIAL DISEASE

EARLY in the twentieth century, officials of the Granite Cutters' Union in Barre, Vermont, complained that consumption, "the white man's scourge," was "claiming almost every granite cutter in this vicinity, before he reaches the age of fifty." It was obvious to the union that the cause of the epidemic was the granite dust inhaled while carving, chipping, and finishing monuments, gravestones, and building facades. The local physicians agreed that the workers were suffering from consumption, but they differed in their understanding of its cause. They believed that the workers' consumption was caused by tiny germs that spread among the work force as a result of poor personal hygiene and unsanitary living conditions.

The physicians, informed by the advances in bacteriology, had begun to refer to consumption as tuberculosis after the tubercle bacillus that had been identified by Robert Koch in the early 1880s. The union and the work force, however, insisted on using the older nineteenth-century terms *consumption* or *phthisis* to describe the condition. From the union's perspective, there was nothing new or complex about what was causing them to cough, wheeze, spit blood, and waste away: Physicians "have given the old-time consumption a new name," the union observed, "and talk learnedly about it, but what does that amount to when men are dying in our midst almost daily of this fell disease?" Writing that the rate of disease should "strike terror to the heart of every granite cutter," the union declared that the focus of attention should be on prevention of the dusty conditions and control over the speed of work because "the men work at a faster clip than the constitution of any human machine is able to stand up to."[1]

The contention over the cause of this disease led to the unmasking of silicosis as an industrial scourge. Despite the fact that the term *silicosis* would not be widely used in the United States until after 1915, dust had been long recognized as a problem for hard-rock miners, cutters, potters, buffers, glassworkers, sandblasters and foundry workers.[2] Since antiquity, observers had recognized that workers developed serious breathing problems when they

---

[1] "Official Correspondence," *Granite Cutters' Journal* 31 (February 1908): n.p.

[2] See Frederick Hoffman, *The Mortality from Consumption in Dusty Trades*, U.S. Bureau of Labor, *Bulletin No. 79* (Washington, D.C.: Government Printing Office, November 1908), 633–875.

inhaled the dust of certain rocks and minerals. In the eighteenth century, Ramazzini noted that marble or stone cutters "are usually troubled with a cough, and some of them turn asthmatic and consumptive."[3] In the early decades of the nineteenth century, Charles Thackrah noted that Derbyshire miners among others could find their health experience substantially improved by removing dust from the air: "Assuredly the wretchedness and mortality of miners may be greatly diminished by reducing the dust of the employ"[4]

Throughout most of the nineteenth century, doctors and laypeople alike had accepted dust as a source of phthisis or, as it was more commonly called, consumption, chronic lung conditions that affected broad cross-sections of Western European and American society. For the previous two centuries, this condition had been the single greatest cause of death in Europe and America. Despite the great attention to epidemics of smallpox, cholera, and typhoid, consumption was "the great white plague" that threatened "the very survival" of European and American society. The symptoms of wasting away, coughing, spitting, and weakening might appear in victims from various classes and social strata. But it was the victim's personal traits and constitutional characteristics that predisposed him or her to the illness, according to the medical experts of that period.[5]

Historians have recognized that Robert Koch's discovery of the tuberculosis bacillus and the development of the germ theory of disease in the 1880s were enormous breakthroughs for medical science. Many leading medical researchers and educators, flushed with confidence as a result of this breakthrough, simply equated consumption with a bacterial disease and looked inward to the laboratory and to science for its diagnosis and treatment. While this movement was crucial to the development of American medicine in general, it served to inhibit developments in the field of occupational medicine. Ironically, the medical profession looked away from the workplace at the very time that changes in the industrial environment created unprecedented health and safety hazards. As America's industrial expansion gained momentum in the late nineteenth century, researchers turned from the study of dust as a cause of illness.

It would not be until the early twentieth century that dust would once again be linked to consumption through a process of negotiation and contention about the causes and nature of illness among statisticians, insurance company actuaries, public health and social reformers, and labor activists. As a result, silica dust was unmasked as a separate and specific cause of industrial disease.

---

[3] Quoted in Hoffman, *Mortality from Consumption*, 682.

[4] Charles Turner Thackrah, *The Effects of Arts, Trades and Professions on Health and Longevity* (originally published, 1832), (Canton, Mass: Science History Publications, 1985), 117. Thackrah has an extended footnote describing dust diseases among other groups of miners.

[5] Rene Dubos and Jean Dubos, *The White Plague, Tuberculosis, Man, and Society* (1952; reprint, New Brunswick, N.J.: Rutgers University Press, 1987), 10.

But because silicosis was a chronic, degenerative disease and took years or even decades to appear, it presented a host of problems to medical researchers and public health workers raised in an intellectual environment dominated by the germ theory. By the end of the Progressive Era, most physicians appreciated that silicosis represented a distinct disease that was rooted in new industrial conditions. Once accepted, silicosis forced a rethinking of the traditional assumptions about personal, industrial, and governmental responsibility for disease.

Phthisis and Tuberculosis

Before the acceptance of the germ theory, practitioners and laypeople alike understood disease in highly personal and idiosyncratic terms. Much of medical therapeutics rested on the belief that disease was a reflection of individuals' special social, personal, hereditary, and economic circumstances. People's maladies were based, in part, on the peculiarities of the individual and his or her life. As Charles Rosenberg has written, "[T]he body was seen, metaphorically, as a system of dynamic interactions with its environment. Health or disease resulted from a cumulative interaction between constitutional endowment and environmental circumstance."[6] It was the special relationship between an individual and a complex, highly particularized environment that was at the root of illness. The practitioner's therapeutic skills were measured by his or her ability to weigh, evaluate, and differentiate the patient from others who might have similar symptoms. Rather than being a technician who administered a universal cure or standardized medical regimen for a set of complaints, medical practitioners for much of the century saw themselves as responsible for adjusting dosages, altering prescriptions, and changing regimens as conditions demanded.

The diagnosis and treatment of consumption, also commonly called phthisis, developed within this general medical milieu. Those suffering from the common symptoms of coughing, wheezing, and spitting blood all had phthisis, a descriptive term derived from the Greek, meaning "to waste away." The disease took on different meanings for different classes and groups in the ever-changing urban and industrial societies of Western Europe and the United States. Physicians "faced with a confusing array of signs and symptoms, bearing no obvious relation to one another" saw these signs as "the expression of different maladies." For middle-class sufferers, the disease was often presented in almost a romantic light. The translucent flush of Victorian ladies suffering from this disease became a standard image in the nineteenth-century

[6] Morris J. Vogel and Charles E. Rosenberg, *The Therapeutic Revolution, Essays in the Social History of American Medicine* (Philadelphia: University of Pennsylvania Press, 1979), 5.

novel. For the working class, however, the disease had a much more threatening aspect: workers and their families huddled together in the slum dwellings of large cities, such as London, Paris, and New York.[7]

The apparent idiosyncracy of the symptoms that marked phthisis among different individuals and social classes during most of the first half of the nineteenth century reinforced standard ideas regarding the nature, course, and treatment of disease. Phthisis could be linked to the ongoing, long-term moral and social environment that predisposed a victim to a disease process. Medical practitioners and the public as well shared a common set of assumptions about the cause and treatment of the disease. Phthisis could be rooted in personal behavior, such as drinking, social position, poor living quarters, the malaise of an urban life-style, or, finally, indoor, unhealthful work: "Treatment was to be sensitively gauged not to a disease entity but to such distinctive features of the patient as age, gender, ethnicity, socioeconomic position, and moral status, and to attributes of place like climate, topography and population density."[8] A practitioner needed to have a complete knowledge of the life history of the patient in order to make an accurate diagnosis and plan of treatment.

Public health practitioners, such as Herman Biggs in New York City, Charles Chapin in Rhode Island, and others had documented the importance of a variety of sources of phthisis. Among them were the home, crowding, impure air, and dust in the workplace. In New York City in 1879, Roger Tracy, the Registrar of Vital Statistics, noted the symptoms of disease among workers in the metal trades: "The disease comes on very gradually . . . and its duration may be extended over four or five years." He described the disease as "begin[ning] with the cough of irritation, dry and hacking at first, with very scanty expectoration, whitish and stringy in character. . . . The expectoration gradually increases in amount and becomes reddish, and soon after this tinge appears there may be haemoptysis."[9] In descriptions of various dusty trades, it was commonly pointed out that phthisis/consumption was caused by the industry. In an *Industrial History of the United States*, published in 1878, the author described the sources of "grinders' consumption" in the axe industry: Because of "the constant inhalation of the grit and bits of steel thrown off in the process . . . a premature death is rarely averted."[10]

Consumption, or *phthisis*, was a term used to denote a wide variety of

[7] Dubos and Dubos, *The White Plague*, 69. Also see F. B. Smith, *The Retreat of Tuberculosis, 1850–1950* (London: Croon-Helm, 1988).

[8] John Harley Warner, *The Therapeutic Perspective, Medical Practice, Knowledge, and Identity in America, 1820–1885* (Cambridge: Harvard University Press, 1986), 58.

[9] Frederick Hoffman, *Mortality from Respiratory Diseases in Dusty Trades*, U.S. Department of Labor, Bureau of Labor Statistics, *Bulletin No. 231* (Washington, D.C.: Government Printing Office, June 1918), 30.

[10] Bolles' *Industrial History of the United States*, quoted in Carey P. McCord, "Grindstones," *Hygeia* 18 (August 1940): 744.

symptoms. The disease could be of an acute nature and "prove fatal in a few weeks." Or it might start with acute symptoms and evolve into a chronic condition. Alternatively, its symptoms might appear slowly, gradually getting worse over many years. Furthermore it could affect lungs, bones, the brain, and other organs of the body. While pulmonary consumption was of primary importance, the variety of symptoms, prognoses, and sites gave medical researchers a basis for developing a complex and all-encompassing nosology. In the United States, the estimates of the prevalence of phthisis, generally understood to mean pulmonary tuberculosis, were higher than similar estimates from England and Wales, where finer differentiations were made to distinguish tuberculosis from pneumoconiosis, bronchitis, or pneumonia.

In the years following Pasteur's work on rabies and yeast, the medical community began to change its views regarding the multiple sources of illness. Increasingly, laboratory science began to hold out the possibility that disease could be explained rationally through the discovery of specific microorganisms. For the elite practitioner, this meant that the detailed life history was no longer as essential for understanding the diagnosis of disease. Although medical practitioners continued to speak of the significance of the "history" in diagnosing patients' illnesses, the concept of a medical history changed.

In the years following Koch's discovery, medical history became a listing of physiological and hereditary factors that might explain the symptoms. "In attempting to arrive at a correct solution of the problem," noted one physician explaining the method of diagnosing tuberculosis in 1904, "the greatest care should always be exercised to ascertain . . . all the facts that can be learned concerning the patient's past history and mode of life." While in the middle years of the nineteenth century this might have meant exploring personal behavior, work history, and living conditions, by now it simply meant examining "the probable duration of the disease, the occurrence of a foregoing haemoptysis, a history of an attack of typhoid pneumonia, pleurisy, or protracted influenza, and, to a certain extent the individual's appearance."[11] The impact of this changing medical culture was critical in the study of phthisis.[12] According to Ludwig Teleky, a noted industrial physician and author of the first history of industrial hygiene, by the year of Koch's discovery, there was "a vast knowledge of [the importance of] dust on the lungs." But now, suddenly, the study of its industrial etiology ceased: "At that time . . . the study of the effects of dust stopped. All cases [of phthisis] were diagnosed as tuberculosis." In Europe, researchers "mocked at all those 'curiosities' of quartz lungs, coal lungs, and iron lungs, 'all of which belong rather in a cabinet of curiosi-

[11] George W. Norris, "The Differential Diagnosis between Incipient Pulmonary Tuberculosis, Healed Cavities, and Non-Tuberculosis Fibrosis," *New York Medical Journal* 80 (July 16, 1904): 103.

[12] Ludwig Teleky, *History of Factory and Mine Hygiene* (New York: Columbia University Press, 1948), 199.

ties than in industrial hygiene.' "[13] All consumption or phthisis came to be understood as tuberculosis, caused by a specific organism and spread like other infectious diseases: "Medical science claims that the presence of the tubercle bacillus in the lungs is the fundamental cause of phthisis, or consumption," trumpeted a New Yorker writing to *Scientific American* in 1904.[14]

For the public health and medical fields, the trick was to reconcile the myriad symptoms of phthisis/consumption with the new "scientific" germ model. After all, the discovery of the bacillus held out the possibility that an effective vaccine could be developed to protect humanity from this age-old scourge. "We are now anxiously waiting the development of Dr. Koch's cure for consumption," said one professor of pathology at the University of Michigan in 1890.[15]

Before the 1880s, public health workers had a different conception of health than did clinicians. While physicians saw sick patients and sought to identify the cause of disease and treat its symptoms, public health workers addressed the problem of environmental control, developing a perspective that emphasized personal and public hygiene. Sanitation, the inspection of meats, sewage, housing, immigration control, and the provision of clean water and air were critical to the mandate of the public health professional.

With the revolution in bacteriology that followed the discoveries of Pasteur, Lister, and Koch in the middle decades of the nineteenth century, a new faith in laboratory science emerged not only among physicians but also among public health workers. "Bacteriology thus became an ideological marker, sharply differentiating the 'old' public health, the province of untrained amateurs from the 'new' public health, which belonged to scientifically trained professionals," points out Elizabeth Fee.[16] Despite the different professional mandates of public health workers and physicians, members of both professions who identified themselves with the science of medicine and public health began to share a common faith in the significance of the disease-specific germ entity in creating consumption. The implication was that the modes of transmission of the bacteria had to be clearly identified if an effective campaign to eliminate the sources of the disease was to be mounted. Why was it that the poor were so likely to be struck by disease? It was because the hot, crowded dwellings in which they lived allowed the germ to propagate and to spread among a

[13] A. Vogt, "*Die Allgemein Sterbelichkeit . . . ,*" quoted in Teleky, *History*, 199.

[14] Correspondence, "Cause and Treatment of Consumption," *Scientific American* 90 (May 21, 1904): 403. Cf. George Rosen, *The History of Miners' Diseases, A Medical and Social Interpretation* (New York: Schuman's, 1943).

[15] Heneage Gibbes, "Is the Unity of Phthisis an Established Fact?" *Boston Medical and Surgical Journal* 123 (December 25, 1890): 608.

[16] Elizabeth Fee, *Disease and Discovery, A History of the Johns Hopkins School of Hygiene and Public Health, 1916–1939* (Baltimore: Johns Hopkins University Press, 1987) 19. See also Barbara Rosenkrantz, *Public Health and the State, Changing Views in Massachusetts, 1842–1936* (Cambridge: Harvard University Press, 1972), especially chs. 3, 4, and 5.

population weakened by inadequate nutrition and horrid living conditions. Why was it that children appeared to be a high-risk group? It was because tainted milk from tubercular cows poisoned children. How was it that individuals outside of any particular risk group came down with the disease? It was because they had a hereditary predisposition that left them vulnerable to infection. Why was it that workers had a higher rate of tuberculosis than did farmers? It was because the closed quarters of factory workers combined with their long hours and inadequate diet to leave them susceptible to phthisis. For the new public health, it was the specificity of the bacterial agent that was important. It seemed that the older generation's emphasis on cleaning up the general environment was misdirected and inefficient. One of the advocates of the new public health summed up the revolution in ideology that overtook the field in the 1880s: "Before 1880 we knew nothing; after 1890 we knew it all; it was a glorious ten years."[17]

There was almost universal agreement among medical and public health personnel about the etiology of phthisis:[18] The bacillus, not dust, made people sick. "Wherever people are collected together, the death rate from consumption is in direct proportion to the degree of crowding together, and the deficiency of ventilation," stated Dr. Arthur Ransome shortly after the discovery of the tuberculosis bacillus. Ransome, an English physician, noted the deleterious effect of dust on workers' lungs but devoted his book, *The Causes and Prevention of Phthisis*, to showing that because consumption was caused by the tuberculosis bacillus, "true" phthisis was caused by germ-laden stagnant air. Although metallic and mineral dusts might be injurious to workers' lungs, they were merely a small problem in comparison to the dangers posed by bacterial infection.[19] Arthur Ransome stated: "Dusts, therefore, although they are a serious danger, and though they ought on this account to be kept away from workpeople, as a preventive measure against consumption, are yet only remotely a cause of the disease."[20]

It was not that the new medical and public health viewpoints completely ignored dust as a factor in the creation of phthisis. But dust's importance was in its role as a vehicle that carried the bacillus from victim to victim. Dust carried the bacteria; dust itself was not the cause of disease. In factories and in the home, stagnant, warm, moist, dust-laden air caused workers and their families to be especially vulnerable to tuberculosis. The slums of large cities came to be seen as "breeding grounds" that were "seeded" with tuberculosis

[17] William Sedgewick, quoted in Fee, *Disease and Discovery*, 19.

[18] This review of the pre-Progressive and European literature is based on Teleky, *History*, 196–210.

[19] Arthur Ransome, *The Causes and Prevention of Phthisis* (London: Smith, Elder, and Co., 1890), 51–67.

[20] Arthur Ransome, *A Campaign against Consumption* (Cambridge: Cambridge University Press, 1915), 27.

bacilli waiting to infect the susceptible victim. Tuberculosis came to be viewed as a disease that could be transmitted to susceptible individuals by means of air impregnated with bacteria from dried sputum, breathing, etc. The dusting of furniture could throw into the air the "dried sputum" of tuberculars. Crowded public spaces and unclean home conditions with moist, warm, and stagnant air were seen as the most likely conduits for the disease.[21] The crisis of phthisis was narrowly defined as a bacterial crisis, and effective means of control were the eradication of sources of infection. In 1898, the Massachusetts Board of Health circulated a pamphlet to all the households in Brookline outlining the sources of infection and the means of preventing tuberculosis. It explained that consumption was caused "by the bacillus of tuberculosis" and the conditions that favored its spread were "defective ventilation, overcrowding of dwellings, factories and workshops, insufficient and badly selected food, dampness of soil, intemperance and undue physical or mental strain, overwork, worry and anxiety."[22]

While authors disagreed about precisely how the disease was communicated between individuals, it was generally accepted that dust could serve as a carrier of the bacillus. One physician summarized the general understanding of the relationship between dust and tuberculosis by noting that "inhalation is probably the common mode of infection, and that indirectly through infected dust with which the air is laden."[23] Others were more alarmist in their description of the significance of dust as a carrier of the tuberculosis bacillus. "A careless or ignorant expectorating consumptive can eliminate and distribute seven billions of bacilli in twenty-four hours," warned S. A. Knopf in the journal *Charities* in 1901. "You know that the expectoration . . . when allowed to dry and pulverize, may, when inhaled with the dust of the atmosphere, give tuberculosis."[24] Dry spittle, capable of producing and mixing with dust, was the dangerous material. "A case of consumption may be made almost harmless to other people by preventing the spit from drying and becoming dust," one editorialist declared. "In cleaning rooms, damp dusters should be used, and wet tea-leaves or sawdust should be put down before sweeping so that the dust will be removed without being spread through the air." It was further suggested that the "dusters should be boiled, and the sawdust or tea-leaves burned" in order to prevent further infection.[25] By encouraging the

[21] George Homan, "The Danger of Dust as a Cause of Tuberculosis," *Journal of the American Medical Association* [hereafter *JAMA*] 48 (March 23, 1907): 1014.

[22] "The Prevention of Tuberculosis in Brookline, Mass.," *Boston Medical and Surgical Journal* 138 (February 10, 1898): 141.

[23] Lester C. Miller, "The Decrease in the Death-Rate of Consumption," *Boston Medical and Surgical Journal* 151 (December 22, 1904): 680.

[24] S. A. Knopf, "Our Duties toward the Consumptive Poor," *Charities* 6 (February 2, 1901): 76.

[25] "Advice about Consumption," *Charities* 3 (September 9, 1899): 8–9.

tuberculosis victim to carry and use flasks to dispose of his or her spittle so that "it cannot dry and be blown about to be inhaled by others," journals declared that responsible tuberculars could stem the disease.[26]

As late as 1913, an article published by the Smithsonian Institution maintained that "no evidence has yet been brought forward which shows that the chemical quality of the air has anything to do with these ill effects [of phthisis], and that, apart from the influence of infecting bacteria, the ventilation problem is essentially one of temperature, relative humidity and movement of the air."[27]

Just as the field had developed unanimity and clarity regarding how to define and explain "true" phthisis Thomas Oliver and British governmental investigators published a series of studies that had a major impact on some American reformers, public health workers, and statisticians. Oliver and others argued that noninfectious cases of lung disorders were more important than previously assumed. In 1902, Oliver in his famous treatise on the *Dangerous Trades*, noted that "the tendency of modern pathology is to look upon all pulmonary phthisis or consumption as tuberculosis, but the fact remains that phthisis can be caused by dust."[28] He cited four specific dust diseases: chalicosis, or silicosis; siderosis, which was due to the inhalation of metallic dusts; anthracosis; and byssinosis. He explained that these pneumoconioses had been neglected but that they were significant for large cross-sections of the working population: "The affected workman is regarded as the victim of consumption, but the disease is not necessarily tuberculosis." He warned, however, that the relationship between pneumoconiosis and tuberculosis was complex, for workers suffering from the former disease were more likely to contract the latter.[29]

By 1906 some British researchers had developed a new theory about phthisis that challenged the bacteriological model. It was not one disease. Rather, there were three distinct conditions producing similar symptoms: "[P]ulmonary disease manifests itself in three kinds or forms—as ordinary tuberculous phthisis, acute or chronic; as 'fibroid phthisis,' and as a mixed form when a tuberculous process is ingrafted sooner or later upon the fibroid."[30] The British Committee on Compensation for Industrial Diseases took pains to distinguish between "fibroid phthisis" and the tuberculous kind.

[26] Editorial, *Charities* 3 (November 18, 1899): 3. See also State of Connecticut, *Report of the Special Commission Appointed to Investigate Tuberculosis* (Hartford, 1908), 40, in which wet mops were also encouraged.

[27] Quoted in Hoffman, *Mortality from Respiratory Diseases*, 33–34.

[28] Thomas Oliver, *Dangerous Trades* (London: E. P. Dutton, 1902), 272. See also Thomas Oliver, "Gold Miner's Phthisis and Some of the Dangers to Health Incidental to Gold Mining in the Transvaal," *Medical Press Circular*, n.s., 76 (1903): 189.

[29] Oliver, *Dangerous Trades*, 272.

[30] "Report of the Departmental Committee on Compensation for Industrial Diseases" (1906), 13, quoted in Hoffman, *Mortality from Consumption*, 638–39.

"The first symptom [of fibroid phthisis] is a cough which insidiously and for a while almost imperceptibly becomes habitual. At first in the morning only, it gradually becomes more frequent during the day, and expectoration, nominal at the beginning, becomes more marked, though not profuse until the latter stages of the disease." While remarking on the atypical and more rapid development of symptoms among the gold and tin miners in South Africa, the committee noted that the development of disabling coughs and serious and disabling shortness of breath could take from ten to fifteen years to develop. In contrast to pulmonary tuberculosis, they pointed out, "there are no signs of fever . . . the flesh does not fall and the muscles retain their strength and volume" even in the last stages of the disease. "Herein fibroid phthisis presents a well-marked difference from pulmonary tuberculosis; and even if, as we have said, the disease becomes complicated with tubercle, yet the rate of progress may be determined rather by the character of the primary than of the secondary disease, though usually the supervention of tubercle hastens the sufferer into a more rapid consumption."[31]

During the first decade of the twentieth century, most medical and public health professionals in the United States were still wedded to a bacteriological model that posited the unity of tuberculosis and phthisis. While some of the leading physicians and public health workers were aware of the growing British, South African, and even German literature on phthisis, it did not influence their understanding of lung disease in the United States. In the United States, competing models of the causes of lung disease arose among lay groups and other professionals, such as social workers, settlement house reformers, and even statisticians.

Workers in the dusty trades, isolated from the new ideology of medicine and public health, were singularly important, for they continued to see their suffering as rooted in the terrible conditions of work. They still accepted the prebacteriological consensus that phthisis was linked to individual circumstance. Rather than emphasizing personal morality, susceptibility, or habit, however, they emphasized social factors, such as work and living conditions. The explosion of job actions, labor unrest, and strikes at the turn of the century cannot be understood without looking into the disintegration of the work environment and concurrent increase in accidents and disease that paralleled the intensification of work and the introduction of power tools in the dusty trades. Miners suffering from constricted breathing called their disease alternately miners' phthisis or miners' consumption; potters called their affliction potters' consumption or phthisis; other workers identified their symptoms as grinders' rot, glassblowers' con, granite cutters' phthisis, etc. There was no attention to the bacteria in the descriptions of their conditions but there was a great deal of

---

[31] "Report of the Departmental Committee on Compensation for Industrial Diseases" (1906), 13, quoted in Hoffman, *Mortality from Consumption*, 639.

attention to the specific industry that caused the sickness. Even industry spokespeople accepted the industrial origins of workers' complaints. They continued to use the terms *phthisis, consumption,* and *tuberculosis* interchangeably, with little regard to the differentiation between bacterial and nonbacterial lung disorders. *The Iron Age,* a trade journal, pronounced, "Miners' phthisis is so great an evil" that it was essential to deal effectively with "this most terrible form of tuberculosis."[32]

The bacteriological consensus was also undermined by a diverse group of Progressive Era reformers who were developing a broader conception of the origins of phthisis. For reformers concerned with the plight of the urban poor, the impact of tuberculosis was obvious and profound and could not be divorced from the terrible conditions of life and work. Charity and settlement house workers, for example, documented that nearly one out of every four dwellings in New York City in 1890 experienced a death from phthisis. In the poorer neighborhoods, it was clear, the toll was much higher, leaving these communities devastated by the disease.[33] For these reformers, phthisis was a disease of poverty, not of germs. One of the leading social welfare reformers of the time, Graham Taylor, declared that tuberculosis was a "disease of the working classes" and that "everything which makes the life of the workingman harder, everything which is attendant upon poverty, makes for the increase of this disease."[34] The interplay of "[h]ousing, playgrounds, diet, income, . . . physical education, and immigration" and even dental hygiene appeared to involve "very diverse if not incongruous topics." But when "grouped about the central idea of promoting immunity their interdependence becomes obvious."[35]

The social reform analysis that intimately linked social conditions to the creation of disease led settlement house workers and labor leaders to emphasize the connection between work and tuberculosis.[36] "Where there is dirt and grime and dust, long hours, foul air and bad pay, the community pays for what

[32] "The Water Drill a Preventive of Miners' Phthisis," *Iron Age* 74 (August 25, 1904): 17. See also John B. Huber, "Occupations With Relation to Tuberculosis," *American Medicine* 9 (January 21, 1905): 112–14; Charles Stover, "The Relation of Tuberculosis to Municipal and Industrial Life," *Buffalo Medical Journal* 62 (May 1907): 583–91; George William Norris, "The Treatment of Pulmonary Tuberculosis," *JAMA* 44 (June 17, 1905): 1893–1897.

[33] "Consumption Widespread," *Charities* 3 (June 17, 1899): 9.

[34] Graham Taylor, "The Industrial Viewpoint," *Charities and the Commons* 16 (May 5, 1906): 205.

[35] Lillian Brandt, "Hygienic, Social, Industrial and Economic Aspects," *Charities and the Commons* 21 (November 7, 1908): 198. See also Livingston Farrand, "Prevention of Tuberculosis," *Charities and the Commons* 19 (November 16, 1907): 1065–66, and Farrand, "To Check the Ravages of Consumption," *Charities and the Commons* 11 (September 5, 1903): 189–190, for a discussion of the implications of the Progressive model of tuberculosis for education and public health campaigns.

[36] See Francis Albert Rollo Russell, "The Atmosphere in Relation to Human Life and Health," quoted in Hoffman, *Mortality from Respiratory Diseases,* 13.

it calls cheap prices by a little money and many lives sacrificed to greed, ignorance and indifference," said a representative of labor in 1906. Labor called
for factory inspection, good wages, "fresh air into our shops," and other factory legislation to address the problem of workers' health.[37] Graham Taylor
saw four "characteristics of employment" that put workers at risk: "insanitary conditions," "[l]ow rate of wages," "[f]atigue," and "long and irregular
hours." Under the heading of insanitary conditions, Taylor identified two major subcategories, "hygienic surroundings which are not inherent in the trade
itself and those conditions which are to a certain extent necessitated by the
character of the trade." Among the latter were those of the dusty trades:
"[T]he dust producing trades each lead as producers of tuberculosis and especially those in which the dust-particles are very irritating." Taylor identified
stonecutters, grinders, cigar workers, lead and copper miners and others as at
risk. Further, he noted that these workers were usually "strong well-developed men" but they suffered from enormous death rates from tuberculosis.[38]
In the hands of reformers in and out of government, statistics and data collection became powerful tools for education, analysis, and agitation.[39]

  This social analysis had an impact on the world view of an elite group of
statisticians and social planners. Frederick L. Hoffman, the statistician for the
Prudential Life Insurance Company, and Louis Dublin, his counterpart at Metropolitan Life, were especially receptive because it helped explain morbidity
and mortality data on the industrial work force that these insurance giants were
accumulating. In the late 1800s, these two companies were the largest and
most important commercial insurers of working-class Americans. They pio-
neered in the provision of "industrial insurance," which provided minimal
life and burial insurance for laborers. Unlike common life insurance, industrial insurance depended on an extensive network of agents, who, on a weekly
basis, would visit workers' homes to collect premiums of five and ten cents
per family member. By 1910, industrial insurance was a three billion dollar
business, with Metropolitan Life and the Prudential handling over 80 percent
of all premiums. In that same year, more than 23 million Americans held industrial policies, with more than 19 million covered by these two companies.[40]

  Because these two insurance giants' success depended on the changing mor-

---

[37] "An Address to the Tuberculosis Committee and to Unionists," *Charities and the Commons*
15 (January 20, 1906): 528.

[38] Graham Taylor, "The Industrial Viewpoint," *Charities and the Commons* 16 (May 5, 1906):
206.

[39] C.F.W. Doehring, *Factory Sanitation and Labor Protection*, U.S. Department of Labor,
Bulletin No. 44 (Washington, D.C.: Government Printing Office, January 1903), 1. C.F.W.
Doehring began one of the earliest government studies of factory hazards by pointing out that
"statistics and clear thinking" were important in that they alerted workers to the dangers of their
jobs.

[40] John F. Dryden, *Industrial Insurance Past and Present* (Newark: Prudential Insurance Company of America, 1912), 10.

tality picture among the various industries and population groups, their statisticians gathered enormous amounts of data documenting disease, disability, and death rates among every conceivable industrial population. They developed actuarial charts for blacks, whites, Native Americans, women, men, children, miners, steelworkers, bakers, quarry workers, white-collar workers, and wage earners in scores of other industries. At the turn of the century, state and federal labor and health departments were just beginning to assume a major role in gathering statistics on the health of the work force. Thus, such statisticians as Hoffman at the Prudential and Louis Dublin at Metropolitan undertook investigations of their own. These became the basis for many state and federal reports, which meant that public agencies had to depend upon the goodwill of the insurance agencies for access to even parts of the data.

Unlike the new public health epidemiologists, who focused their attention on the diseased as a source of infection, Hoffman sought to understand disease as a reflection of community structure and organization. For example, Frederick Hoffman found it necessary to take extended tours of the communities in which the Prudential had extensive interests in order to document the industrial, home, and community factors that affected mortality and morbidity rates. In towns all along the way, he would conduct what we would today recognize as detailed epidemiological and ecological studies of the relationship between health and community development. He would arrive in a community in the afternoon and begin developing a detailed profile of that town's health experience. Sometimes he would begin by heading directly to the cemetery, where he would spend several hours noting the dates of birth and death on the tombstones. In his hotel in the evening, he would develop a detailed actuarial chart on the age-specific mortality of different populations over time. He would spend the next day visiting the local mine, mill, or smelter. He would travel into the shaft of a mine, chronicling the safety and health risks associated with every phase of production. He talked to company officials, gathering data about the number of accidents and the incidence of sickness, including pneumonia, tuberculosis, and lead poisoning. He would follow up on this by visiting local physicians, coroners, and funeral homes and the local library to corroborate the picture that he heretofore had developed. If the Prudential already insured workers in that community, he would compare this information with data that he had gathered through his own claims department. If the company had not yet moved into the town, he would make a recommendation to the company president as to whether or not to move into the community and, if so, which groups of workers to insure.[41]

Hoffman's work was critical to the unmasking of silicosis as a distinct con-

[41] See Frederick L. Hoffman Manuscripts, Columbia University, particularly Box 5, Folder 16, which contains the correspondence from his second Western trip. Hoffman took a similar trip in 1913. Together, correspondence from these trips provides a fascinating glimpse into the methods of the Prudential Life Insurance Company.

dition in the United States. His detailed studies and reading of the European and South African literature had convinced him that the interests of the insurance industry were diverging from those of the medical and public health professionals. These experts' commitment to the germ theory had blinded them to the industrial causes of phthisis. In his pathbreaking 1908 study, "The Mortality from Consumption in Dusty Trades," Hoffman pointed out that "human health was much influenced by the character of the air breathed and that its purity [was] a matter of very considerable sanitary and economic importance."[42] He directly contradicted the prevalent assumption among clinicians that tuberculosis and other infectious diseases were the primary threat to the average worker. "The sanitary dangers of air contaminated by disease-breeding germs are probably not so serious as generally assumed," he began. Rather, "the destructive effects of the dust-laden atmosphere of factories and workshops are a decidedly serious menace to health and life." He maintained that there was actually a "paucity of bacteria in very dusty air," but that "dust in any form, when inhaled continuously and in considerable quantities, is prejudicial to health because of its inherent mechanical properties, destructive to the delicate membrane of the respiratory passages and the lungs."[43]

Hoffman alluded to the earlier studies of Sir James Crichton-Browne, which had compared workers in the "principal dust-producing occupations" with agricultural workers, who worked in a "practically dustless atmosphere." The former suffered disproportionately from various respiratory diseases when compared with the latter. He also referred extensively to the work of J. T. Arlidge, who in 1892 "published a treatise on The Hygiene, Diseases, and Mortality of Occupations." In that work Arlidge had challenged the assumptions of clinicians and pathologists who assumed that the presence of tuberculosis bacilli in the lungs of dead workers indicated that the bacilli were the primary cause of their disease. He had called this at best a "half truth":

> I doubt if these bacilli actually develop phthisis unless there be some antecedent change in the vitality of the affected tissue. . . . In other words, I look upon a phthisical lung as one prepared for the germination and multiplication of bacilli [by dust], and not a primary product of those microscopic organisms. . . .[44]

Hoffman's 1908 study of "Consumption in the Dusty Trades" built on the evidence presented in the foreign studies and the progressive social analysis as developed by the reformers. Hoffman also used statistical materials to challenge the clinical viewpoint of the medical and public health professions. In doing so, he was providing a new tool that gave legitimacy to the popular view

[42] Hoffman, "Mortality from Consumption," 633. For an earlier piece describing the plight of stonecutters, see Frederick L. Hoffman, "Industrial Insurance and the Prevention of Tuberculosis," *Medical Examiner* 11 (1901): 694.

[43] Hoffman, "Mortality from Consumption," 633–34.

[44] Hoffman, "Mortality from Consumption," 638.

that dust was dangerous to health. Although the British, and especially Thomas Oliver, had used statistical and epidemiological data, Hoffman was the first American to use such methods to document the prevalence and scope of industrially created lung diseases and to use this material to decipher the implications about the work environment. Hoffman began by establishing the number of workers over the age of sixty-five in a variety of industries. Drawing on a sample of nearly 23,000 deaths among industrial workers, he sought to establish "the true rate of mortality from all causes or specific causes such as consumption." He did this by ascertaining the "number of deaths in every thousand persons of any particular trade . . . for any single year." He then compared the industrial mortality rates with the overall mortality rates for specific diseases, such as consumption, and then established age-specific death rates for each disease.[45]

Statisticians for the insurance industry played a major role in uncovering the impact of industrial conditions on workers' health. In addition to Hoffman, Louis Dublin, the statistician for the Prudential's major competitor in the field of industrial insurance, Metropolitan Life Insurance Company, also was engrossed in investigating the relationship between work and disease. Dublin's access to the enormous wealth of statistical materials garnered from his policyholders provided a unique view of this intricate relationship. "The records that pass through my office," Dublin explained, "permit me to observe the forces that tend either to extend or to diminish the life span of" industrial workers. Statistics offered reform-minded public health advocates and profit-conscious insurance executives an important tool for shifting the focus of research into phthisis from the germ to the factory.[46]

The statisticians' methods were used to link industrial dust and tuberculosis. Hoffman noted that "in the group of occupations exposing chiefly to the inhalation of metallic dust" the mortality from consumption was over a third greater than overall mortality among industrial workers. His detailed age-specific analysis of the mortality data led him to conclude that different types of

---

[45] Hoffman, "Mortality from Consumption," 641–43. Thomas Oliver, upon whom Hoffman depended for his British data, had recognized the importance of social and health statistics in unmasking most occupational diseases. In an address delivered in 1913, he began by saying that "little was thought of the relation of disease in employment until statistics came to be collected." See Thomas Oliver, "Dust and Fume, Foes of Industrial Life, Plenary Address," in *Transactions of the Fifteenth International Congress on Hygiene and Demography*, vol. 1 (1913), 303. See also some examples of authors concerned with the influence of industrial dust on workers health: John B. Andrews, "Diseases of Occupation," *American Federationist* 18 (June 1911): 455–57; "Labor Unions' Health Conference," *Charities and the Commons* 23 (October 9, 1909): 69–70; "Permission Given to Build Sanitarium," *Charities and the Commons* 23 (November 6, 1909): 159.

[46] Louis I. Dublin, "Conditions of Industry which Unfavorably Affect the Health of Workers," in Eighth Annual New York State Industrial Conference, *Proceedings* (Albany: J. B. Lyon Co., 1925), 201.

dust created different patterns of mortality from consumption. "Dust from any hard stone (such as flint, granite, sandstone, etc.) is undoubtedly very injurious to the lungs, producing a marked predisposition to phthisis." However, he noted that other dusts produced in coal mines and cement factories did not have the same effect on the work force. While the case for the significance of dust as a cause of pneumoconiosis was building, Hoffman's focus in this 1908 report remained on the impact of industrial dusts on tuberculosis.[47]

The strength of the European labor movement, the existence of workers' social and health insurance plans in Germany, and the Welsh miners' experience in South African gold mines combined to force European and British investigators to recognize a link between work and disease. But clinicians and pathologists in the United States largely ignored this analysis. While Hoffman in his 1908 report was building a powerful case documenting the complexity of the problem of the relationship between phthisis and dust, his analysis reached only a portion of the medical and public health community. For the bulk of the American medical profession, phthisis was still synonymous with tuberculosis. Concerned primarily with the pervasive impact of tuberculosis among individual patients and working with a heterogenous clientele from diverse occupations and backgrounds, doctors saw little significance in this new model of lung disease. Within such important medical journals as the *Journal of the American Medical Association*, the *Boston Medical and Surgical Journal*, and the *Pennsylvania Medical Journal*, there was barely a mention of the new paradigm arising from Hoffman's research and the British literature.

Even the public health profession, which had a greater familiarity with population-based statistics, was slow to understand the significance of the data emerging from the statisticians. In the early years of the century, the profession was isolated from the social turmoil created by the new industrial conditions. Unlike the insurance industry or the social reformers, whose interests and activities forced them to confront the impact of industrialization on the life of the work force, the public health profession was still primarily concerned with the problems of infectious disease among populations in the urban centers and ports. There was little attention to the problems of the industrial worker at the worksite and no attention to dust diseases, which were noninfectious. Industrial hygiene was not even a recognized field. Campaigns against "phossy jaw"—a disfiguring disease caused by the ingestion of phosphorus among matchmakers and others—and for safety in factories and mines were carried out by labor unions, muckrakers, social welfare reformers, and settle-

---

[47] Hoffman, *Mortality from Consumption*, 830, 836. The significance of Hoffman's findings can be understood by looking at the number of workers in the dusty trades. Out of a total work force estimated by Hoffman at 45 million in 1910, trades producing metallic dusts accounted for over 291,000; those producing mineral dusts, 529,000; and mineral extractive industries, 845,000.

ment house workers rather than medical and public health professionals. In an article published in the popular progressive weekly *The Outlook*, one author described the "work that kills," noting particularly that census reports should specify the occupations that expose "the worker to the constant inhalation of irritating dust."[48] In Illinois, the State Factory Inspector pointed to the deleterious effects of dust on workers in the metal polishing, buffing, and grinding trades, and in New York State, the Factory Investigating Commission that was organized following the Triangle Shirtwaist fire held hearings on the dust conditions in a number of upstate industrial concerns.[49]

While individuals in the public health movement such as C.-E.A. Winslow and Alice Hamilton, participated in these larger movements, industrial hygiene was not seen as an intrinsic part of the mandate of public health.[50] It was only in the second decade of the twentieth century, well after Hoffman's first study was published, that the public health profession took official notice of industrial hygiene, and even then it rarely incorporated factory conditions into its campaigns to control tuberculosis and other infectious diseases among the industrial work force.[51] As late as 1922, Hoffman complained that there was too much emphasis on treatment of tuberculosis and too little on prevention. He noted that among the numerous recommendations of the committee on tuberculosis policy of the Conference of State and Provincial Boards of Health

[48] Earl Mayo, "The Work That Kills," *The Outlook* 99 (September 23, 1911): 205.

[49] Oscar F. Nelson, *Twentieth Annual Report of the Chief Factory Inspector of Illinois* (July 1, 1912–June 30, 1913); New York State, *Second Report of the Factory Investigating Commission*, vol. 3, *Minutes of Public Hearings* (1913), 662–711; New York State, *Preliminary Report of the Factory Investigating Commission*, vol. 1, *The Diseases of the Bakers* (1912), 225–33; "How to Prevent Consumption," *The International Wood-Worker* 16 (May 1906): 137–139; Shelby M. Harrison, "Second National Conference on Industrial Diseases," *Survey* 28 (June 15, 1912): 448–51; Frederick L. Hoffman, "Industrial Diseases in America," *American Labor Legislation Review* 1 (1911): 35–39; Frederick L. Hoffman, "Legal Protection from Injurious Dusts," *American Labor Legislation Review* 1 (June 1911): 110–12; Frederick L. Hoffman, *Problem and Extent of Industrial Diseases*, American Association of Labor Legislation, Publication No. 10, 1910, 35–51.

[50] C.-E.A. Winslow, "Occupational Disease and Economic Waste," *Atlantic* 103 (May 1909): 679.

[51] In the 1910s, a series of reports and studies was published by the U.S. Public Health Service and state departments of health and labor documenting the problem of dust, tuberculosis, and their relationship to work. See U.S. Treasury Department, Public Health Service, *Tuberculosis among Industrial Workers, Public Health Bulletin No. 73*, March 1916; U.S. Department of Labor, Working Conditions Service, *Preliminary Report on Mortality from Tuberculosis in Dusty Trades* (Washington, D.C.: Government Printing Office, 1919); "The Hazards to Health from Industrial Dusts," *Pennsylvania Labor and Industry Department Monthly Bulletin* 3 (February 1916): 4–9; George L. Apfelbach, "The Dusty Trades," in *Twenty-fourth Annual Report of the Chief State Factory Inspector of Illinois* (July 1, 1916–June 30, 1917), 75–77; Robert Northrup, "Development in the Removal of Dust, Fumes and Gases," in *Proceedings of the Industrial Safety Congress of New York State*, vol. 4 (1919), 206–18; U.S. Department of Labor, Bureau of Labor Statistics, *Bulletin No. 207, Causes of Death by Occupation*, March 1917.

in 1919, "there is not a single reference to the dust problem. . . . Until the industrial aspects of the disease, and particularly the dust question, are more clearly realized, there is little hope of a reduction of tuberculosis frequency among industrial workers."[52] Hoffman, the statistician, challenged the prevalent assumptions of the new public health workers who maintained that "to control tuberculosis, it was not necessary to improve the living conditions of the one hundred million people in the United States, only to prevent the 200,000 active tuberculosis cases from infecting others."[53]

It is only in 1915 that the mainstream journals and publications in public health began to accept interpretations promoted by the statisticians and social reformers. As the United States became more involved in supplying European combatants with munitions and matériel after the outbreak of World War I, the U.S. Public Health Service was first granted authority to investigate "occupational diseases and the relation of occupations to disease" and organized a Section of Industrial Hygiene and Sanitation. Shortly thereafter, the American Public Health Association formed its own section of Industrial Hygiene.[54] By the end of the Progressive Era, officers in the U.S. Public Health Service were increasingly struck by the importance of the workplace, in addition to the home, as a major predisposing factor affecting workers' health. In a major study of health insurance conducted by two senior U.S. Public Health Service officials, B. S. Warren and Edgar Sydenstricker, the Service concluded that "there is no longer any doubt that modern industry is responsible for a considerable proportion of workingmen's physical ills."[55] In their study they cited statistics developed by Lee Frankl of Metropolitan Life that illustrated the problems workers in silica dust industries were experiencing. In terms of lost days of work due to illness, laborers in foundries, quarries, and machine shops had a sickness rate of between twelve and fourteen days per year, in contrast to clerks, bookkeepers, and butchers, who were out sick between four and six days per year.[56] A few of the state departments of health took an active and sustained interest in occupational diseases, most notably that of Ohio under the leadership of Emery R. Hayhurst. In a massive study of industrial hygiene

[52] Frederick L. Hoffman, *The Problem of Dust Phthisis in the Granite-Stone Industry*, U.S. Department of Labor, Bureau of Labor Statistics, *Bulletin No. 293* (Washington, D.C.: Government Printing Office, 1922), 6.

[53] Fee, *Disease and Discovery*, 20–21.

[54] J. W. Schereshewsky, "Industrial Hygiene," *Public Health Reports* 30 (October 1, 1915): 2928; W. S. Bean, "The Role of the Federal Government in Promoting Industrial Hygiene," *American Journal of Public Health* 15 (July 1925): 626; David Rosner, "American Public Health Association," in P. Romanofsky, ed., *Social Service Organizations*, vol. 1 (Westport, Conn.: Greenwood Press, 1978), 128.

[55] B.S. Warren and Edgar Sydenstricker, *Health Insurance, Its Relation to the Public Health*, U.S. Treasury Department, Public Health Service, *Public Health Bulletin No. 76* (Washington, D.C.: Government Printing Office, 1916), 8.

[56] *Ibid.*, 13.

in Ohio published in 1915, Hayhurst pointed to the problem of dust in producing pneumoconioses, independent of tuberculosis. Citing the dangers of iron dust, coal dust, cotton dust, and silica dust, Hayhurst drew on Hoffman and Oliver to conclude that these dusts produced a fibrosis that resulted "in the end, in a condition called *phthisis*, which is usually complicated by the presence of the *bacillus tuberculosis*."[57]

The Acceptance of Silicosis as a Separate Disease

Although the term *silicosis* was not generally used in the United States until 1917, the recognition of this as a separate and distinct condition had slowly gained acceptance following the publication of an article identifying silica dust as the cause of the fibroid form of phthisis in 1900 in the *Journal of the American Medical Association*. Reporting on the experience of one Nevada gold-milling operation that had recently introduced new mechanical milling techniques, William Winthrop Betts told of the extraordinary death rates from "chalicosus pulmonum" that had been "induced by stone dust."[58] The studies of British workers in South African gold mines attracted widespread attention to the devastating effects of industrial dusts and specifically silicosis on the health of the work force. Researchers such as Edgar Collis, J. S. Haldane, and the Miners' Phthisis Commission in South Africa illustrated that not all dusts resulted in tuberculosis and that some dusts, particularly silica, could cause serious lung disease in their own right. Shortly after the Boer War, silicosis gained wider public notice as English miners who had worked in the South African mines returned to Great Britain. Thomas Oliver, the authoritative British expert on occupational disease, described the fate of "young miners in the bloom of health." After working in the South African gold fields for only a few years, they "returned to Northumberland and elsewhere broken in health."[59] Because of the unusually hard nature of the rock from which gold

[57] Emery R. Hayhurst, *Industrial Health Hazards and Occupational Diseases in Ohio* (Columbus: Ohio State Board of Health, February 1915), 18. We would like to thank Saul Benison for providing us with this citation. For an earlier study, see Emery R. Hayhurst, *Consumption and Preventable Deaths in American Occupations*, (Columbus: F. J. Heer Printing Company, 1914), 10, which stated: "Consumption is the principal terminal occupational disease. . . . Conservatively put, over 50 per cent of all deaths among occupied persons are preventable. This amounts to about a quarter of a million lives a year in the United States."

[58] William Winthrop Betts, "Chalicosis Pulmonum or Chronic Interstitial Pneumonia Induced by Stone Dust," *JAMA* 34 (January 13, 1900): 70–74. See also Daniel E. Banks, "Silicosis Epidemic Reported in 1900," *JAMA* 251 (January 13, 1984): 217.

[59] Thomas Oliver, *Diseases of Occupation*, 279, quoted in George S. Rice, "Historical Review of Silicosis," in Edwin Higgins et al., eds., *Siliceous Dust in Relation to Pulmonary Disease among Miners in the Joplin District, Missouri*, U.S. Bureau of Mines, *Bulletin No. 132* (Washington, D.C.: Government Printing Office, 1917), 84–85. In 1902, the British government ap-

ore was extracted, the use of dry drilling and blasting created hazards for South African workers and their overseers.

In 1902, the British appointed a commission to study the nature and prevalence of lung diseases in the mines. One of the commission's clearest pathological findings was that victims of Rand miners' phthisis, as it was called, were not suffering from tuberculosis. The commission concluded that it was "in the first instance a purely local affection of the lungs, the result of irritation by dust, and without tubercle." In contrast to tuberculosis victims, there was "neither the rise of temperature nor the evening sweating that are present in tuberculosis phthisis, and 'blood spitting' is an extremely rare event." The report continued by noting the distinctions between tuberculosis and this new form of phthisis: "So markedly absent is expectoration in uncomplicated cases that it is difficult to obtain sputum for bacteriological examination."[60] In 1907 and again in 1911, new South African commissions further documented the extent of gold miners' phthisis. By 1912, a new commission had concluded that "all true cases of miners' phthisis are thus primarily cases of silicosis."[61]

Throughout the early decades of the century, the desire to differentiate tuberculosis from fibroid phthisis was frustrated by the problems associated with new medical technologies, which often provided compromised information to interested investigators. By the early 1900s, the invention of the x-ray combined with the development of the tuberculin test and bacterial analysis of sputum could provide evidence for distinguishing between infectious and fibroid forms of phthisis: "Less than a year after William Conrad Roentgen . . . had discovered [x-]rays in 1895, Francis H. Williams of the Massachusetts General Hospital demonstrated x-ray films of patients' chests."[62] Over the course of the first two decades of the century, the tuberculin test was gradually introduced as a tool for distinguishing those exposed to the bacillus and those not exposed. However, even with the improvements in technology, differential diagnosis of these lung conditions was fraught with uncertainty. X-ray readings were an inexact science at best. As late as 1941, textbooks noted the difficulty in distinguishing silicosis from tuberculosis by use of x-rays, even in conjunction with other diagnostic tools. "If there have been no previous films of the patient's chest," remarked Holmes and Ruggles in their standard text *Roentgen Interpretation*, "it may be very difficult, after a frank tubercu-

---

pointed a commission, which reported the widespread existence of a disease that sometimes mimicked tuberculosis but was caused solely by the dust of the mines. In England itself, only two years later, J. S. Haldane conducted a study of Cornish miners, discovering similar symptoms of silicosis among them as well.

[60] Report of the South Africa Miners' Phthisis Commission as quoted in Rice, "Historical Review of Silicosis," 85.

[61] "Report of a Commission on Miners' Phthisis and Pulmonary Tuberculosis, Pretoria, 1912," quoted in Rice, "Historical Review of Silicosis," 88.

[62] Harry F. Dowling, *Fighting Infection* (Cambridge: Harvard University Press, 1977), 79.

losis with cavitation has developed in such an individual, to determine how much of the picture is fibrous tuberculosis and how much is a preexisting silicosis."[63] Others noted the "difficulties of diagnosing tuberculosis in the presence of silicosis" and that "the incidence of tuberculosis appears to vary considerably depending on methods used by different investigators."[64] Furthermore, the extraordinary exposure of the general population to tuberculosis made the tuberculin test little more than a confirmation of an individual's presence in a society plagued by tuberculosis.[65] Also, work histories were never routinely taken, and even when they were, their interpretation depended upon a medical profession that was largely unaware of the issue of pneumoconiosis.[66]

The differentiation of tuberculosis and silicosis was established in the United States in spite of the weaknesses of the new technologies. The European and South African studies together with the statistical materials about mortality of metal miners in the United States aroused so much concern that in 1911 the U.S. Public Health Service and the Bureau of Mines initiated an investigation of the lung diseases of metal miners. This effort resulted in the identification of silicosis as a major health hazard for metal miners and other industrial workers. Frederick Hoffman had intended to conduct a study for the Prudential but, pressed by other demands on his time, was unable to do so. He therefore pushed for "the National Association for the Study and Prevention of Tuberculosis to pass a resolution suggesting to the Federal Government an investigation into the health of metal miners."[67] Although the assistant surgeon general, S. C. Hotchkiss, died before completing his work,[68] in 1912 he published a preliminary report of his examination of the health risks in the Colorado mines, noting that "the inhalation of dust, known as silicosis among metal miners and as anthrocosis among coal miners" was a constant hazard. He found that it was "difficult to ascertain the actual amount of miners' phthisis."[69]

In 1914, two federal agencies, the U.S. Public Health Service and the

---

[63] George W. Holmes and Howard E. Ruggles, *Roentgen Interpretation*, 6th ed. (Philadelphia: Lea and Febiger, 1941), 254.

[64] Leonard Greenburg, "The Incidence and Causation of Tuberculosis in the Foundry Industry," in *Tuberculosis in Industry, Symposium on Silicosis* (Saranac Laboratory, June 1941), 264.

[65] Barbara Rosenkrantz, Introduction, in Rene Dubos and Jean Dubos, *The White Plague, Tuberculosis, Man, and Society* (1952; reprint, New Brunswick, N.J.: Rutgers University Press, 1987).

[66] Charles L. Minor, "Symptomotology of Pulmonary Tuberculosis," in Arnold C. Klebs, ed., *Tuberculosis* (New York: D. Appleton and Co., 1909), 150.

[67] "Annual Report of the Statistician's Department for 1911," Frederick L. Hoffman Papers, Box 1, Folder 3, Columbia University Manuscripts Division.

[68] Rice, "Historical Review of Silicosis," 97–98.

[69] S. C. Hotchkiss, "Occupational Diseases in the Mining Industry," *American Labor Legislation Review* 2 (1912): 131–39.

Bureau of Mines, initiated the first detailed community study of the disease that would prove to be a landmark in the discovery of chronic industrial disease. Conducted by Anthony J. Lanza who would become a major figure in industrial hygiene in the years to come, the study focused on the Tri-State lead- and zinc-mining region of Missouri, Kansas, and Oklahoma. Although public health workers had accepted that heavy metal poisoning could produce chronic diseases, the significance of Lanza's study was that he documented that symptoms from toxic exposures could and did occur years and sometimes decades afterwards. This extremely long period between exposure and disease added a whole new dimension to the understanding of chronic disease in general and industrial lung disease in particular. Coming during the heady period when research scientists had accepted the primacy of bacteriological agents as the cause of disease, this new perspective brought into question many of the assumptions that then governed medical science. The accepted methodology relied on laboratory procedures to discover the germ or specific agent that created disease symptoms. By identifying the germ or poison in the blood, urine, or sputum, diagnosis could be exact and conclusive, even without corroborating evidence from patients themselves. But Lanza relied on a constellation of indirect indicators, which had to substitute for the seeming precision of the laboratory. To diagnose silicosis or other occupational lung diseases, he depended upon the testimony of the worker that he or she had been employed in a dusty trade, and used x-rays and evidence of shortness of breath. Unless a patient died and an autopsy was performed, it was impossible to develop the direct evidence that the bacteriological revolution had trained physicians to depend upon for a diagnosis.

The methods of the occupational diagnostician diverged even further from those of the clinical medical model in that the long latency period between exposure and symptoms clouded the significance of the victim's work history. Only in industrial communities where the population depended upon a single dusty trade could a direct relationship be drawn between a particular dust and disease. This new model of diagnosis of chronic disease clashed with the bacteriological model of public health and medical personnel. In subsequent decades of the twentieth century, infectious disease subsided as the major health threat to the American population, and chronic disease increased in significance. And the reluctance of many in the profession to incorporate chronic conditions of long latency into their model became problematic for medicine.

Given the tendency within the public health community to accept the bacteriological perspective, it is not surprising that Lanza began his study by documenting the extraordinarily high rates of tuberculosis among miners and their families.[70] In Jasper County, Missouri, the death rate from this disease was

---

[70] A. J. Lanza and Edwin Higgins, eds., *Pulmonary Disease among Miners in the Joplin District, Missouri, and Its Relation to the Rock-Dust in the Mines; A Preliminary Report*, U.S. Bu-

over 200 per 100,000 residents in 1912, which was substantially higher than anywhere else in the state. By 1913 the rate would rise to 229 per 100,000. But at the same time, Lanza showed that there was also a high incidence of nontubercular lung disease, which he initially called miners' consumption: "It is possible for a miner to have his lungs injured by rock dust, producing a condition that is not tuberculosis." Its symptoms were thickened and inelastic lung tissue, which led to shortness of breath, constant cough, lessened working ability, and loss of weight. He noted the close relationship between miner's "con" and tuberculosis and remarked on the role that tuberculosis played in accelerating the death of workers with "the con":[71] "While the cause of miners' consumption is found entirely in the underground work of the miners," it was "the poor and often wretched conditions under which so many live, and the presence of tuberculosis foci" that reduced workers' "vitality and resistance, on the one hand, and [led] directly to increase their chances of tuberculosis infection on the other."[72] Using a public health model that stressed the relationship between poor living conditions and infectious disease, the Public Health Service report emphasized the importance of poor living conditions as the factor responsible for the high rate of tuberculosis.[73]

reau of Mines Technical Paper No. 105 (Washington, D.C.: Government Printing Office, 1915), 37, 40. See also A. J. Lanza, "Prevention of Illness among Employees in Mines," *Transactions of the American Institute of Mining Engineers*, American Association for Labor Legislation Manuscripts, Industrial and Labor Relations Archives, Cornell University, Pamphlet Collection, Occupational Diseases, 1919–1922. During this period, others began to note that lung disease was "even more important than accidents [in decreasing the life span of workers] and is responsible for a loss of between eighteen months and two years in the longevity of workers. . . . When we consider those occupations which have long been associated with an unusually high incidence of tuberculosis we find a mortality eight, ten and even twelve times the rate for farmers, who hardly ever suffer from tuberculosis as a result of their occupation." See Louis I. Dublin, "Conditions of Industry which Unfavorably Affect the Health of Workers," in *Eighth Annual New York State Industrial Conference Proceedings* (Albany: J. B. Lyon Co., 1925), 203.

[71] A.J. Lanza, *Miners Consumption*, U.S. Treasury Department, Public Health Service, *Public Health Bulletin No. 85* (Washington, D.C.: Government Printing Office, 1917), 25, 28.

[72] Lanza, *Miners Consumption*, 25, 28. See also Lanza and Higgins, *Pulmonary Disease*, 36–37.

[73] By the end of the decade, many public health officials fundamentally accepted Hoffman's formulation, noting that tuberculosis among many groups of workers was brought on by the occupational hazard of silicosis. A critical study carried out by the U.S. Public Health Service in 1929 noted exactly the same epidemiological data as did Hoffman: Workers in the granite industry were experiencing a tuberculosis rate far in excess of that of the general population, and the disease seemed to be rising for these workers, while the rate for the general population appeared to be on a decline. The study explained this phenomena much as had Hoffman eight years earlier. Furthermore, it noted "the rapid rise in mortality from tuberculosis among granite cutters since the adoption of the hand pneumatic hammer" thereby acknowledging for the first time the relationship between changing work technology and the creation of an epidemic of an organic disease, tuberculosis. Finally, it concluded that tuberculosis usually manifested itself twenty years after exposure to silica dust. Even after workers were removed from the dusty workplace, silicosis and tuberculosis continued to develop. It warned that "even if adequate local exhaust ventilation were

The study exposed the horrendous toll of nontubercular lung diseases.[74] The report noted that of the approximately 9,000 workers employed in the area, about 30 percent had some form of silicosis. Further, it defined three stages of the disease, with the first being characterized by "slight or moderate dyspnea [shortness of breath] on exertion" and the third marked by total or very severe disability. It graphically described the suffering that many of the miners experienced as the disease progressed: "If we can imagine a man with his chest bound with transparent adhesive plaster, we can form a mental picture of how useless were the efforts at deep inhalation made by these patients."[75]

Lanza examined 720 miners. Of these, 120 were diagnosed as having first-stage silicosis. Their average age was only 31 years, and they had been employed in the mines only 3½ to 4½ years on average. The Service investigators found another 142 men suffering from second-stage silicosis. This group had averaged 11.6 years on the job and were, on the average, 32.7 years old. The group in the third and most serious stage numbered 68, and their average age was 37.8 years; they had been working on average 15.9 years as miners.[76] The report concluded that "five years' steady work with exposure to flint dust is fairly certain to find the miner in at least the first stage of silicosis."[77] The study also included a house-to-house survey to obtain information on miners who had already died. It concluded that "9.6 years . . . may be taken as the average expectancy of life in a miner with silicosis, dating from the time he commenced hard-rock mining."[78] The report summarized the horrible conditions of work and life in an area that later would be called "a virtual hellhole."[79] Not only were workers suffering from silicosis, but they and their families had an extraordinarily high rate of tuberculosis, due to the wretched working conditions. Of the sample of 720 miners, the Service found that over 100 had both silicosis and tuberculosis, and 39 had uncomplicated tuberculo-

---

immediately provided . . . it seems evident that the deaths from tuberculosis among workers who have used the hand pneumatic hammer for a long period would continue to occur and that perhaps the death rate would rise much beyond its present level." A. E. Russell, R. H. Britten, L. R. Thompson, and J. J. Bloomfield, *The Health of Workers in Dusty Trades, II. Exposure to Silica Dust (Granite Industry)*, U.S. Public Health Service, *Public Health Bulletin No. 187* (Washington, D.C.: Government Printing Office, 1929), 205–06; see also Oscar A. Sander, *A Practical Discussion of the Silicosis Problem*, U.S. Department of Labor, Division of Labor Standards *Bulletin No. 10* (Washington, D.C.: Government Printing Office, 1936), 253.

[74] Anthony Lanza, "Physiological Effects of Siliceous Dust on the Miners of the Joplin District," in U.S. Bureau of Mines, *Bulletin No. 132* (Washington, D.C.: Government Printing Office, 1917), 65.

[75] Lanza, "Physiological Effects," 8–9.

[76] Lanza, "Physiological Effects," 15–21.

[77] Lanza, "Physiological Effects," 25.

[78] Lanza, "Physiological Effects," 27.

[79] Quoted in Verne Zimmer to Secretary of Labor Frances Perkins, Memorandum, October 25, 1939, National Archives, Record Group 100, Records of the Division of Labor Standards, 7-0-6-13.

sis.[80] At the same time that the federal government was studying the Tri-State region, Lanza and Daniel Harrington were also investigating the health of metal miners in Butte, Montana. In 1916, they commenced a study of this community, which confirmed the frightening findings of the studies of the Tri-State region.[81] In one study of the death rates of metal miners in a number of states, including Missouri, R. R. Sayers of the Bureau of Mines documented the enormous toll of silicosis and tuberculosis. Between 1917 and 1920, these two diseases combined to claim nearly 2,000 of every 100,000 people in the state. This compared with Colorado, another state with an important mining industry, where these two diseases claimed only 750 deaths for every 100,000 residents.[82] By the end of the Progressive Era, researchers accepted that silica created a serious chronic lung disease for significant groups of workers in critical American industries.[83]

Lanza's work studies were carried out among industrial workers living in the most horrendous conditions in the country. He therefore assumed that the high rate of tuberculosis among metal miners and their families was primarily caused by their wretched living conditions and only secondarily by the weakened conditions of miners' fibrotic lungs. Although he recognized the importance of industrial conditions in producing the new disease of silicosis, he continued to rely on the bacteriological model to account for the elevated rates of tuberculosis. Frederick Hoffman, however, shattered this easy assumption in his work among granite cutters in Barre, Vermont.

The general decline of tuberculosis rates in the decades around the turn of the century unmasked for Hoffman the special nature of silicosis. Silicosis predisposed workers to tuberculosis even in the absence of poor living conditions. Throughout most of the nineteenth century, the death rate from consumption fluctuated between 30 and 40 per 10,000 population. In Massachusetts, at the end of the Civil War consumption accounted for 35 deaths for every 10,000 people in the state. Beginning in the mid-1880s, the death rate from consumption began to decline rapidly. By the beginning of the twentieth century, there were only 18.5 deaths from consumption for every 10,000 people.[84] In the country generally, the death rate also declined, from 19.5 per

[80] Lanza, "Physiological Effects," 28.

[81] Daniel Harrington and A. J. Lanza, "Miners' Consumption in the Mines of Butte, Montana," in U.S. Bureau of Mines Technical Paper No. 260 (Washington, D.C.: Government Printing Office, 1921).

[82] R. R. Sayers, "Silicosis among Miners," in U.S. Bureau of Mines Technical Paper 372 (Washington, D.C.: Government Printing Office, 1925), 5.

[83] See Frederick Hoffman, *Mortality from Respiratory Diseases in Dusty Trades*, U.S. Department of Labor, Bureau of Labor Statistics, *Bulletin No. 231* (Washington, D.C.: Government Printing Office, 1918), 33–34.

[84] Lester C. Miller, "The Decrease in the Death Rate of Consumption," *Boston Medical and Surgical Journal* 151 (December 22, 1904): 679.

10,000 in 1900 to 9.7 in 1921.[85] In Barre, Vermont, however, the death rate from pulmonary tuberculosis was, as late as 1919, over 23.3 per 10,000 persons, compared with 9 per 10,000 for the rest of the state, despite the relatively healthful living conditions of the granite workers.[86]

Granite Cutters and the Unmasking of the
Industrial Source of Tuberculosis

Hoffman's uncovering of the intricate relationship between tuberculosis and silicosis illustrates the interaction of social movements and professional analysis. It was the long history of changing work conditions and labor unrest that brought Hoffman to the area in the first place and alerted him to the impact of changing work processes on the health of the work force.[87]

In the first two decades of the twentieth century, steam-driven equipment replaced hand drills and sledgehammers in granite quarries throughout the nation. These quarries produced the large blocks of granite that would be chipped, carved, and crafted into the ornamental stone used for building facades, monuments and gravestones, columns, mantlepieces, doorsteps, and hearthstones. From deep, cavernous pits in the earth's surface, workers would cut giant blocks of stone, which would be hoisted, loaded, and transported to the carving sheds, where the artisans and operatives would cut, shape, and engrave the stone. In these sheds, power tools were introduced in the late nineteenth century, leading to increased production, speedups, dust, disease,[88]

[85] U.S. Bureau of Census, *Historical Statistics of the United States, Colonial Times to 1957* (Washington, D.C.: Government Printing Office, 1960), 26.

[86] Hoffman to David Lyman, President, National Tuberculosis Association, May 12, 1919, quoted in Frederick Hoffman, *Second Preliminary Report of Committee on Mortality from Tuberculosis in Dusty Trades* (New York: National Tuberculosis Association, 1919), 15, 21.

[87] "Workmen of Italian, Scotch and Spanish descent constitute 74.6 per cent of the granite cutters of the Barre district." Frederick L. Hoffman, *The Problem of Dust Phthisis in the Granite-Stone Industry*, U.S. Department of Labor, Bureau of Labor Statistics, *Bulletin No. 293* (Washington, D.C.: Government Printing Office, 1922), 49. See also Paul Demers, "Labor and the Social Relations of the Granite Industry in Barre" (unpublished paper, Goddard College, 1974); Bernard Sanders, "Vermont Labor Agitator," *Labor History* 15 (Spring 1974): 261–63. See Linda Bryder, "Tuberculosis, Silicosis, and the Slate Industry in North Wales, 1927–1939," in Paul Weindling, ed., *The Social History of Occupational Health* (London: Croom Helm, 1985), 108–26, for a discussion of the tuberculosis—silicosis relationship in Great Britain.

[88] Bedford Stone Club Auxiliary to J. W. Schereschewsky, November 1, 1917, National Archives, Record Group 90, Records of the Public Health Service; see also Schereschewsky to Surgeon General, November 9, 1917, National Archives, Record Group 90, where Schereschewsky writes that "the use of these tools is accompanied by a shower of fine siliceous dust particles, which have an injurious effect on the lungs if inhaled continuously over a protracted period." See also David Edsall to Surgeon General Rupert Blue, January 31, 1918, National Archives, Record Group 90.

and, ultimately, labor unrest.[89] In the first decade of the twentieth century, the *Granite Cutters Journal*, the publication of the granite workers' union, contained numerous articles about "stone cutters' consumption," closely linking its increase to the recent introduction of power tools and the continuing problem of poor ventilation in the sheds. In contrast to prevalent medical opinion in the early years of the century, which emphasized the bacterial origins of consumption, for granite cutters, it was the dust in the sheds where the granite was cut that was at the root of the scourge. In July 1905, an article "About The Dust Question" stressed the importance of better ventilation in the sheds: "The constant breathing of stone dust is unquestionably highly detrimental to health and it should be incumbent upon employers to install the means of reducing such risks to a minimum."[90] Toward the end of the first decade of the century, it was apparent to all that "granite cutters' consumption" was a serious threat to the health of all workers in the sheds. During the course of the next year, the workers of the area had decided that conditions in the sheds were reason for action. During the summer, when the sheds were open, the use of the pneumatic tools that had been introduced over the course of the past decade was tolerable. But during the winter months, when the windows were closed in the sheds in order to conserve heat, dust was everywhere. The workers in Northfield, a granite center about ten miles from Barre, voted in November 1909 that they would not use the pneumatic tool until the warmer weather, May 1, 1910, when the sheds would be opened up and ventilated. In response, the owners fired and locked out the workers, leading to a much wider job action in the granite sheds throughout the Barre area.[91] The specific demand of the workers was that use of pneumatic tools be eliminated during the winter months and that efforts be made to keep the shed free of dust at all times.[92] An agreement reached in February provided for an immediate pay increase and for the pneumatic tools not to be used until April 1. Employers had until June 1 to install dust removal equipment or the tool was to be permanently retired. Just before the June 1st deadline, the Barre granite cutters wrote to the national union that "it will be good-bye to the notorious trouble-making disease-breeding, hand surfacer tomorrow, unless properly equipped with suction fan or other device to remove the dust. . . . The hand surfacer is only a man killer at

[89] Andrew D. Hosey, Victoria M. Trasko, and Henry B. Ashe, *Control of Silicosis in Vermont Granite Industry*, Progress Report, U.S. Department of Health, Education and Welfare, Public Health Service (Washington, D.C.: Government Printing Office, 1958), 5–7.

[90] "About the Dust Question," *Granite Cutters' Journal* 29 (July 1905): 1. See also Letter to the Editor, *ibid.* (January 1905): 8; James McAdam, Note, *ibid.* (June 1905): 1; Letter to Editor, *ibid.* 30 (March 1906): 3; and "Fighting Tuberculosis," *ibid.* (September 1906): 1, which stated: "All are agreed that there is too much dust in the stone shed and everyone, employers as well as workmen, wish the evil remedied."

[91] Paul Demers, "Labor and the Social Relations of the Granite Industry in Barre" (unpublished paper, Goddard College, 1974), 54–63.

[92] Correspondence, *Granite Cutters' Journal* 34 (April 1910): 7.

best, and the scrap heap where many of them will be consigned to is a fitting end for all such inventions."[93]

The strike over pneumatic tools was part of a much larger struggle over control of the work process, not only in the granite trade but also in a host of other industries during the late nineteenth and early twentieth century. During the Progressive Era, popular perception of the deleterious effect of changing production processes in a host of industries reinforced epidemiological studies. In a discussion of the axe industry, one commentator described the decreasing time it took different nationalities to recognize its health hazards: "When I came here 40 years ago [1880] I found the victims among the Yankees who had ground some 20 years before. Those could grind 18 or 20 years before having to give it up. The French-Canadians were then grinding. They could work 12 to 16 years. They became frightened off and the Swedes took up the work. They would get the disease in 8 or 10 years. Now the Finns and Polanders are at it, and they last only 3 to 5 years, and the disease is more common among them."[94] As we will see later in the foundry and metal-mining industry, this general conflict, which has been described by David Montgomery and others, was fought out around health and disease as well as around other issues.[95]

The significance of the granite cutters' objections to pneumatic tools as a source of disease and the resultant labor strife surrounding workplace control did not escape investigators. Frederick Hoffman, the noted statistician and vice president of the Prudential Life Insurance Company, began to follow the health experience of these workers shortly following the severe labor unrest among the granite cutters. Hoffman helped organize a study for the U.S. Department of Labor Working Conditions Service on the prevalence of tuberculosis and silicosis, and his preliminary report began with an acknowledgment of the importance of labor in bringing the issue to his attention by quoting from a letter from Walter W. Drayer, general secretary and treasurer of the Journeymen Stone Cutters' Association of North America. In his letter, Drayer noted that during the second decade of the twentieth century there had been an "almost universal installation" of the air hammer in the limestone and granite industries. He went on to detail the devastating effects of the use of this new technology on the health of the workers: "The use of the pneumatic hammer subjects our members to more danger in the contracting of tuberculosis than do the tools of our trade—the mallet and hammer—inasmuch as the vibration or stroke of this hammer is constant, thus emitting a steady stream of this fine dust into the face and nostrils of the operator, while with

[93] Correspondence, *Granite Cutters' Journal* 34 (June 1910): 9.

[94] Quoted in Cary P. McCord, "Grindstones," *Hygeia* 18 (August 1940): 744.

[95] David Montgomery, *The Fall of the House of Labor* (Cambridge: Cambridge University Press, 1987); and Montgomery, *Workers' Control in America* (Cambridge: Cambridge University Press, 1979).

the tools of the trade there was, of course, an interval between the blows which gave the dust some opportunity of being carried away in the air."[96] Hoffman agreed with their assessment about the effect of the introduction of high-speed drills on the health of stonecutters. Those workers who used the pneumatic tools were at considerably higher risk than those who did not: "Surfacing and carving and cutting with pneumatic tools are the most dangerous employments, and the risk is less in polishing, grinding, sawing, and lathe work, most of which is carried on by the wet process." Surfacing, the process by which stone is removed from the ground, was now especially dangerous: "The greatest amount of dust comes from the surfacing machines which are operated with compressed air. The tool is either a large hammer or instrument which presents four smaller separate faces . . . [creating] the finest dust of all." He contrasted the experience of those employing jackhammers—often called "widowmakers" by the workers[97]—in granite quarries with that of other workers who did not employ the new devices. In Aberdeen, Scotland, for example, granite cutters used hand tools, thereby lowering substantially their own exposure to dust and hence nearly eliminating "industrial phthisis." In 1919, while preparing to join in this health investigation of the quarry workers in Barre, Vermont, Alice Hamilton wrote, "There is an interesting dust problem out here [in Barre], so confused with labor difficulties that it is impossible to obtain any impartial information on it."[98]

But research into the health problems of this group revealed an even more troubling aspect. Granite cutters in Vermont and Massachusetts, while experiencing high silicosis rates, rarely died of that disease. Rather, despite the prevalence of silicosis, they died of tuberculosis.[99] Frederick L. Hoffman and

[96] U.S. Department of Labor, Working Conditions Service, *Preliminary Report of Committee on Mortality from Tuberculosis in Dusty Trades* (Washington, D.C.: Government Printing Office, 1919), 13–14. Hoffman continued by quoting the minutes of the committee, where it was generally concluded that the excess mortality from tuberculosis in Vermont was largely due to the introduction of the pneumatic tools. See also Hoffman to Dryden, January 7, 1918, Frederick Hoffman Papers, Folder 22, for Hoffman's urging on Royal Meeker of the Bureau of Labor Statistics the need for such a study.

[97] Script for *Stop Silicosis*, National Archives, Record Group 100, Motion Picture Division, 84–91.

[98] Alice Hamilton to the Chairman, January 19, 1919, quoted in Frederick Hoffman, *Second Preliminary Report of Committee on Mortality from Tuberculosis in Dusty Trades* (New York: National Tuberculosis Association, 1919), 9.

[99] Frederick L. Hoffman, "Problem of Dust Phthisis in the Granite-Stone Industry," *Monthly Labor Review* 15 (September 1922): 178–79; William McFarland, "Silicosis and Tuberculosis among Granite Workers in Barre, Vt.," *Monthly Labor Review* 25 (September 1927): 67–69; Daniel J. Kindel and Emery R. Hayhurst, "Stereoscopic X-Ray Examination of Sandstone Quarry Workers," *American Journal of Public Health* 17 (August 1927): 820–21; A. J. Lanza and Robert J. Lane, "The Prevalence of Silicosis in the General Population and Its Effects upon the Incidence of Tuberculosis," *American Review of Tuberculosis* 29 (January 1934): 8–16; A. E. Russell, R. H. Britten, L. R. Thompson, and J. J. Bloomfield, *The Health of Workers in Dusty Trades,*

Louis Dublin, Hoffman's counterpart at the Metropolitan Life Insurance Company, established as early as 1908 that workers exposed to mineral dusts had high rates of tuberculosis.[100]

But Frederick Hoffman in the early 1920s showed that silicosis alone, in the absence of poor living conditions, was sufficient to lead to elevated rates of tuberculosis. In a study for the Bureau of Labor Statistics of the Department of Labor of the granite stone workers of Vermont, Hoffman identified the factors responsible for their inordinately high tuberculosis rates. He showed that between the late nineteenth century and World War I, there had been an extraordinary rise of tuberculosis among granite cutters at the same time that its prevalence had declined in the broader population. Between 1896 and 1918, granite cutters saw the rate of tuberculosis rise from 257.7 per 100,000 to 953.4 per 100,000 despite a decline among the general population for the same period from 207.5 to 96.4 per 100,000. Despite nearly identical rates in 1896, the granite cutters' rate rose 400 percent, while the general population's declined more than 50 percent. Hoffman took issue with the public health community's perspective, which emphasized poor living conditions as a necessary precondition for tuberculosis, by noting that the granite cutters had among the best living conditions and physical appearance of all industrial workers. He remarked that they lived "under sanitary conditions above the average" and that their "housing conditions . . . are also above the average" of most workers, "so that the possibly unfavorable environmental factors are of decidedly secondary importance." Furthermore, the workers had "a superior physique, indicative of a higher degree of disease resistance." How then could one explain their devastating health experience, especially the excessive deaths due to tuberculosis? Given the favorable general living conditions of the work force, one should expect improved longevity and lowered tuberculosis rates. Hoffman believed that disease was proportionate to the length of time workers

---

II. Exposure to Siliceous Dust (Granite Industry), U.S. Public Health Service, *Public Health Bulletin No. 187* (Washington, D.C.: Government Printing Office, 1929); L. R. Thompson and Rollo H. Britten, "The Silica Dust Hazard in the Granite Cutting Industry," *Journal of Industrial Hygiene* 12 (April 1930): 145–47; Leroy U. Gardner, Edward R. Baldwin, Trudeau Foundation, statement on silicosis [1924], C.-E.A. Winslow Manuscripts, Box 102, Folder 1838, Yale University Archives; James A. Britton, "Silicosis: A Modern Factory Health Hazard," *Journal of Industrial Hygiene* 6 (September 1924): 201–02; Charles Badham, "The International Silicosis Conference Held at Johannesburg, August, 1930," *Journal of Industrial Hygiene* 13 (May 1931): 169–82; "Silicosis in the Abrasive Powder Industry," *American Journal of Public Health* 21 (December 1931): 1390–92; "Industrial Hygiene," *American Journal of Public Health* 22 (July 1932): 762–63; Adelaide Ross Smith, "Silicosis among Rock Drillers, Blasters and Excavators in New York City Based on a Study of 208 Examinations," *Journal of Industrial Hygiene* 9 (February 1929): 37–81; A. J. Lanza, "Occupational Diseases: Their Prevalence and Relative Importance," *Safety Engineering* 67 (May 1934): 212.

[100] Hoffman, *Mortality from Consumption*, 633–875; and Louis Dublin, "Dust and Pulmonary Tuberculosis," *The Survey* 29 (March 22, 1913): 864–65.

were exposed to silica on the job rather than to their exposure to germs at home.[101]

By the mid-1920s, few doubted Hoffman's conclusion that silicosis in and of itself was the primary problem affecting the workers of Barre, Vermont. A slew of investigators from the Public Health Service, Vermont Department of Health, Vermont Industrial Hygiene Division, and the union began exhaustive studies documenting the prevalence of this disease.[102] The Public Health Service and others would continue studying the occurrence of silicosis among granite workers for decades to come,[103] but effective reform of working conditions would not be initiated until the late 1930s, after evidence of excess death among granite workers had become overwhelming (see Table 1), and after a series of crises had affected not only the granite industry but the nation's foundry workers, metal miners, potters, glassblowers, and metal grinders as well. Between 1924 and 1926, the U.S. Public Health Service made "an exhaustive environmental and clinical study in Barre," which attempted to set limits for dust exposure in the sheds. A later Public Health Service report noted that "at that time practically every pneumatic tool operator could be expected to develop the disease after 15 years of exposure to granite dust." In 1937–1938, the Public Health Service returned to Barre and confirmed its earlier findings. This was not surprising because the Industrial Hygiene Division of the Vermont Department of Health had found "little, if any, improvement in the dustiness of the sheds up to that time."[104]

[101] Frederick L. Hoffman, *The Problem of Dust Phthisis in the Granite-Stone Industry*, U.S. Department of Labor, Bureau of Labor Statistics, *Bulletin No. 293* (Washington, D.C.: Government Printing Office, 1922), 1. See also Frederick L. Hoffman, "Problem of Dust Phthisis in the Granite-Stone Industry," *Monthly Labor Review* 15 (September 1922): 178–79; U.S. Bureau of Mines, "Reports of Investigations" (February 1921, mimeo, Serial No. 2213).

[102] A. E. Russell, R. H. Britten, L. R. Thompson, and J. J. Bloomfield, *The Health of Workers in Dusty Trades, II. Exposure to Siliceous Dust (Granite Industry)*, U.S. Public Health Service, *Bulletin No. 187* (Washington, D.C.: Government Printing Office, 1929); William McFarland, "Silicosis and Tuberculosis as Seen in the Granite Workers in Barre, Vt.," *Journal of Industrial Hygiene* 9 (August 1927): 315–30.

[103] Edward J. Rogers, "Silicosis or Pneumoconiosis in Vermont Granite Cutters and Slate Workers," *New England Journal of Medicine* 207 (August 4, 1932): 203–08; Edward C. J. Urban, "Ventilation in the Granite Industry," *Journal of Industrial Hygiene and Toxicology* 21 (March 1939): 57–66; Louis Benson, "Pulmonary Tuberculosis in Granite and Marble Workers of Vermont," in *Symposium on Silicosis in Industry* (Saranac Laboratories, 1941), 279–89; Albert E. Russell, "The Health of Workers in Dusty Trades, VII. Restudy of a Group of Granite Workers," in Federal Security Agency, U.S. Public Health Service, *Bulletin No. 269* (Washington, D.C.: Government Printing Office, 1941).

[104] Andrew D. Hosey, Harry B. Ashe, and Victoria M. Trasko, *Control of Silicosis in Vermont Granite Industry* (U.S. Department of Health, Education and Welfare, Public Health Service, 1958), x. See also D. C. Jarvis, "The Upper Respiratory Tract in Granite Dust Inhalation," *Ann. Otol. and Rhinol. and Laryngol.* 32 (June 1923): 405–12; D. C. Jarvis, "A Roentgen Study of Dust Inhalation in the Granite Industry," *American Journal of Roentgenology*, n.s., 8 (May

TABLE 1
Percentage of Deaths from Tuberculosis

Age Group	Granite Workers	All Males
20–29	20.0	30.1
30–39	37.5	23.8
40–49	53.7	14.8
50–59	45.6	10.4
60–69	30.9	3.3
70 and over	8.4	0.8
Total	34.4	7.6

Source: Commonwealth of Massachusetts, *Report to the General Court of the Special Industrial Disease Commission* (Boston: Wright and Potter Co., 1934), 90, 91.

Industrial Hygiene in the 1920s

To the extent that silicosis was seen as an important public health problem, it was that it predisposed its victims to tuberculosis. But physicians, insurance statisticians, workers and public health officials all saw these conditions from very different perspectives. Tuberculosis, particularly, came to take on different meanings for all the different groups who played a role in defining it. For many clinicians, tuberculosis was understood to be produced by the bacillus; for some Progressive Era public health workers, the disease was linked to poor living conditions; laborers used the term *tuberculosis* to denote a wide variety of industry-related lung conditions.

In the 1920s, a new field emerged that integrated several different traditions and perspectives. Industrial hygiene assumed a varied character in the 1920s that reflected the various traditions from which it arose during the Progressive Era. Industrial hygienists counted among their number public health and urban reformers, the new medical and public health bench scientists and professionals, and, finally, physicians, engineers, and other personnel employed by industry. The reformers emphasized working conditions, wages, and hours in their fight for better health. The newer generation of industrial hygienists were primarily physicians whose training led them to see industrial disease in much narrower terms. This group emphasized personal hygiene, the laboratory, and identification of specific toxins or germs in their attempt to improve workers' health. The third group, drawn from the ranks of company doctors, industrial

1921): 248–58; D. C. Jarvis, "A Conception of Chest X-Ray Densities Based on a Study of Granite Dust Inhalation," *American Journal of Roentgenology*, n.s., 9 (May 1922): 226–34.

engineers, and newly emerging industrial welfare departments, also tended to emphasize individual responsibility and susceptibility rather than corporate or societal factors in their analysis. Throughout the book we will explore how these different perspectives interacted in defining the disease of silicosis. During the 1920s, all three groups agreed that tuberculosis was the major problem affecting the industrial work force. But even here, there were differing interpretations of what the problem of tuberculosis really was. Progressive public health workers, such as Alice Hamilton and C.-E.A. Winslow believed that tuberculosis was closely related to poor working conditions. Industry spokespeople and the new group of industrial hygienists saw tuberculosis as a problem of poor personal hygiene and unhygienic living conditions. Because tuberculosis disabled the work force, it had become a significant problem for industry, accentuating labor shortages created by the immigration restriction acts of 1921 and 1924.

The chief of the Department of Safety of the Westinghouse Electric and Manufacturing Company exemplified the corporate viewpoint by complaining that tuberculosis caused absenteeism at the plant.[105] Emery R. Hayhurst, perhaps the foremost exponent of the new public health professionals, represented the conflicting approaches to industrial hygiene that became apparent in the 1920s. Earlier, during the Progressive Era, he had conducted a massive survey of industrial conditions in Ohio that began by pointing out that industrial diseases were produced by the "attempted or forced adaptations to unnatural environments" of which the modern factory was the most obvious symbol. Yet, in the 1920s, in his discussion of industry and tuberculosis, he emphasized the positive uses to which the factory could be put. The factory could be used by epidemiologists to identify the sick worker and play a useful public health service by introducing preemployment physicals, periodic screening and tracking services. Rather than see the industrial establishment as a source of the high rates of tuberculosis as he did in his earlier years, his new approach was to see the factory as an extension of the public health clinic, where diseased workers could be identified and treated.[106] Most of those who considered themselves to be public health scientists wanted to use the factory for disease treatment and prevention despite the fact that many workers "considered themselves well and had never had a sick day in their lives." For these representatives of the growing industrial hygiene movement, medical and

---

[105] "Industries and Tuberculosis," *American Journal of Public Health* 17 (April 1927): 410.

[106] "Tuberculosis as an Industrial Health Problem," *Monthly Labor Review* 22 (April 1926): 880–82, which stated: "The question is not one of tracing industrial tuberculosis back from the dispensary to the workplace, but preferably one of tracing industrial and personal health hazards forward into health complaints and nipping both before tuberculosis develops." See also "The Greatest Toll of Tuberculosis is from Men in Industry," *American Journal of Public Health* 17 (July 1927): 759; Bernard S. Coleman, "Extension of Industrial Hygiene by Tuberculosis Associations in the United States," *American Journal of Public Health* 19 (February 1929): 157–65.

industrial hygiene departments could be used to uncover this public health danger.[107] The new industrial hygienists and the company physicians agreed on one basic point: The primary problems of the shop floor were related to the immediate danger from accidents and acute, especially infectious diseases that spread among the work force. They were not interested in chronic conditions that could appear years later, when a mobile work force would no longer be their responsibility. Thus, silicosis as a disease that predisposed workers to tuberculosis years and even decades after they had left the plant was of minor concern throughout the 1920s.

Not all respected public health leaders in the 1920s adopted this view regarding silicosis and tuberculosis. Louis Dublin, the statistician for the Metropolitan Life Insurance Company, reared in the traditions of the Progressive Era public health movement, pointed out that by the mid-1920s the lives of industrial workers on average were eight years shorter than those of workers engaged in other forms of employment:

> The handicap of eight years in the expectation of life is in the nature of attacks which millions of men who are engaged in industry pay under present conditions. It is a measurable and very real burden which might readily be expected from the very nature of industrial employment and the mode of life of workers.

While the focus of the nation was fixed on industrial accidents and industry's "safety first" movement, Dublin pointed out that "tuberculosis is even more important than accidents" in that it was a major factor in shortening lives as well as a significant source of disability and suffering. By the mid-1920s, as technicians and industry took over responsibility for industrial hygiene, Dublin believed that he was representing a tradition that was under siege. "I have for years held," Dublin remarked, "that industrial employment is probably the most important single factor in the tuberculosis death rate." Dublin was less concerned with the bacteriological agent and its specific means of transmission than he was with the problem of dust and poor working conditions that allowed disease to flourish. Dublin included in his concept of industrial sources of disease "the effects of the dusts inevitable in certain trades, excessive fatigue, bad posture, crowded workrooms and other conditions of employment which make the worker more susceptible to deleterious home influences."

Dublin's position reflected the older Progressive notions regarding the intimate relationship between work and home life as well as Metropolitan's increasing involvement in using clinics as a means of identifying diseased workers.[108] Disease could not be addressed simply by protecting the worker from a

[107] "New Jersey Health Service for Industry," *American Journal of Public Health* 17 (August 1927): 868–69.

[108] See Chapter V; and Alan Derickson, " 'On the Dump Heap': Employee Medical Screening in the Tri-State Zinc-Lead Industry, 1924–1932," *Business History Review* 62 (Winter 1988):

specific germ. Rather, conditions in the plant, and specifically dusts, undermined workers' resistance and also caused disease.[109] C.-E.A. Winslow also spoke against the rising tide of conservative thought that saw the high incidence of tuberculosis in the industrial population as due to poor living habits and unhealthful living conditions. Just as the decline in the rate of tuberculosis had helped to expose silicosis, during the 1920s Winslow and others pressed the point that silica itself was responsible for the high tuberculosis rates among industrial workers.

> There has been argument, of late, to the relative weight of various factors in the determination of the prevalence of tuberculosis. I am familiar with no single factor in the entire list, whether hereditary or environmental, which shows so clear and so striking a statistical relation to the tuberculosis death rate as exposure to the inhalation of siliceous dusts.[110]

Dublin's and Winslow's argument brought the history of workers' lung diseases full circle. In the mid-nineteenth century, before the discovery of the tuberculosis bacillus, medical and popular opinion saw a variety of workers' lung conditions as one disease, phthisis, whose origins lay in the individual's circumstances and personal characteristics. By the 1920s, armed with a reform ideology and better sources of information, the medical community once again focused on the relationship of consumption to industry and the special circumstances of workers' lives. Science might have distinguished between silicosis and tuberculosis. But there was a greater understanding of how complex and intertwined was their relationship. Over the course of the next half-century, researchers would achieve clarity and specificity about the origins of silicosis in the American workplace. Yet the issues that Dublin, Hayhurst, C.-E.A. Winslow, and Westinghouse spokesmen raised regarding individual and corporate responsibility for its occurrence would constantly reemerge. In this debate, the differing interpretations of the causes of lung diseases, whether silicosis, tuberculosis, bronchitis, emphysema, or asthma, would shape public and industrial policy and even medical and public health specialties.

656–77, for discussion of the Metropolitan's role in the creation of a clinic used in the diagnosis of tuberculosis and silicosis.

[109] Louis I. Dublin, "Conditions of Industry which Unfavorably Affect the Health of Workers," in Eighth Annual New York State Industrial Conference, *Proceedings*, (Albany: J. B. Lyon Co., 1925), 202–03. See also Louis I. Dublin, "Health of Workers," reprinted from *Monthly Labor Review* 20 (January 1925) (Washington, D.C.: Government Printing Office, 1925), 8–14; "Special Aspects of the Declining Tuberculosis Rate in the United States," *Monthly Labor Review* 26 (March 1928): 520–22; Louis I. Dublin, "Incidence of Tuberculosis in the Industrial Population," *American Journal of Public Health* 22 (March 1932): 281–91. See also Louis I. Dublin, *Health and Wealth, A Survey of the Economics of World Health*, (New York: Harper and Brothers, 1928), 109–33.

[110] C.-E. A. Winslow, "Tuberculosis in Dusty Trades," *The Survey* 54 (June 15, 1925): 355.

By the 1920s, silicosis was established as an important industrial disease.[111] No longer merely an idiosyncratic industrial dust disease in a "cabinet of curiosities," it clearly affected important American industries. But silicosis was perceived as a problem affecting rural, relatively isolated populations in widely scattered communities. Joplin, Missouri, Couer D'Alene, Idaho, Barre, Vermont, or Rockport, Massachusetts, was not likely to gain national attention because its population was being devastated by an obscure disease. One indication of the lack of political concern about the disease was that none of the workers' compensation legislation passed between 1911 and 1925 included silicosis as a compensable condition. Silicosis had been created as a disease category but was not yet understood to be a national health problem. It would take a crisis in an industry critical to the national economy to make this a condition capable of capturing the attention of the vast majority of practitioners or the imagination of the American public.

[111] See, in addition to other works by Hoffman, S. H. Katz, "Investigation of Dust in the Air of Granite-Working Plants," in *Reports of Investigations* (U.S. Bureau of Mines, February 1921, Mimeo, Serial No. 2213); and S. H. Katz and L. J. Trostel, "Dustiness of the Air in Granite-Cutting Plants," *Transactions of the American Society of Heating and Ventilating Engineers* 28 (1922): 235–63.

II

FOUNDRIES AND THE SILICOSIS PROBLEM

THE COMMON IMAGE of a foundry is the large cauldron of molten metal, pouring into molds of various sizes and shapes. The heat of the furnace and the fumes of lead, zinc, iron, and bronze as they pour out are what define the popular image of these factories in which thousands of laborers toiled. Yet perhaps the most threatening and dangerous aspect of these institutions has hardly penetrated the popular imagination.

To walk into a foundry is to walk through sand. Even today, sand is used in every process in a plant. Black or green, mixed with a wide variety of other substances, scattered over the floors, the workbenches, the instruments and casts themselves, sand is ever present. It is in the air foundry workers breathe. Large plumes of sand dust, created in the myriad of processes necessary to produce a finished product, permeate the atmosphere. Usually the dust is easily seen as it floats from one part of the plant to the other. Sometimes it is only a shaft of light, penetrating the foundry from a small widow or shaft high above the work floor that illuminates the immense amount of dust that workers breathed. Sand found its way into every crevice or crease in workers' clothing, on their shoes and in their socks. When workers left after a day's toil, they would spit it from their mouthes, blow it from their noses, clear it from their throats—and cough it up from their lungs.

Foundries, plants where tools and major machine parts are cast, have always been highly individualized concerns that produced a wide range of cast metal products. Everything from farm machinery to potbellied stoves to automotive engines or parts were cast in these ubiquitous and varied plants. The basic process of casting iron and other metals has remained relatively constant over the course of the last century, although the technology has changed. At every stage of foundry work, sand is involved. Workers build a model of the object to be cast and use these as patterns to create a sand mold. In casts that have interior openings or holes, a sand "core" is made as well. Melted metal is poured into the sand mold, around the core, to create the object. After cooling, the mold and core are removed from the casting during the "shakeout"—the process of breaking up the sand mold and core with hammers, chisels, or mechanical vibration. After this, the castings are ready for final cleaning and finishing by means of grinding, chipping, sanding, brushing, and, by the early twentieth century, sandblasting.

During the first quarter of the twentieth century, a small group of public health workers, industrial hygienists, insurance spokespeople, and isolated unions and communities became aware of silicosis. Public health and medical professionals framed the scientific understanding about the complex relationship between silicosis and tuberculosis. But this professional recognition was itself shaped by the industrial transformation that the country was undergoing. Silicosis not only affected workers in isolated communities but now created disease, dependence, and suffering for workers and their families in one of the most important national industries—the foundry—which in turn formed the basis for the metal-fabricating and toolmaking industries. Because the foundry was crucial to the economic health of thousands of communities, large and small, rural and urban, all across America, the emergence of silicosis as a problem in the foundry forged a new understanding of this disease and shaped the environment within which these professionals operated. This chapter will trace the changing labor and production processes in the foundry, changes that greatly increased the number of diseased workers and in the context of the Depression would allow for the national recognition of a crisis. The very debates about the nature of industrially caused chronic disease that were at the intellectual core of medical and public health controversies during this period would emerge as critical political controversies as lung disease threatened an industry of national significance, for seemingly academic questions had profound political and economic consequences:

> Founding is a trade that involves some knowledge of almost every operation required in the making of machines; and men well versed in the mechanic arts assert that the art of founding demands a greater mechanical skill, caution, and good judgement than any other of the allied trades. The art of founding is largely dependent on the hand and mind for results, machinery having played but a small part in the work of molders compared to what it has done for workers in most other trades.[1]

The local crises over silicosis that affected scattered towns and villages in Idaho, Missouri, Montana, and Vermont became a national problem with the recognition that foundries all over the country exposed their workers to massive amounts of silica dust. Closely linked to every major heavy industry in the country, foundries were scattered throughout the nation but were concentrated in the industrial heartland of the East and Midwest. The number of employees and the size of the plants varied tremendously from fewer than a dozen workers in the smaller, rural enterprises that produced the farming implements and tools to about 175 employees in the large foundries producing machinery and engine parts. In 1880, there were 145,000 workers employed in almost 5,000 foundries. By 1900, there were over 350,000 employees in 9,300 shops nationwide. The average foundry had between 30 and 35 employees during

---

[1] International Correspondence Schools, *Shop and Foundry Practice*, vol. 4 (Scranton, Pa.: Colliery Engineer Company, 1901), 47.

these years; the vast majority were small shops with fewer than 30 workers.[2]
By 1914, there were over 18,000 foundries in the United States employing
660,000 wage earners.[3] Major manufacturing and commercial centers, such
as Chicago, New York, Philadelphia, Pittsburgh, Detroit, Cleveland, and Cincinnati, had large numbers of foundries. Foundries were also essential to the
growth and development of rural farming communities, for it was in the small
foundries set up on the riverbanks that iron tools and machinery were manu-
factured for local agricultural markets. In 1910, every state except Wyoming
had at least two foundries. Mississippi, for example, had twenty-two foundries, North Dakota had five, Oregon had forty-five, South Carolina had
thirty-one, and Utah had twenty.[4] By 1909, foundries and related machine
shop products "were the second most important manufacturing industry in the
United States, in both the number of wage earners employed and in the value
of the finished goods."[5]

Although sand dust was understood to be a hazard in the nineteenth-century
foundry, the severity of the problem grew as a result of fundamental changes
in the work methods, technology, and organization of foundries in the early
twentieth century. Three basic processes accounted for the intensification of
the silicosis hazard. First, binders were mixed with sand so that the mold could
hold the shape of a pattern to be cast. Sand was the basic ingredient used in
creating the mold because of its relative abundance in nearly every community, its physical strength, and its chemical ability to resist breakdown or burn-
ing under exposure to the intense heat of molten metal. No other substance
had the chemical, physical, and economic attributes of this common substance, and it is still a mainstay of metal foundries today. In order to provide
sand with the right consistency necessary to hold its shape, other commonly
used "binders," such as water, wheat flour, linseed oil, rosin, molasses,
and—more recently—synthetic glues, would be mixed with the sand to meet
the various requirements necessary for the creation of different molds of varying sizes, shapes, and depths. In the nineteenth century, the mixing of sand
and its various binders was performed by workers using shovels, sieves, rid-
dles, rakes, and other common hand tools. At the beginning of the century,
these relatively simple tools were replaced with power sand-mixing, -screen-
ing, and -cutting machines that greatly increased the amount of sand that could

[2] U.S. Bureau of the Census, *Census of Manufacturing, 1900*, vol. 2, pt. 1 (Washington, D.C.:
Government Printing Office, 1901), 8.

[3] William Huston Chartener, "The Molders' and Foundry Workers' Union: A Study of Union
Development" (unpublished Ph.D. diss., Harvard University, 1952), 218. His estimates of the
number of shops and the number of workers are somewhat larger than those of the Census: for
1890, 8,075 shops and 287,000 wage earners; for 1914, 18,076 shops and 660,000 wage earners.

[4] "The Foundry Industry of the United States and Canada in 1910," *The Iron Trade Review* 46
(May 5, 1910): 870.

[5] Margaret Loomis Stecker, "The Founders, Molders, and the Molding Machine," *Quarterly
Journal of Economics* 32 (February 1918): 279.

be mixed. By the early years of the century, one worker running a machine mixer for two hours could mix as much sand as two workers mixing by hand for an entire day. This greatly increased the dust hazard that the workers were exposed to.[6]

After the metal was poured into the sand cast and allowed to cool for a period of thirty minutes or so, the second dust-producing process began as the mold and core were removed. This process, commonly called the shake-out, required workers first to break apart the mold with a sledgehammer or other tools, depending on the size, shape, and fragility of the casting. Since the sand was dried by the heat of the metal, the process of removal was a difficult task, requiring workers to chip, pound, and shake out the sand imbedded in the various crevices and holes in the casting. If a large core had been used to create hollowed areas in, for example, a cast-iron potbellied stove, a sledgehammer would be used to break apart the sand inside the casting. As pneumatic tools became more common, greater quantities of fine dust were thrown into the air workers breathed.

The third process was essentially a continuation of the shake-out, in which the casting was freed from all residue sand and, if necessary, ground, polished, or given a specific finish. During most of the nineteenth century, workers cleaned and smoothed large and small castings by hand with wire brushes. Toward the end of the century, more sophisticated and mechanical means of cleaning were devised employing "tumbling" machinery in which sand was used as an abrasive to clean the molds. While small, sturdy casts could be placed in dust-tight "tumbling mills," larger and more delicate molds could not. By the early teens, these objects were sandblasted by workers using compressed air and sand mixtures through hoses hand held by the employee.[7] Especially with the introduction of pneumatic tools, such as those used in sandblasting, the amount of dust generated in the foundry increased manyfold.[8]

By tracing the history of the foundry trade in the late nineteenth and early twentieth centuries, it is possible to see the intertwining relationship between

[6] W. J. McConnell and J. W. Fehnel, "Health Hazards in the Foundry Industry," *The Journal of Industrial Hygiene* 16 (July 1934): 232.

[7] Magnus W. Alexander, *Safety in the Foundry* (Chicago: National Founders Association, 1915), 135–40; E. O. Jones, "Cleaner Air for the Foundry," *National Safety News* 30 (September 1934): 21–22; Dr. E. G. Meiter, "The Dust Problem in the Foundry Industry," *Safety Engineering* 66 (September, October 1933): 101–04, 141–43; Carey P. McCord, "Health Hazards in the Foundry," *National Safety News* 29 (January 1934): 34–35.

[8] See, for example, Industrial Correspondence Schools, *Shop and Foundry Practice* (Scranton, Pa.: Colliery Engineer Company, 1901), sec. 35. See also, William C. Stimpson, *Foundry Work* (Chicago: American Technical Society, 1916), 6–22; U.S. Department of Labor, Bureau of Labor Statistics, *Safety Code for the Protection of Industrial Workers in Foundries, Bulletin No. 336* (Washington, D.C.: Government Printing Office, 1923), 6–8; James M. Tate and Melvin O. Stone, *Foundry Practice* (New York: John Wiley and Sons, 1909), 189; G. P. Fisher, "25 Years of Progress in Mechanical Equipment for Foundries," *Iron Age* 115 (January 1, 1925): 41–42.

struggles around workers' control and conflict over workers' health. Although some may argue that the increased dust hazard can be understood as the unfortunate result of a necessary technological change in the production process, the more fundamental explanation is that the quest for profit undermined both workers' autonomy and workers' health. In foundries (as in other industries), the increase in dust was intimately linked to the decline in status and power of skilled workers.

The Growth of American Foundries

For most of the nineteenth century, foundry work was a skilled trade, requiring relatively few tools and arduous training in a variety of areas. Molders, the mainstay of the foundry work force, depended upon little more than the awl, the hammer, clamps, wedges, wrench, and "rammer," a tool used in pressing the sand evenly around the pattern to create a mold. Besides these relatively simple instruments, most of the work of molding depended upon the skill, knowledge, and strength of a work force that prided itself on its ability to judge the quality of sand, to mix sand to a proper consistency, and to create patterns that under the intense pressure exerted by exposure to tremendous heat and weight would hold their shape and produce a perfect cast. Cast-metal objects in the nineteenth century were often fragile pieces. Any mistake on the part of a molder could produce fatal flaws in the shape or integrity of the finished product. Given the uneven quality of much of the iron used in production, a slight flaw in the sand mold might create a fissure that would make an entire locomotive engine useless. Too much moisture in the sand mixture could produce scaling or cracks in ornamental objects that would reduce their value. A large casting for a cast-iron building could be rendered worthless or even dangerous by a poorly trained molder. In the nineteenth century, objects of the highest quality tended to be cast in as few pieces as absolutely necessary, thereby increasing the importance of the worker's skill. The entire body of the highest quality potbellied stove, for example, would generally be cast as one unit. The intricate grillwork design and the lettering on the front, as well as the strength of the body and its ability to withstand high temperatures, depended on the skill and intelligence of the molder, who controlled every aspect of the production process.[9] The nineteenth-century molder was an artisan, skilled in a wide range of techniques necessary to artistic creation.

The most critical skill of nineteenth-century molders was their responsibility in preparing the sand mold. Each half of the mold would be created by

[9] Nineteenth-century molders are good examples of the skilled artisans who David Montgomery discusses at length in his book, *The Fall of the House of Labor, The Workplace, the State and American Labor Activism, 1865–1925* (Cambridge: Cambridge University Press, 1987), esp. ch. 1, "The Manager's Brain Under The Workman's Cap."

packing sand around a pattern, usually a wooden model of the finished cast. The sand mixture would be shoveled or poured into a wooden frame called a flask that would contain the pattern to be replicated. The molder was responsible for "ramming" the sand tightly around the pattern. An early twentieth-century text described the importance of ramming: "The success of making the mold and obtaining a good casting is dependent mainly upon the manner of ramming . . . to form the mold. Hard spots in the sand cause scabs, and soft spots cause swells. Unevenness of ramming causes similar unevenness in the casting."[10] In the case of a complex pattern with creases and crevices, angles and curves, the ability of the molder to guarantee the integrity of the sand mold was central to the whole foundry process. "Ramming is a very important operation and the art should be learned thoroughly, as no amount of finishing will rectify faulty ramming," warned one late nineteenth century text.[11]

The nineteenth-century molders saw themselves as artists as well as artisans. In an era when iron castings were used for everything from locomotive engines, gears, and pipes to ornate potbellied stoves, ornamental fixtures, and cast-iron building facades, their artistry was visible to everyone. They were cautioned to remember that "along with strength beauty must be combined," and even the detail on the common manhole cover used for urban sewer and water supplies bore their distinctive imprint.[12] Molders' apprentices were advised to examine the cast iron in lower Manhattan and elsewhere throughout the nation to inspect the imperfections in the detail that were the result of the use of inadequately prepared sand, or poorly rammed molds: "To one acquainted with the tricks of the trade, it is easy to find lifter and tool-marks in abundance; places where scabs and swells have been imperfectly removed with a chisel can be readily traced; moldings and figures imperfectly finished."[13] One molder wrote to the union journal in 1900 that "to be a good molder a man must have been educated in the art (for it is an art), must have an eye for beauty, take an interest in his work, must know when it is done right or discover the wrong."[14]

For most of the nineteenth century, foundry owners were forced to contend with the power of the molder, who was the fulcrum of the foundry shop floor. It was the skilled molder who controlled the pace of work, the quality of the crafting, the number of objects produced. Using a relatively few hand-held tools, which were often their own, it was the molders who were in charge of production. In a shop of ten molders, the molders would hire two or three

[10] James M. Tate and Melvin O. Stone, *Foundry Practice* (New York: John Wiley and Sons, 1909), 77.
[11] Simpson Bolland, *The Iron-Founder* (New York: John Wiley and Sons, 1892), 29.
[12] Bolland, *Iron-Founder*, 172.
[13] Bolland, *Iron-Founder*, 172.
[14] "Ironmonger," "Self-Respect," *Iron Molders' Journal* 36 (1900): 457.

apprentices and ten laborers, often called helpers, "berkshires," or "bucks." These laborers would perform all the ancillary tasks necessary to keep the molders working at their determined pace. They would cart the sand to the molders, pour the metal into the mold, break open the molds and free the cores after a pouring, and remove excess sand from the finished casting.

From the earliest days of the Molders' Union in the mid-nineteenth century, the "helpter" (*sic*), or berkshire, system and the piece rate system of payment created tensions between the union and the foundry owner. The piece rate system, in which molders were paid a negotiated amount for each casting, allowed individual molders a certain degree of control over the production process. Molders could hire their own sets of helpers to produce larger numbers of castings and thereby increase their income. But the piece rate system also had severe disadvantages, which led the Molders' Union to campaign against it throughout the nineteenth and early twentieth centuries. Specifically, by encouraging individual molders to increase production by hiring larger and larger numbers of helpers, the union believed that the overall effect was to reduce the piece rate and to increase the pace of work. As production increased, foundry owners could point to the molders' growing income as a rationale for lowering the piece rate.[15]

Second, the molders employed two different types of helpers. Unskilled workers performed ancillary tasks, such as mixing and hauling sand, moving castings, and chipping and cleaning them. The other group of helpers worked directly with the molders in a variety of more critical tasks. The former group of helpers had no opportunity to learn critical elements of the molding process, but the latter could and did learn all essential skills. While individual molders had a short-term interest in employing these helpers in order to increase their income, the union recognized that as helpers acquired skills, they could and were used by management to undermine the hegemony of journeymen molders over production. In a study of the molders published in 1921, the author noted that "while the journeymen have been able to restrict the helper in larger degree to work requiring little skill, they have not found it feasible to 'clear the boards.' "[16]

The molders also pressed for the abandonment of another one of the central characteristics of the older craft system: They sought and generally achieved agreements with the owners to have helpers paid wages by the owners rather

[15] The union often tried to balance the self-interest of individuals against the general understanding that the piece rate system hurt all skilled molders. See, for example, Editorial, "Piece Work and Eight Hours," *Iron Molders' Journal* 36 (1900): 206, in which the editors seek to head off conflict between older workers, who recognize the speed-up effects of piece work, and younger, healthier members, who still believe that the system benefits them.

[16] Frank T. Stockton, "The International Molders Union of North America," *Johns Hopkins University Studies in Historical and Political Science*, series 39, no.3 (Baltimore: The Johns Hopkins Press, 1921), 185.

than out of their own pockets. They also demanded that molders be responsible only for skilled work within the shop, with other tasks to be performed by nonunionized, unskilled labor. In the increasingly specialized plant and the tumultuous economic conditions of the late nineteenth century, the skilled molders sought to shift the costs of labor back onto management. In so doing, they further participated in undermining their hegemony over the production process.[17]

At the same time, many foundry owners sought to undermine the autonomy of the molders by introducing a variety of devices that lessened owners' dependence on skilled workers. From the 1870s through the early part of the twentieth century, foundries introduced power sand-mixing, -screening, and -cutting machines, core-making machines, electric frames, conveyors, trolley systems, tumbling mills, and sandblasting machinery. Together, these innovations allowed managers and foundry owners to hire laborers to perform specific tasks formerly controlled by the molders.[18] As the foundry was increasingly mechanized and specialized, the older system of craft control declined. By 1918, one observer remarked that "the brains which formerly had vested in the molder were transferred entirely . . . to the machine."[19]

One of the biggest changes was the introduction of molding machines, which undercut the very skill that the molders sought to protect. These new machines were powered rammers that exerted an even and uniform pressure on molds that were being mass produced. In a few plants controlled by large national corporations, skilled molders were virtually eliminated from the whole process. Singer Sewing Machine Company produced the "Singer New Family" machine in its own foundry:

> On its floor molds could be laid out for more than thirty tons of melted pig iron. Singer took pride in having adopted a foundry system that dispensed with skilled molders. It had a dual basis—a special press or molding machine which packed the sand around the pattern in one operation, plus intensive division of labor.

Standardization and mass production permitted the adoption of new means of organizing work that undercut the need for skilled molders and replaced them with semiskilled operatives capable of learning repetitive tasks that no longer required a knowledge of the entire production process. While such mass production techniques were taking place in only a minority of "captured" foundries—foundries that were owned by or producing solely for mass production industries—they augured poorly for the future of the artisan molders. By the

[17] Stockton, "The International Molders," 176–85.

[18] G. P. Fisher, "25 Years of Progress in Mechanical Equipment for Foundries," *Iron Age* 115 (January 1, 1925): 41–42; Chartener, "The Molders' and Foundry Workers'," 214.

[19] Margaret Loomis Stecker, "The Founders, the Molders, and the Molding Machine," *Quarterly Journal of Economics* 32 (February 1918): 284.

early twentieth century, machinery was being adopted throughout the foundry industry in both large or small plants.[20]

Molders' opposition to the mechanization of the foundry was of long standing. As early as 1866, William Sylvis, the founder of the newly organized Molders' Union and one of the organizers and leaders of the National Labor Union, had captured the opposition of most skilled molders to machinery. He assured a union convention (with a confidence not borne out by later events) that the molders were "one of those trades that can never be interfered with by machinery, for the reason that it requires a *thinking machine* to make castings." Nearly twenty years later, Terence Powderly, grand master workman of the Knights of Labor, voiced the growing recognition of the threat that machinery posed to molders and others in the larger labor movement. In 1885 he described how "one iron man, who does not feel, sleep, eat, or drink, who never tires and never rests" displaces "three flesh-and-blood men, who have children depending upon them for bread" and who are "thrown out of employment through the introduction of these agents."[21]

But by 1900 the union had recognized that it was inevitable that machinery would be introduced and so they needed to gain control of its use. The union negotiated with foundry owners to limit the operation of the machines to the skilled molders.[22] Because the introduction of machinery was accompanied by a tremendous expansion of foundries throughout the nation, there was an increase in the number of skilled molders between 1890 and 1920. But their relative position both in their power and as a proportion of the work force declined. Between 1900 and 1913, the percentage of skilled molders in the foundry industry declined from about 60 percent to 40 percent.[23]

The Impact on Workers' Health

The relative decline of the skilled artisans paralleled a deterioration in their working conditions. Whereas in the nineteenth century the molders controlled the pace and nature of work, in the twentieth century owners asserted their authority through the introduction of mechanical devices and the segmentation of the work process. By 1911, the foundries had become a primary focus of the scientific management movement, leading to the famous strike among molders at the foundry of the Watertown Arsenal in Massachusetts. Similar conflicts in small private factories might elicit local concern, but because the

---

[20] David A. Hounshell, *From the American System to Mass Production, 1800–1932* (Baltimore: Johns Hopkins University Press, 1984), 105.

[21] Quoted in Chartener, "The Molders' and Foundry Workers'," 212–13, 216.

[22] Editorial, "Our Attitude to the Machine," *Iron Molders' Journal* 36 (1900): 594–97.

[23] Chartener, "The Molders' and Foundry Workers'," 219. See also Stockton, "The International Molders," 186–98.

arsenal produced arms for the government, it became a focus of national attention, leading Congress to investigate the use of scientific management as a tool by management against labor.[24] One contemporary remarked that the new machine molder "became himself a mere machine, with none of the variety to his work that characterized the skilled hand worker."[25]

Similar changes in many industries led to the degradation of skill and the loss of control over shop floor conditions. These, in turn, had a significant impact on the health and welfare of the workers, as disease and disability strained the resources of working-class families. In the early years of this century, it was apparent to labor, government, and even management that conditions in the nation's foundries were deplorable. Even before the introduction of mechanized equipment, the heat of the plant, the long hours of work, the inadequate safety precautions, the sudden changes in temperature, and the dust created by various processes all combined to make work in the early twentieth century foundry an enormously hazardous occupation. Burns from molten metal, explosions when water struck extremely hot molds, poisonings from metallic fumes and exposure, and injuries from falling metal objects were constant dangers to all employees.

During the early twentieth century, the acute hazards of the foundry dominated most investigations, and substantial improvements were effected that cut down on the accident rate and amount of heavy metal poisoning. But, as technological innovation reduced the number of accidents, it increased the danger of other, longer-term threats to workers' health. The impetus for the uncovering of the dust hazard came from a New York State investigation that had been prompted by the worst tragedy in New York industrial history. In the aftermath of the Triangle Shirtwaist Factory fire on March 25, 1911, which claimed the lives of 143 immigrant women, New York State established a Factory Commission to investigate industrial working conditions and recommend legislation. In its four years of work, the commission held hearings throughout the state, which resulted in the enactment of fifty-six laws on various aspects of factory regulation, including foundries.

The New York State Factory Commission that conducted these hearings was remarkable in its composition. Chaired by Robert F. Wagner, and including Vice-Chair Alfred E. Smith and Mary Drier, the commission undertook the most exhaustive investigation of factory conditions in the United States until that time. All of the commissioners would play leading roles in future labor and reform movements: Wagner as a U.S. senator, Smith as governor of New York State, and Drier as head of the Women's Trade Union League. The commission echoed the union's recommendations for the redesign of the foundry,

[24] "The Strike at the Watertown Arsenal," *International Molders Journal* 47 (1911): 695.
[25] Margaret Loomis Stecker, "The Founders, the Molders, and the Molding Machine," *Quarterly Journal of Economics* 32 (February 1918): 285.

but, more important, for the first time it defined the problem of the factory in terms that would resonate more strongly during the New Deal. Reflecting the Progressive Era reform movement's assumptions about relative responsibility for workplace hazards, the commission pointed to the responsibilities of management in controling disease hazards and in protecting workers from the excesses of industrialization. The commission extended the analysis of accidents and acute disease to the issue of long-term degenerative lung disorders.

In the course of the hearings, it became apparent that it was not just accidents that worried laborers and officials from the Molders' Union. In 1912 and 1913, the commission heard from a number of officials of the Molders' Union, who declared that "the dust proposition is one that the moulders have been trying to get rid of for some time." The commission asked William Buchanan, who was treasurer of the Rochester Molders' Union local, how the dust was created, and he explained that "the dust is generated by shaking out castings and mixing up the sand in the place, and by cleaning castings and knocking the cores out of them."[26] From the self-interested perspective of the skilled molders, the problem was that the physical structure of the foundry exposed all workers, despite their actual responsibility, to a constant dust hazard.

In the early twentieth century foundry, dust produced by common laborers in the sand-mixing and shake-out departments floated freely throughout the plant. In order to cut down on the amount of dust, shake-outs in some plants were done at night, after most of the workers had left. Workers on the night shift were unskilled, unorganized, and, according to the molders' spokespeople, "pretty nearly all foreigners, Polish and Italian." Everyone acknowledged that the shake-out was "very unhealthy work."[27] Furthermore, the intense nightly shake-outs left the atmosphere of the large, open space of the foundry saturated with dust even the next morning, when the skilled unionized laborers returned: "When the molders come to work in the morning the sand is practically scraped out, and it fills the place with that dust," remarked Buchanan to the state investigator.[28] Thus, even before the widespread introduction of mechanical equipment, a large foundry was understood to be an intrinsically dusty place.

The testimony of public officials as well as industry spokespeople illustrated common assumptions of the time regarding responsibility for risk from foundry work. Most local officials believed that little could be done to change fundamentally the polluted environment in which workers toiled. Hollister Hessler, the commissioner of public safety of Syracuse, whose department conducted factory inspections in the area, reflected the common assumption prevalent at the time. When asked by Robert Wagner himself why so little had

[26] New York State, *Preliminary Report of the Factory Investigating Commission*, vol. 3 (Albany, 1912), 987.

[27] New York State, *Preliminary Report*, vol. 3, 1174.

[28] New York State, *Preliminary Report*, vol. 3, 987.

been done to correct the dust hazard in foundries inspected by the commissioner and his staff, Hessler responded, "I would think it would be practically impossible to have a foundry that would not be very dusty and very smokey."[29]

County and city politicians saw the conditions of work as an intractable problem inherent to the foundry. Workers argued, however, that they should not be made to bear the burden of mechanization. One labor representative noted that "something like 45 or 47 per cent of [New York State molders] died of tuberculosis or pulmonary diseases" and that this placed a substantial financial burden on the welfare funds of the union. "We have to pay thousands of dollars every year because of the fact that the men's health becomes impaired because of these conditions," testified John H. O'Leary, the vice president of the international.[30] Daniel O'Connor, the secretary of the union local in Albany, described how the Molders had organized a "legislative conference" in April of 1912 to develop a bill to protect the health of the "moulders of the State." This action was necessary, he told the commission, because there had been "considerable complaint around the State that the conditions were so that their health was in danger."[31] The union's point was that it was management that should bear primary responsibility for safeguarding workers from the dust hazard. The shake-out and cleaning of castings should be done in separate rooms to confine the dust arising from the process. The union defined its mandate quite narrowly, with the result that it accepted the fundamental position of local officials and management that dust was an essential ingredient of foundry work. In seeking to confine the dust hazard to the shake-out and cleaning rooms, it also was willing to leave the unskilled, unorganized, and largely immigrant workers unprotected. The burdens of disease and disability would be left to the newcomers.

The Impact on Women and Immigrant Workers

The union used the health issue in three separate ways: first, by trying to protect its own members by isolating the dusty processes in separate quarters; second, by allowing immigrants to bear the most intense health risks from the dust; and finally, by eliminating women from the shop floor.[32] In the late nine-

[29] New York State, *Preliminary Report*, vol. 3, 1199.

[30] New York State, *Second Report of the Factory Investigations Commission*, vol. 3 (Albany, 1913), 904, 910.

[31] New York State, *Second Report*, vol. 3, 895.

[32] See also Pennsylvania Foundry Act of June 7, 1911, *Pennsylvania Labor and History Department Monthly Bulletin* 3: 79–80; U.S. Congress, *Report on Condition of Women and Child Wage-Earners in the United States*, 61st Cong., 2d sess., 1911, S. Doc. 645, vol. 11: *Employment of Women in the Metal Tradess*, 43–44.

teenth century, as many of the core-making operations became mechanized, young boys were employed in the core rooms at greatly reduced wages. It was not uncommon in the bigger foundries to see ''long rooms filled with boys as early as 1888.''[33] At the turn of the century, foundries also began to employ immigrant women in these departments at even lower wages than those of the boys. One union official related that in Syracuse, union molders received $3.15 per day but that women, who were excluded from the union, were being hired at from $4 to $8 per week and forced to work under the same deplorable conditions.[34] Commissioner Mary Drier, who was most concerned about working women's rights, described ''the tremendous speed, the tremendous pressure that they were working under in the foundry.''[35] Contemporary accounts of the lives of women foundry workers give vivid testimony to the trying conditions that Drier referred to:

> At one bench is a group of Polish girls, round featured, with high foreheads and fair hair, but the rest are of the Hungarian type, its dark skin and muscular poise seeming for the moment the incarnation of the activities of smoking ovens, boiling crucibles and iron molten with fierce heat. The dim light through the window clouded with black dust hardly reaches the center of the room where the rows of ovens are, and even the glare of an electric bulb cannot dispel the impression of unreality, of remoteness, the notion that these are creatures of a race born underground to work on the metals of the earth.[36]

The women core makers were paid by the piece, ten cents per one thousand simple finger-shaped cores. In a good day, ''the quick girls can make three a minute, or 10,000 a day.''[37] Although the women suffered from the same unhealthful conditions as the men, the union believed that it was preferable to exclude them from the foundry rather than include them in the union's demands for higher wages and better working conditions.

In fact, union officials used paternalistic arguments to exclude women from the foundry by emphasizing their fragile nature and the ''intrinsic'' unsanitary nature of foundry work. At its annual convention in 1912, the union resolved ''to use every effort to bring about the elimination'' of the employment of women in foundries because ''twentieth century civilization is not in favor of the dragging down of American womanhood so that the foundrymen can increase their profits.'' More specifically, the resolution proclaimed, ''[W]e believe that the foundry is no place for females, because of the brutal character of the work and the unhealthy and unhygienic conditions surrounding such

[33] Chartener, ''The Molders' and Foundry Workers','' 199.

[34] New York State, *Preliminary Report*, vol. 3, 1165.

[35] New York State, *Preliminary Report*, vol. 3, 1204.

[36] Elizabeth Beardsley Butler, ''Pittsburgh Women in the Metal Trades,'' *Charities and the Commons* 21 (October 3, 1908): 34–35.

[37] Butler, ''Pittsburgh Women,'' 35.

employment.''[38] New York State's Factory Investigating Commission report sought to lead the union away from its narrow conception of the problem while maintaining its own protectionist stance. They did not support the absolute prohibition of the employment of women in core making because that would place an extreme burden on them. But the commission did recommend that foundry work for women "should be discouraged and ultimately suppressed." "Instincts of chivalry and decency as well as concern for the preservation of the race, demand that we should not permit women to engage in work detrimental to their health, that overtaxes their strength, and impairs their vitality as wives and mothers," the commissioners declared.[39]

The debate on the dangers for women foundry workers took place within the context of the deterioration in health conditions for all workers. Mechanization and the deskilling of the molders' trade had fundamentally altered work relations as well as working conditions. The dust hazard in the foundry was serious enough in the years before mechanization. But the introduction of sandblasting to clean and polish castings accentuated the problem. By literally shooting sand at cast-iron objects, the larger crystals of sand were broken into even finer crystals, creating immense quantities of minute particles that permeated every corner of the foundry. These particles, unlike the larger dust particles produced by using a hand-held wire brush, were less likely to be filtered out by the labyrinthian canals of the nasal sinuses and cilia and mucous membranes of a worker's nose, throat, and bronchi. As a result, a much larger percentage of the crystalline silica reached the fragile air sacs, which became the locus of silica disease. In short, workers in foundries were exposed to greater risk as more and more dust penetrated their lungs.

Health as a Labor-Management Issue

As labor itself became aware of the dust hazard, the debate entered into a new arena. Once limited to the discussions among statisticians, public health professionals, and a few local groups of workers in quarrying and mining, the attention of the Molders' Union forced the dust debate into the larger context of labor-management conflict. Significantly, as labor and management would enter into the debate, they would introduce issues and questions regarding the extent of the dust hazard, the efficiency of protective equipment, the type of protection that should be provided for workers, and who should bear the responsibility for risk. Some of these problems were practical issues that could be negotiated between labor and management. But other issues were more fundamental and went to the very core of the intellectual debate about what

[38] New York State, *Second Report*, vol. 3, 813.
[39] New York State, *Second Report*, vol. 1, 262–63.

disease was and what caused it. Although these issues were discussed in terms that laypeople commonly used, they ultimately affected the medical and professional debates that were going on simultaneously. It was in the context of differing conceptions of responsibility and obligation for workers' suffering that the academic debates took place.

By the beginning of the second decade of the twentieth century, the Molders' Union had identified sandblasting as a major threat to health. While Hoffman, Dublin, and other statisticians and public health professionals recognized the general problem of dust for workers, it was the union itself that heightened awareness of the increased dangers brought on by new technologies in the foundry. One union official complained as early as 1914 that foundry managers "are getting up more devilish arrangements every day for cleaning castings" and that "sand blast cleaning should be prohibited in the foundry." Further, John O'Leary of the union international suggested that all dust-producing processes, especially those using explosives in the "breaking of castings" or the destruction of the hardened cores inside the castings, should be prohibited in the foundry buildings, where workers could be exposed to the new, dangerous forms of dust created by these new technologies.[40]

The union's complaints forced industry to begin to develop a rationale for defending their introduction of new technologies. Industry's first response was to argue that the problem had been exaggerated and that the industry was correcting the few unhealthful worksites. In a book published in 1915 by the National Founder's Association, *Safety in the Foundry*, Magnus W. Alexander argued that mechanization had actually decreased the health hazard to workers: "In the early history of foundry work, it was the ordinary custom to hand clean the burnt sand and scale . . . [and] in this process large volumes of dust were thrown into the air close to the cleaners' head where he could not avoid breathing it." To meet this hazard, the industry had developed the "tumbling mill," in which small castings could be cleaned by use of sand abrasive in containers. By enclosing the sand, workers were ostensibly protected from dust exposure. For larger, or more delicate castings, the industry developed the "hose type sandblast apparatus." To protect the workers, Alexander maintained, the industry made all sandblasters wear respirators and other protective clothing and separated the process in "sandblast rooms" with exhaust and ventilation systems.[41]

---

[40] New York State, *Second Report*, vol. 3, 909; John R. O'Leary, "Foundry Regulations," *Pennsylvania Labor and Industry Department Monthly Bulletin*, June 1915, 42–43.

[41] Magnus W. Alexander, *Safety in the Foundry* (Chicago: National Founders' Association, 1915), 135–39. See also John Arthur Turner and L. R. Thompson, *Health Hazards of Brass Foundries*, U.S. Treasury Department, Public Health Service, *Public Health Bulletin No. 157* (August 1925; Washington, D.C.: Government Printing Office, 1926). Note that the major focus of the hazards is on zinc ague rather than silicosis.

Despite the general argument that industry had made the workplace safe and healthful by the introduction of mechanical cleaning machinery, industry spokespeople acknowledged that dust still pervaded the atmosphere of the foundry. Further, they agreed that some workers still became diseased from the foundry dust. Even though the formal medical and public health studies were just appearing, they granted that individuals suffered from lung disorders. However, their concession to the unhealthfulness of the foundry was quite limited. Workers did get sick. But they became ill because of their own hereditary or constitutional predisposition to disease rather than because of any systematic exposure to dust. Regarding the workers in the sandblast rooms, Alexander wrote:

> Inasmuch . . . as some apparently strong men have a predisposition to certain diseases of the lungs if they work in a confined place or where there is much dust floating in the air, it behooves the employer for his own protection as well as that of the employees to select only such men for this work whose physical condition fits them for it.[42]

Industry maintained that it had used technologies to improve the conditions of work and done all it could to reduce the risks of the job. If workers became sick, therefore, it was individual characteristics that predisposed workers to certain illnesses. Disease did not result from general conditions of work but from individual susceptibility.

The assurances of industry representatives that the foundry could be easily made safe for its work force studiously ignored some of the countervailing pressures that were transforming the health environment. First, in the late nineteenth and early twentieth centuries, the number and size of foundries were expanding rapidly. The vast majority of these foundries were small, competitive shops that stood in stark contrast to the giant foundries "captured" by major national corporations, such as General Electric, International Harvester, and U.S. Steel. Although the smaller foundries were using more machinery and sandblast operations, there was little incentive or interest in renovating foundry space to isolate sandblasters. In fact, in the highly competitive "job shops," which often operated on a small margin of profit, safety measures were generally too costly to adopt. Thus, despite the fact that industry journals pointed the way to the safe adoption of this new equipment,[43] most

---

[42] Magnus W. Alexander, *Safety in the Foundry* (Chicago: National Founders' Association, 1915), 139.

[43] In a tentative American standard adopted by the National Founders' Association and the American Foundrymen's Association in 1923, Rule 215 on Sandblasting declared: "Sand Blasting by hand-operated apparatus shall be carried on in suitable sand-blast room or outside the foundry. . . . Dust shall not be exhausted into the open air but into a collector." U.S. Department of Labor, Bureau of Labor Statistics, *Safety Code for the Protection of Industrial Workers in Foundries, Bulletin No. 336* (Washington, D.C.: Government Printing Office, 1923), 6.

small foundries could not afford to adhere to these strict safety standards. Rather, the foundry was generally a building with large open spaces in which casts and molds could be easily moved from one operation to the next. Within this type of structure dust generated by one process such as the shake-out or sandblasting would easily permeate the air of every part of the plant.[44] While industry touted the ability of new technologies to adequately ventilate the foundry, one survey in Ohio found that such technologies were rarely employed: "Especially devised health appliances such as hoods and exhausts over furnaces, and exhausts and air conditioning systems for the foundry quarters, were good in 6 places, fair in 4 more, poor in 1, and absent in 31."[45]

Another factor undermined the adoption of safety precautions even in the newer foundries. As large national corporations developed their own foundries, they began producing larger and larger castings in greater and greater volume. Engine blocks, large machine parts, and gears demanded greater space and very careful handling. Tumbling mills were frequently too small and too violent to handle such castings. Sandblasting, with its adaptability and maneuverability, was better suited for cleaning larger, more intricate products. The huge quantities of dust produced by the sandblasting of numerous objects in the "captured" foundries for steel, farming implements, and, later, automobiles permeated the larger plants as well. In addition, the larger castings, especially in steel, needed more sand chipping by hand and with pneumatic tools, thereby creating more direct exposure of workers. Just the process of shaking-out large castings created much more dust in unconfined spaces.[46]

Public Health and the Politics of Silicosis in the Foundry

The labor unrest in Barre, Vermont, and Joplin, Missouri, had already focused public health professionals' attention on the deleterious effects of pneumatic

[44] For discussions of the introduction of mechanical devices in the foundry and their generation of dust, see, for example, C.-E.A. Winslow, Leonard Greenburg, and E. H. Reeves, "The Efficiency of Certain Devices Used for the Protection of Sandblasters against the Dust Hazard," *Public Health Reports* 35 (March 5, 1920): 518–35; James M. Betton, "How to Operate the Sandblast Efficiently," *Foundry* 43 (May 1915): 182–83; "Safety in Tumbling Mill Operations," *Foundry* 43 (April 1915): 144–45; E. C. Barringer, "Cleans Castings Hydrolically," *Foundry* 53 (December 1, 1925): 951–954; "Cleaning Room Progress Aids Production of Quality Castings," *Foundry* 56 (July 15, 1928): 546–48; Charles Boultman, "Dust Prevention and Suppression in Sandblasting," *Safety Engineering* 62 (July 1931): 19–23; "Sand Mixing Plant for a Large Foundry," *Iron Age* 94 (December 3, 1914): 1273–75; "Mixes Sand Mechanically," *Foundry* 53 (November 1, 1925): 882–84.

[45] Emery R. Hayhurst, *Industrial Health-Hazards and Occupational Diseases in Ohio* (Columbus: Ohio State Board of Health, 1915), 129.

[46] O. A. Sander, "Lung Findings in Foundry Workers, A Four Year Survey," *American Journal of Public Health* 28 (May 1938): 603.

drills. But the foundry led eminent public health leaders reared in the Progressive Era reform efforts to turn their attention to the sandblaster. In 1920, C.-E.A. Winslow, the Yale professor who was soon to be president of the American Public Health Association, concluded that, as in these other enterprises, sandblasters were particularly exposed to dust and, therefore, disease:

> Since the dust in this case is chiefly composed of particles of crystalline silica, a dust known to cause distinctive changes in the lung tissue which predispose to pulmonary tuberculosis, it is evident that the workers in the sand-blasting industry are exposed to a serious hazard from which they should be protected by the most effective possible means.[47]

As sandblasting became critical in the foundries, it was increasingly perceived as the major source of silicosis.[48]

Despite their relatively conservative outlook, by the 1920s public health investigators had documented the dangers posed by silica dust in a host of industries. While their studies rarely touched on the political and economic implications of this fact, the implications were clear to industry leaders.[49] Furthermore, the glimmerings of a massive crisis for industry could be discerned by the fact that workers themselves were beginning to bring cases of disease to the courts in the form of liability suits. In the early years of the Depression, as workers in foundries found themselves laid off from their jobs, the number of such suits reached epidemic proportions, as we will describe in the next chapter. Industry representatives recognized that the information gathered through the relatively independent researchers in universities and the Public Health Service could have a tremendous impact in court, especially if the De-

[47] C.-E.A. Winslow, Leonard Greenburg, and E. H. Reeves, "The Efficiency of Certain Devices Used for the Protection of Sandblasters Against the Dust Hazard," *Public Health Reports* 35 (March 5, 1920): 531–32. See also the summaries of this influential report in: "Protection of Sandblasters against the Dust Hazard," *Monthly Labor Review* 10 (May 1920): 154–57; and "Devices to Protect Sandblaster against Dust Hazard," *American Journal of Public Health* 10 (August 1920): 631.

[48] See John Arthur Turner and L. R. Thompson, Health Hazards of *Brass Foundries*, U.S. Treasury Department, Public Health Service, *Public Health Bulletin No. 157* (Washington, D.C.: Government Printing Office, 1926), for a discussion of the brass foundries' health problems. Although the authors acknowledged that silica dust was a problem in the cleaning departments, the major problems that they identified related to metal dusts and fumes.

[49] W. E. Watters, "Protected Sand-Blasters Do More Work," *National Safety News* 22 (July 1930): 27. "Among the many hazards common to steel and iron foundries," began this article in the organization's newsletter in 1930, "sandblasting has received comparatively little attention until quite recently." The author, a representative of a foundry in Melrose Park, Illinois, took a generally self-congratulatory tone in that he reported that his company had virtually eliminated the dust hazard for its workers. But he reported quite openly that "it is an unquestionable fact that in the sand-blast operation the operator is generally exposed to extremely fine silica dust." He noted that "with the increased use of sand blasting for cleaning castings, the hazards inherent in this operation naturally become more noticeable."

pression and its resulting unemployment increased. Fears that suits for liability for disease could become a substitute for an as yet nonexistent welfare system haunted insurance and industry spokespeople as the Depression intensified.

In 1931, the National Safety Council, a private organization originally established with the support of industry during the waning years of the Progressive Era, sought to shape the scientific discourse by hiring C.-E.A. Winslow, perhaps the most prestigious and independent public health leader, and Leonard Greenburg, then an officer in the Public Health Service and an assistant professor at Yale, to prepare a report on sandblasting and the danger of silicosis in foundries. Together, they formed a technical committee that produced a report warning about the dangers to sandblasters from silica dust and recommending that metallic abrasive should be substituted wherever possible for silica on emery wheels and other polishers. While the committee did not formulate any standards for minimal dust levels, they did quote previously published standards, thereby acknowledging the danger of exposure to silica dust. In strictly technical language, Winslow and Greenburg showed that when modern equipment was properly used, exposure to silica dust could be kept well below the previous standards of the era. But they concluded that such standards were rarely met: "The air of the workroom [where self-enclosed barrels, tables and cabinets for sandblasting were used] generally contains a highly hazardous dust concentration," they pointed out, and "such an atmosphere cannot fail to predispose in a high degree to silicosis."[50]

After delivering the report, the council indicated to Winslow that given the increased number of lawsuits, many in the foundry industry would not be happy with his findings. Winslow acknowledged this but sought to convince the council of the technical accuracy of his findings, which could "not possibly be avoided." Maintaining that the council had hired him to conduct an independent investigation, not a propaganda piece for industry, he held that he and the council "shall have to stand for the criticism involved." He felt that, with relatively minor changes, few could argue with the report's scientific observations, although he recognized that the foundry owners were worried "that any mention of the fact that there is a hazard in sandblasting will stir up legislation and litigation and like the ostrich they want to hide their heads in the sand and pretend that nothing is going on."[51]

Winslow was correct: Industry was not willing to accept the report. When news of the draft report's contents was revealed, hundreds of telegrams and letters were sent by industry groups demanding the right to inspect and amend the report.[52] The Steel Founders' Society of America wrote to the council

[50] Leonard Greenburg and C.-E.A. Winslow, "The Dust Hazard in Air-Pressure Abrasive Blasting (Sandblasting)," *Archiv für Gewerbepathologie und Gewerbehygiene* 3 (1932): 598.

[51] Winslow to Cameron, January 12, 1932, Winslow Manuscripts, Box 88, Folder 1429.

[52] Cameron to C.-E.A. Winslow and Leonard Greenburg, March 19, 1932, Winslow Manuscripts, Box 88, Folder 1429.

requesting that "any final action be deferred until those industries affected . . . have a chance to be heard." While the letter acknowledged the desirability of "suggestions designed to protect workers from dust conditions," it cautioned that the industry would suffer if the recommendations were "not most carefully prepared or made too broad."[53] The American Foundrymen's Association representative, L. W. Olson, prepared the most detailed critique of Winslow's report, claiming that workers could be rotated into and out of dusty jobs with little impact on their health. Olson revealed that such a rotation system was in place in his own company, the Ohio Brass Company of Mansfield, Ohio. "We have now for a number of years followed a plan of limiting employment in sandblast operations for any one individual to a period of one year," he wrote. He confidently asserted that "this plan seems to quite effectively remove any health hazard that there may be with our apparatus."[54] The conflict over the report revealed industry's ideas about the nature of disease. Building on the idea of time-limited acute infections, the industry spokesman refused to recognize the gathering evidence that indicated that once silicosis began it was progressive and not reversible. For industry, if symptoms did not appear within a year, any subsequent disease could not be ascribed to industrial conditions. A disease of long latency was a disease of personal habit, individual susceptibility, and, ultimately, personal responsibility.

Even though Winslow and Greenburg's report did not raise these issues explicitly, foundry industry representatives feared any report that even indirectly implicated silica dust in long-term disease. After setting up a review committee, the council decided to shelve the report until it could be rewritten. Winslow wrote a stinging letter denouncing the suppression of the report:

> The basic issue is that they [industry spokesmen] do not want any publication from the Council to imply that silica dust is hazardous under any conditions. They know

[53] Granville P. Rogers to W. H. Cameron, Managing Director, National Safety Council, February 8, 1932, Winslow Papers, Box 88, Folder 1429.

[54] L. W. Olson to Leonard Greenburg, February 9, 1932, Winslow Manuscripts, Box 88, Folder 1429. The rotation of workers through dusty production processes was a commonly accepted practice and was generally accepted through the late 1930s as a reasonable way of protecting workers from silicosis. This was in spite of the recognition by many that silicosis, once contracted, was a chronic condition that would get worse with time. Removing a worker from a site once the silica was lodged in the lungs, would not stop or cure the disease. A 1939 letter from Verne Zimmer, the director of the Division of Labor Standards, to R. R. Sayers of the U.S. Public Health Service raised this issue: "Heretofore . . . we have put forward what seemed to be the consensus of medical opinion . . . that, if a worker with non-disabling silicosis, uncomplicated with infection, is removed from dusty employment, there is no probability of the disease progressing further. . . . Recently, however, there seems some reason to believe that medical opinion is more divided on this point and that there is ground for believing that in a substantial number of cases silicosis progresses despite removal of workers from the hazard, and despite removal or control of the dust exposure." Sayers maintained that such rotation practices were still acceptable. See Zimmer to Sayers, April 25, 1939, and Sayers to Zimmer, May 1, 1939, National Archives, Record Group 100, 7-1-5-1.

that it is, but they don't want any authoritative body to say so. Now you cannot very well discuss protection against silica dust without the implication that silica dust is undesirable.[55]

The final resolution of this confrontation reflects the enormous influence that private industry had on ostensibly objective scientific research in the early 1930s. Ultimately, two versions of the report appeared in print. The first, authored by Winslow and Greenburg, was not published in the United States but rather in a German periodical, *Archiv für Gewerbepathologie und Gewerbehygiene*, in late 1932. Submitted on March 18, 1932, in the midst of the controversy within the National Safety Council, the article makes clear the relationship between sandblasting and silicosis: "The essential hazard involved in air-pressure abrasive blasting is, of course, exposure to chrystalline silica in the form of quartz sand used as an abrasive, which, when taken into the lungs, causes silicosis and predisposes towards tuberculosis." Although the report concluded that it was possible to make the sandblasting operations safe, in most of the foundries where sand was used for abrasive blasting, the air was dusty and the danger of silicosis was severe.[56]

A second version was published in an American journal, the *Journal of Industrial Hygiene*, and represented the results of the negotiations within the National Safety Council. In contrast to the European version, Winslow was not listed as an author, although two other prominent public health investigators, J. J. Bloomfield and Leonard Greenburg, were. The article never explicitly says that silicosis is a problem in the foundries. In fact, the word *silicosis* only appears once in the entire twenty journal pages and that is in reference to quarry workers in Barre, Vermont. Furthermore, while reporting the same technical findings about the levels of dust to which workers were exposed in the nation's foundries, it was "quartz" that was identified as the cause of lung "fibrosis" among workers. No conclusions were reached despite the fact that the stated purpose of the article was to "predict the relative hazard of this occupation and to attempt to devise means for the protection of the worker."[57]

---

[55] Winslow to J. I. Banash, December 3, 1932, Winslow Manuscripts, Box 88, Folder 1429. The final report is referred to in Ludwig Teleky, *History of Factory and Mine Hygiene* (New York: Columbia University Press, 1948), 206. The foundry industry was not the only one to seek to downplay or ignore the significance of the emerging silicosis problem in the early 1930s. The head of the Massachusetts Division of Occupational Hygiene, Manfred Bowditch, later related how the president of the Granite Association disputed "the value of dust control at the source, saying that 'small respirators' are all that is required, and capping the argument with the statement that silicosis is not 'recognized in our industry as a disease.' " Manfred Bowditch, "Functions of the State in the Control of Silicosis," in B. E. Kuechle, ed., *Fourth Saranac Laboratory Symposium on Silicosis* (Wassau, Wisc.: Employers Mutual Liability Insurance Company, 1939), 310.

[56] Leonard Greenburg and C.-E.A. Winslow, "The Dust Hazard in Air-Pressure Abrasive Blasting (Sandblasting)," *Archiv für Gewerbepathologie und Gewerbehygiene* 3 (1932): 577, 598.

[57] J. J. Bloomfield and Leonard Greenburg, "Sand and Metallic Abrasive Blasting as an Industrial Health Hazard," *Journal of Industrial Hygiene* 15 (July 1933): 184–204.

Acknowledging Silicosis in the 1930s Foundry

By the mid-1930s the national associations and their journals were publicizing the industry's efforts to put its house in order. With numerous studies that documented the hazards of silica in foundries, and under pressure from the insurance industry, which was threatening to withdraw its liability coverage, foundry owners largely abandoned their earlier position that there was no significant dust problem in the industry. The new tactic was to claim that they had developed and implemented new technologies to prevent future disease and that the cases that continued to appear were the legacy of an earlier period before reform. Their only major difficulty with this approach was that the actual studies of foundry operations, as documented by commissions in North Carolina and Massachusetts, found that most foundries had not implemented the changes. This is not surprising given the facts that most of the foundries were small, the vast majority employing fewer than sixty workers, and that the Depression had put added financial pressures on these marginal operations.

Furthermore, during the 1920s, the work force of the foundry had changed markedly, further lessening industry's interest in protecting its work force. What had been before the war an overwhelmingly white, native, and immigrant male work force was now increasingly black. Especially during the 1920s, as immigration from Europe was severely restricted, blacks found that the foundry was one of the "dirty, hot, and unpleasant" industries that "had an almost spectacular increase in the proportion of Negroes." From a negligible percentage before 1915, African-Americans came to represent over a third of all foundry workers and over two-thirds in some Southern cities, such as Birmingham, Alabama.[58]

What few improvements did occur in the industry were clearly not evident in foundries employing primarily black workers. In fact, there is little published material from the 1920s on the especially harsh conditions under which blacks toiled. Only in case reports of deaths do we get an occasional glimpse. In 1937, one pathology report from the Saranac Laboratory in upstate New York detailed the case history of its subject. The worker had been employed as a sandblaster, polishing metal castings from August 1934 to October 1935—only fourteen months. The case record notes that this worker was never supplied with masks, ventilating equipment, or the suction devices then being touted as the answer to the industry's silicosis problem. He was forced to give up his job in October because of increasingly severe shortness of breath, and a year later he entered the local hospital because his condition had deteriorated markedly. He was diagnosed as having silico-tuberculosis, and he died in December 1936, only "twenty-eight months after the beginning of exposure to

---

[58] Sterling D. Spero and Abram L. Harris, *The Black Worker, The Negro and the Labor Movement* (New York: Atheneum, 1931, 1974), 155–56.

silica, after an illness of fourteen months."[59] For black workers employed in the most hazardous jobs and provided with little protection, silicosis was an acute and life-threatening disease, not a long-term chronic disablement.

During the Depression, the industry underwent a dramatic decline. In 1932 and 1933, unemployed Molders' Union members averaged more than 7,000, which was more than the number of active members.[60] Furthermore, with the number of foundries decreasing in the early 1930s, few of the older job shops spread out across the country could afford to invest in expensive new ventilating equipment and positive air respirators. Even fewer could afford to reconstruct their plants to separate the sandblasting and chipping operations that placed all their workers at risk.

Simultaneous with the widespread acknowledgment that there was a silicosis hazard in foundries,[61] foundry representatives developed a rationale for

[59] Case Files P-37-178, Vorwald Collection, Box 123.

[60] Chartener, "The Molders' and Foundry Workers'," 250.

[61] W. J. McConnell and J. William Fehnel, "Health Hazards in the Foundry Industry," *Journal of Industrial Hygiene* 16 (July 1934): 227–51. Early attempts by industry to suppress the issue were replaced in the early 1930s by a concerted effort to capture the research effort and define the dangers. Beginning in the early 1930s, industry-sponsored reports that documented the significance of silicosis and tuberculosis among foundry workers appeared in Wisconsin, New York, North Carolina, and Pennsylvania. In Wisconsin, the industrial insurer Metropolitan Life conducted a study for the Wisconsin Manufacturers Association that was a damning indictment of foundry practices. See O. A. Sander, "Lung Findings in Foundry Workers, A Four Year Survey," *American Journal of Public Health* 28 (May 1938): 601–09. Beginning in 1931, the study examined working conditions in twenty-one foundries in the state and found that of 215 workers exposed to high levels of silica dust, 31 percent had first- or second-stage silicosis. The study concluded that although foundries presented a serious hazard, modern engineering techniques could effectively be employed to eliminate the hazard. The problem was not inherent in the industry, only in the traditions of managers and owners who resisted technological changes. A year later, O. A. Sander began a four-year longitudinal study in Wisconsin, which confirmed that there was a potential hazard and that the larger foundries appeared to have a larger percentage of silicotic workers when compared to smaller operations. See also, for industry studies of silicosis, "Silicosis in the Foundry," *American Journal of Public Health* 23 (April 1933): 372–73; Carey P. McCord, "Health Hazards in the Foundry," *National Safety News* 29 (January 1934): 34–36. In the mid-1930s, as a result of New York's inclusion of silicosis in workers' compensation legislation, foundry owners in the area around Utica conducted a study of the prevalence of silicosis. While acknowledging the presence of a hazard, especially for workers engaged in the shake-out, the authors concluded that "the occurrence of silicosis in foundry workers . . . is relatively low compared to other dusty industries and was not as great a hazard as was felt both by the employers and the insurance carriers at the time this condition was incorporated in the compensation law." See John F. Kelley and Robert C. Hall, "Silicosis in Modern Foundries," *New York State Journal of Medicine* 37 (1937): 480–81.

In addition to the insurance- and industry-sponsored studies, various states also began to document the health risks of foundry silica dust. In February 1934, the Massachusetts Special Industrial Disease Commission published the results of its examination of granite and foundry workers. See Commonwealth of Massachusetts, *Report to the General Court of the Special Industrial Disease Commission*, February 1934, House Report No. 1350, 42–43. Regarding the foundries, the commission found that despite the understanding that technological means were available to stem

industry inactivity, which they maintained until the mid-1930s. Just as labor had argued nearly two decades before, industry spokespeople now blamed the mechanization process between 1915 and 1925 for the widespread hazard. It was "the great increase in concentration of the dust generated during the industrial boom" of those years that created the real danger: "During those years machine methods were replacing the old hand methods with the resulting excessive exposures." Furthermore, "Most cases of silicosis developed during this speed-up era did not begin to manifest themselves until after 1925." The industry position subtly shifted during the middle years of the Depression. Earlier arguments about the nonexistence of diseases of long latency now became part of the explanation for the current silicosis problem. At the same time, the industry rejected the view that silicosis was still a problem, claiming that improvements in working conditions had eliminated any new silicosis cases. Theodore Hatch, for example, writing in the trade journal *Factory and Industrial Management*, acknowledged that the control of dust had not yet been solved. But "great strides had been made toward its solution." He claimed in 1928 that there were no longer "grinding and polishing rooms filled with dust, nor processes like sand-blasting carried on in the corner of an open factory room." It was the "cooperation of manufacturer, doctor, engineer"

---

the silicosis hazard, only a minority of the state's foundries invested in the necessary equipment. Furthermore, those foundries that did have adequate ventilation equipment rarely maintained it properly, thereby defeating its purpose. The commission concluded: "There is an absence of effective isolation of the particularly dirty processes, such as sand blasting, sand chipping, sand preparation and shake-out work, resulting in general air dustiness." The report continued: "[T]he careless use of compressed air in cleaning molds and the careless application of parting sand create an unnecessary exposure for molders who represent approximately 45 per cent of the employees in the foundry industry." New York State also sponsored a study of the foundry industry in 1938. See Leonard Greenburg, William Siegal, and Adelaide R. Smith, *Silicosis in the Foundry Industry*, State of New York, *Special Bulletin No. 197* (1938), 39; for a more detailed discussion of the need to prevent silicosis in a wide range of industries, see *Special Bulletin No. 198* (1938). In the midst of the heated debate over workers' compensation then going on, the focus was not on the conditions in the industry, but on the degree of silicosis among the work force. The study concluded that the "silicosis hazard in the foundry industry in New York State while existent, is of a mild degree of severity and may be expected to yield satisfactorily to appropriate measures of control." In North Carolina, a state commission found that silicosis among foundry workers was less than in other industries. See "Report of a Study of the Foundry Industry in North Carolina," [about 1938], Industrial and Labor Relations Archives, Cornell University, 5. However, the commission found that the atmosphere of the foundries was extremely dusty and that the longer a worker was employed in the industry, the more likely he or she was to contract silicosis. Further, the commission documented that few of the engineering devices necessary for the prevention of the disease were appropriately used in the foundries of the state. For example, despite the fact that everyone acknowledged that simple cloth or sponge respirators were inadequate, and that the only effective means of stopping the inhalation of dust was a forced air respirator, the commission reported: "Sandblasting is employed for cleaning castings in many of the plants, but in no instance is the worker adequately protected to prevent inhalation of silica dust. . . . The universally employed safeguard is a canvas helmet with which, in a few plants a common type filter pad respirator is used. In none of the plants is the positive pressure air line helmet employed."

that had "brought about wonderful improvement."[62] It was not conceivable to Hatch and other industry spokespeople that there might be silicosis cases appearing twenty years hence.[63] Industry maintained that when it recognized the severity of the disease in the early 1930s, foundry owners took action to reform their plants. The founders' trade association noted, "Since 1930 we, and other allied foundry associations have been preparing and furnishing information with regard to the potential occupational disease hazards in the Foundry Industry."[64]

In general, founders and their allies maintained that the apparent tardiness in addressing the hazard was because of a lack of information on the founders' part: "To any one not familiar with the exact situation in industry, it may seem strange that employers did not act years ago to attempt a better control of the silica-dust hazard," noted Frederick Willson, a physician who was president of Willson Products in Reading, Pennsylvania. "This undoubtedly would have been done by most employers if they had been aware of the danger, but unfortunately the subject, although under investigation and fairly well understood in scientific circles, was largely unknown to industry."[65] It was easy to maintain this fiction even during the Depression since the general public was unaware of the internal debates among Winslow, foundry owners, and the National Safety Council. Nor were most people aware that a special Massachusetts commission in 1934 found that conditions in most plants had not changed in twenty years: "[I]n all but one or two establishments visited, the complete foundry process is carried out on one floor, with no isolation of the extremely dusty processes."[66]

In the years between 1900 and 1930, silicosis emerged from the "cabinet of curiosities" to become a condition of national concern. From the rural, remote regions of Vermont, Missouri, and Montana, it was forced onto a truly national agenda. This did not occur solely because of the internal logic of scientific discovery or because of the activities of professionals. Rather, it emerged from the activities of laborers struggling to control the conditions of work in a rapidly changing industry. Labor and management defined silicosis in terms increasingly removed from the discourse of public health and medicine. Yet they raised problems about the definition of disease and the respon-

[62] Theodore Hatch, "The Dust Hazard in Industry," *Factory and Industrial Management* 75 (February 1928): 320.

[63] O. A. Sander, "Lung Findings in Foundry Workers, A Four Year Survey," *American Journal of Public Health* 28 (May 1938): 601.

[64] E. O. Jones, Director, Safety and Hygiene Section, American Foundrymen's Association, to Frances Perkins, February 29, 1936, National Archives, Record Group 100, 7-0-4(1).

[65] Frederick Willson, "Dust in Industry, Shop Methods and Equipment Effective in Controlling Dust Hazards," *Mechanical Engineering* 55 (February 1933): 80.

[66] Commonwealth of Massachusetts, *Report to the General Court of the Special Industrial Disease Commission*, February 1934, House Report 1350 (Boston: Wright and Potter Printing Co., 1934), 35.

sibility of society that ultimately had to be integrated into the professional models of disease causation. In the years of the Depression, a new ingredient was added to the social conditions in which scientific and technical arguments took place. The severe economic decline that took its toll on both labor and industry alike would force a parochial concern to become a full-blown crisis.

III

"THIS KING OF OCCUPATIONAL DISEASES—

SILICOSIS"

Nineteen thirty-five. A wave of fear was sweeping the
country. Silicosis was taking its toll from the ranks of American
workers. Cause of the disease, dust. Results of the disease,
disablement, poverty, death. Cure for the disease, none.
Throughout America, workers exposed to dust grew fearful
of their health and of their very lives.
(*Opening narration of* Stop Silicosis, *a film produced by the
Department of Labor in 1938*)

Out of a clear sky and with dramatic suddenness, the insurance
companies were faced with a situation that was in many respects
terrifying. They naturally found themselves in a very
uncomfortable position. The success of silicosis damage suits was
appalling and there was enough in the situation to retard at times
the ordinary flow of common sense. Many employers found
themselves with employees on their payroll who already had
silicosis and in respect to whom a liability already existed, a
liability not previously covered by insurance and for which no
reserves had been accumulated. It is not to be wondered at if
difficulties arose in trying to solve this knotty problem which had
social as well as economic aspects.
(*Anthony J. Lanza, 1939*)

IN 1931, Michael Farina, a sandblaster for the General Electric Company
in Schenectady, New York, was laid off. Although hundreds of thousands
of workers all across the country were losing their jobs at this time, Farina
was told that it was not just the Depression that had led to his hardship. A
company physician had diagnosed him as "a victim of Silicosis" on the basis
of an x-ray the company had forced upon him. General Electric promised him
another job, but, as days dragged into weeks, Farina found "that they forgot
about it," and he had not been able to find work since. Finally, in 1936, he
wrote to Frances Perkins about his plight, for he believed that he was "entitled
to another job or should receive compensation [for] silicosis since [his] illness

was the result of the work [he] had been doing."[1] We do not know what happened to Farina. But thousands of others in a similar situation did more than ask for relief. They turned to the courts as a means of seeking compensation for the disease that had cost them their jobs. This simple act so necessary for survival set off a chain of events that provoked the worst legal crisis involving workers' safety and health up to that time.

The stock market crash of October 1929 and the subsequent depression fundamentally altered many aspects of American life. With at least a quarter of the labor force unemployed and a much larger percentage of the population struggling to survive on reduced wages and the threat of layoffs, Americans had to confront a social and economic crisis of massive proportions. Prior to 1933, there were no federal welfare programs, no social security payments, no unemployment benefits—no safety net to catch men and women, children and elderly, sick and disabled. The few social programs that did exist were run by private charity organizations, city welfare bureaus, or state emergency relief agencies. Vast regions of the country did not even have minimal programs to support starving citizens in rural and urban communities. People were forced to develop their own networks for social support through families or friends. Workers and families organized self-help organizations, councils of the unemployed, and unions to find ways of controlling their own fate. They were forced to reformulate their assumptions about how to survive without work, social and familial support, or state or private mechanisms for guaranteeing basic necessities. Breadlines, riots, marches, rent strikes, sit-ins, and labor strife were the most obvious signs of the desperation of the times. But they also reflected the new range of options that working-class Americans believed were legitimate for survival.

It was in this new, tumultuous social environment that the issue of social responsibility for chronic industrial illness and disease was now discussed. As workers were thrown out of work and families forced to support the disabled on meager or no income, the arguments about responsibility for industrial disease and disability took on a new urgency and meaning. Responsibility for sickness now emerged as a highly politicized issue, for upon this seemingly academic debate would hinge the economic survival of families. The social and economic circumstances of the Depression transformed the question of who was sick and who was well. Before the Depression, doctors, public health, industry, and labor were willing to cede to medical experts the right to diagnose dust disease. Although groups disagreed about who was responsible for the risks of work and how extensive the dangers were, it was generally

[1] Michael Farina to Frances Perkins, July 28, 1936, National Archives, Record Group 100, 7-2-1-5-1.

agreed that experts could and should reach a consensus on the defining features of the disease itself.

During the Depression, however, this consensus broke down. Different interest groups now debated how sickness should be defined and who should diagnose it. On the one hand, some professionals demanded "objective" proof in the form of laboratory tests and x-ray evidence to establish the existence of disease. It was the diagnostician, they felt, depending on these technological tools who was to define disease. Laborers, on the other hand, were concerned with how they felt and whether their physical condition allowed them to maintain a normal life. For the laborer, a normal life included recreation, longevity, a role in the family as well as a job. Furthermore, workers wanted to define when and if they were able to work. In the context of the Depression, sickness became a legitimate means by which to address the problems of dependence in a society without a social welfare system. Business and insurance companies feared that private capital would be forced to absorb the financial costs of an increasingly dependent population. These differing perspectives existed before the Great Depression, but now a worker's ability or inability to draw a deep breath meant more than the difference between a job and destitution.

Workers thrown out of work used any means necessary to survive, and many workers in the dusty trades turned to the courts. Those who suspected that they were fired because of their impairments argued that industry bore the responsibility for their plight. They argued that their plight was not the result of individual failings or bad luck but was, rather, due to the inadequate protection offered them by their employers. The social crisis of the Depression created personal tragedies. But as larger and larger numbers of workers in foundries and other silica industries turned to the courts for redress, their personal suffering became a national crisis. For the first time, the problem of silicosis moved out of the domain of professionals and a few labor unions into the arenas of popular culture and public policy. Before the Depression would end, novels and movies, national magazine exposés, and intense media attention would force the issue of industrially caused chronic disease onto the national agenda. In turn, the attention of the popular media redefined the social conditions in which the debate about silicosis took shape. The public now debated what had been the preserve of a small cadre of lawyers, doctors, and public health professionals. Labor, management, industry, and insurance representatives argued in terms accessible to laypeople. Later, professionals would reclaim their turf and preside over arguments about "latency," "time of onset," and "disease process." However, during the Depression decade the very definition of disease was not the preserve of the elite but was part of a wider public dialogue.

Lawsuits Create a Silicosis Crisis

As late as 1929, silicosis had assumed a great deal of "importance in the minds of those concerned with public health"[2] but had not become part of public discourse. In New York, a study done by the Columbia University School of Public Health and supported by Harry Hopkins, soon to become head of the Works Progress Administration, revealed that rockdrillers, blasters, and excavators constructing the city's subways were subject to a serious hazard. In an article entitled "Silicosis Denounced as 'Murder' of Labor," the New York *Times* reported that organized labor in the state had begun to take notice. The vice president of the state's Federation of Labor, Thomas J. Curtis, told a committee of the legislature that "with all the work now going on in New York City the drilling of rock is putting the dust into the lungs of hundreds who are being diseased, and there is no redress for them."[3] The head of New York State's Division of Industrial Hygiene, James Hackett, remarked in 1932 that silicosis "would continue to exist unnoticed in the community were it not for the fact that workers suffering from the disease, or the relatives of people who had died from the disease, have recently taken civil action against employers and have recovered considerable amounts of money therefore." The lawsuits brought "silicosis within the rage of practical politics."[4] By September 1933, *Business Week* commented that an "epidemic of lawsuits" was "giving serious concern to the construction, quarry, and mining industries and to foundries and glass works. . . ."[5]

Insurance companies were the first to understand the potential problems that the flood of lawsuits was creating because they were insuring foundries and other industries against liability suits through general comprehensive liability policies. In 1932, the first issue of *Industrial Medicine*, soon to become the central journal in the field, featured a long review essay by Andrew J. Farrell, head of the claims and legal department of a major Chicago insurance com-

---

[2] "Effect of Dust on the Lungs," *American Journal of Public Health* 20 (April 1930): 368.

[3] "Silicosis Denounced as 'Murder' of Labor," *New York Times*, March 7, 1929.

[4] James D. Hackett, "Silicosis," *New York Department of Labor Industrial Bulletin* 11 (December 1932): 475. See also, for early 1930s discussions of silicosis, Adelaide Ross Smith, "Review of Silicosis," *New York Department of Labor Industrial Bulletin* 12 (February, April, June, July, 1933): 32–33; 90–92; 144–46; 176–78; and John Campbell, "The Conference Discussion of Industrial Disease," *Pennsylvania Department of Labor and Industry Monthly Report*, June 1932, 24–28. The latter reported that "Doctor Hamilton also made the point that industries causing the largest amount of danger are those in which there is silica dust present."

[5] "Silicosis Menace," *Business Week*, September 1933, 19–20. See also "Silicosis Menace," *Literary Digest*, December 15, 1934, 118; *New York Times*, December 5, 1934, for a report on a symposium on this problem before the American Society of Mechanical Engineers; "Silicosis," *Time*, January 6, 1936, 27. See Anthony Bale, *Compensation Crisis: The Value and Meaning of Work-Related Injuries and Illnesses in the United States, 1842–1932* (Ph.D. diss., Brandeis University, 1986), for an extended and incisive discussion of the liability system.

pany. He argued that the problem was not that silicosis caused disability, but that unemployment caused workers to use the legal system as a welfare system and that unscrupulous lawyers were taking advantage of ignorant workers. The result was not justice for the work force but rather the "closing of industrial plants and a vast economic loss."[6] Another insurance company representative later affirmed Farrell's predictions when he declared that silicosis "has all but paralyzed the [insurance] industry in many cases."[7] Employers Mutual, a company that had a large industrial clientele, reported in its twenty-fifth annual report to policyholders that silicosis suits resulted in "the most serious claim problem ever encountered . . . in its entire history." In the social context of the Depression, the insurance industry proclaimed that silicosis was "probably the most serious occupational disease hazard in existence today." This view was not based on epidemiological studies, medical opinion, or research. Rather it flowed from logic of social upheaval during the worst industrial and economic crisis in American history.[8]

The crisis for the insurance industry soon became a crisis for the various industries and the work force as well. Insurance companies sought means by which to limit their risks through selectively insuring or canceling industrial liability policies. High-risk companies, such as foundries, metal mines, glassworks, potteries, and quarries were told that they had to examine all employees for signs of silicosis and to terminate those who showed any symptoms of disease. In the midst of the Depression, when jobs were scarce, many of the employed were faced with unemployment if industry or insurance company physicians, utilizing x-rays, found suspicious signs of silicosis on the films. Industry itself was pressed by the insurance companies to fire employees, thereby creating further antagonism and labor strife during these turbulent years of labor organizing. Further, certain industries, such as glassblowing and foundries, were forced to lay off highly skilled workers upon whom they depended. The president of the National Founders Association described how this process worked in his industry: "The insurance carriers demanded in many instances that all the employees of their foundry risks submit to a medical examination. If the employer refused to accept this demand, they received notice their policy would not be renewed at its termination, and in some instances policies were cancelled immediately." He blamed the insurance companies, not heavy industry, for the hardships that workers faced: The foundries "found themselves in a very embarrassing position when the carriers de-

[6] Andrew J. Farrell, "Silicosis in Certain of Its Legal Aspects," *Industrial Medicine* 1 (October 1932): 35.

[7] "Cause and Effect of Silicosis Explained by Medical Experts," *National Underwriter* 38 (April 19, 1934): 31–32.

[8] "Silica Dust Declared Biggest Claim Problem," *Weekly Underwriter* 134 (May 2, 1936): 936.

manded that men whose x-ray examinations revealed that they had accumulated certain amounts of fibrosis should be eliminated from the pay-roll."[9]

The effect of these new policies on the work force was dramatic and immediate. For example, the wife of a worker in Barberton, Ohio, wrote to the
federal government that her husband had been laid off from the Ohio Insulation Company in 1935 because the managers suspected that he had silicosis.
The company had "all persons in the factory examined at Springfield Sanitarium to find out" if they suffered from lung disease. Despite the fact that her
husband did not believe that he was ill, he was "unable to get work anyplace."
She believed that her husband had given "fifteen of the best years of his life
and they surely ought to have a place in their organization for him."[10] Silicosis
had become a social problem of immense proportions:

> The problem of silicosis presenting the specter of disability and death to a large
> group of labor, incalculable risks to casualty insurance companies, financial ruin
> to many dusty industries, unplumbed complexities to doctors, engineers, lawyers,
> industrial commissions and public health authorities blazed into prominence in the
> U.S. when fanned by the ill-wind of depression after having smoldered peacefully
> for decades.[11]

As social issues around silicosis entered the legal arena, professional dis-
agreement, previously relegated to obscure technical journals, became a matter for contentious public debate. Because of the legal system's adversarial
nature, the lawsuits highlighted the conflicting opinions of scientists, doctors,
and engineers about occupational lung diseases. Judges and juries, who in
other circumstances would have preferred to defer to the "objective experts"
in highly technical matters, found themselves in the position of having to decide which expert testimony to believe. Lawyers for workers and lawyers for
insurance companies and industries each presented juries with their own
groups of experts. Faced by conflicting medical testimony about the nature
and causes of the plaintiff's lung condition, and faced with the worker's often
obvious suffering, jurors in the early years of the Depression frequently
brought judgments against insurance companies and industry alike. Because
there were so many lawsuits, especially in the industrial states, and because

[9] E. O. Jones to U.S. Department of Labor, November 29, 1935, National Archives, Record
Group 100, 7-2-1-5-1.

[10] Beryl McDonald to Mrs. Roosevelt, April 10, 1936, National Archives, Record Group 100,
7-2-1-5-1. See also Norman A. Buending to Alice Hamilton, May 14, 1936, National Archives,
Record Group 100, 7-2-1-5-1 and reply, in which Buending describes the plight of fluorspar
miners in Hardin County, Illinois.

[11] D. E. Cummings, "Administrative Aspects of Silicosis," in B. E. Kuechle, ed., *Third Symposium on Silicosis* (June 21–25, 1937), 225–34. "The fury with which this blaze flared when
finally touched off can be partially attributed to the general resentment which had accumulated
over many years from the failure of managements to acknowledge, guard against or compensate
for the disease." *Ibid.*

so much hinged on the decisions of juries and judges, the public could see in a very concrete way that medical analysis and diagnoses were subject to conflicting interpretations and were the result of differing values and assumptions. Further, the fact that expert opinion could be bought by plaintiff and defendant alike demystified professional arguments. The very fact that foundries were such a ubiquitous part of America's industrial and agricultural base meant that friends and relatives of disabled foundry workers were educated about the workings of the professions. As C. O. Sappington, an industrial hygienist associated with industry, pointed out, "so much emphasis has been placed on silicosis that the entire population has become silicosis-conscious."[12]

For the foundry industry it was as if a "plague . . . arose in the industrial centers of the Atlantic coast and worked westward, causing an excitment in this country that verged on hysteria." According to the medical director of a foundry in Chicago,

> [I]ndustrialists were dumbfounded and grasping for advice and guidance to meet the plague. Medical men and research workers were caught unaware. . . . Attorneys and legislators saw a field for action in the interests of the workingclass— and themselves. News commentators and reporters recognized "an interest story" that would make the frontline. This entire state of confusion arose in a time of business recession which reached an economic depression of magnitude such as this country had never experienced.[13]

The circumstances of the Depression brought into high relief the suffering of workers suing for liability. And as workers won their suits, it emboldened more of the unemployed and their lawyers. In New York State alone, the foundry industry faced over $30 million in lawsuits in 1933.[14] In the face of obvious suffering, judges, furthermore, were more and more likely to hold companies accountable for death and disability resulting from known risks. In contrast to earlier decades, when the doctrine of assumed risk and the fellow-servant rule tended to favor employers, the rash of lawsuits and the circumstances of the Depression changed the rules of the game. In 1931, one company owner sought to inform his fellow corporate heads about the changing legal environment in which dust cases were being decided. He quoted from one New Jersey Supreme Court opinion that companies had a responsibility to

[12] C. O. Sappington, "What Price Occupational Diseases?" *Pit and Quarry* 29 (September 1936): 48.

[13] Dr. J. H. Chivers, "Discussion," in Leonard Greenburg, ed., *Silicosis in the Foundry Industry* (Chicago: American Foundrymen's Association, 1938), 30.

[14] "Silicosis Menace," *Business Week*, September 1933, 19–20. See also Benjamin F. Tillson, "Silicosis: Its Economic Aspects," *Engineering and Mining Journal* 135 (June 1934): 263, who pointed out: "Several years ago the damage claims ran from $5,000 to $10,000 but now $100,000 is not an uncommon claim for an individual." He estimated that "at least $300,000,000 in silicosis claims have originated in the last few years."

maintain a safe environment for the work force, "free from latent dangers known to the defendant company, or discoverable by an ordinary prudent master." The assumption of risk on the part of the employee was now the exception rather than the rule in the new industrial setting.[15]

Workers' Compensation and the Containment of the Silicosis Issue

It became clear that it was in the interest of a broad range of groups to try to defuse the social crisis surrounding silicosis. The insurance industry took the lead, but state government, labor unions, and the professional community all saw the social crisis of silicosis suits as a threat. It was necessary to remove the disease from the political arena and return it to the stewardship of the professionals. By doing so, internal debates based upon the differing views of experts could be contained within professional journals and forums rather than aired in public court and in the public media.

As early as 1932, the insurance industry representatives began to press for the inclusion of silicosis in states' workers' compensation systems. Theodore C. Waters, a lawyer who was expert in occupational disease litigation, suggested that the flood of lawsuits had at least "served the fortunate purpose of proving the inadequacy of common-law procedure to adjust disputes between employer and employee, arising from this type of occupational-disease injury." He maintained that a viable alternative existed within the workers' compensation system, which was still largely reserved for industrial accident compensation. From the insurance industry's perspective, the advantage of covering silicosis through workers' compensation was that administrative tribunals handled the claims—employees could no longer use the courts to recover large sums of money for their disease. Workers' compensation removed contention over responsibility for industrial disease from the public arena of the courts.[16] Other insurance executives agreed, but they recognized the difficulty of enacting favorable compensation legislation in each of the separate states. They noted that in states where there were provisions for occupational diseases in the workers' compensation laws, "there is not so much activity in stirring up claims" through a workers' compensation system that "limited by statute" the amount that could be recovered. In addition to the smaller claims, the insurance industry was attracted by the fact that the "rights of the claimant are still subservient to the powers of the industrial commission, even after

---

[15] Frederick Willson, "The Very Least an Employer Should Know about Dust and Fume Diseases," *Safety Engineering* 62 (November 1931): 317.

[16] Theodore C. Waters, "Legal Aspects of the Dust Diseases," *Pit and Quarry* 30 (December 1937): 59.

trial."[17] Even though a few states provided coverage under their workers' compensation laws for silicosis claims and the number of such claims also increased dramatically in the early 1930s, the average awards through the compensation system were dramatically lower than under the liability system. The U.S. Commissioner of Labor Statistics estimated that the average award in New York State for other occupational diseases was only $325 in 1929.[18] As late as 1935, Wisconsin's relatively progressive system awarded an average of only $430 per occupational disease claim.[19]

Since the Progressive Era, workers' compensation had proven extremely effective in ameliorating the conflict between workers and management over disabling accidents that cost workers their earning power as well as their physical integrity.[20] However, because the compensation system had been devised to address the issue of acute accidents, not long-term chronic industrial disease, it was not clear to those advocating a broader approach exactly how to proceed. The history of the inclusion of occupational disease in the state compensation systems was neither smooth nor obvious.

Although Great Britain, Germany, and other European societies had established various workers' compensation programs in the late nineteenth century, the American system developed gradually through state legislative action during the period 1911 to 1925. First in the most industrialized states and gradually extending to nearly all of the states, workers' compensation systems became the bedrock legislation that addressed the immense social and economic costs to workers and their families of rapid and relatively unrestrained industrialization. While each state developed different mechanisms for judging the extent of workplace injury and the amount of money to be awarded for particular accidents and the types of injuries incurred, all these laws had certain features in common. First, they were framed as "no-fault" systems in which awards were made irrespective of responsibility for injury. Second, the workers' compensation laws were framed to address the problem of accidents and injuries, not disease. Finally, the workers' compensation systems were generally voluntary mechanisms that substituted relatively small awards for many workplace injuries in exchange for exclusion of covered risks from the liability tort system, where awards were potentially much larger. Generally adminis-

---

[17] Andrew J. Farrell, "Silicosis in Certain of Its Legal Aspects," *Industrial Medicine* 1 (October 1932): 35.

[18] Ethelbert Stuart, U.S. Commissioner of Labor Statistics, "Occupational Diseases and Workmen's Compensation Laws," *Monthly Labor Review* 30 (February 1930): 93–94.

[19] See A. Z. Skelding to R. Campbell Starr, September 28, 1936, National Archives, Record Group 100, 7-0-4(1).

[20] Anthony Bale, "Compensation Crisis: The Value and Meaning of Work-Related Injuries and Illnesses in the United States, 1842–1932" (Ph.D. diss., Brandeis University, 1986), ch. 16, for a discussion of the relationship between the growing silicosis suits and the movement to include disease in workers' compensation legislation.

tered through insurance companies, a crisis in the workers' compensation system could directly affect both industry and insurance carriers alike.

In the early legislation, the issue of work-related disease was hardly addressed. The sociologist Anthony Bale has outlined two basic objections that were widely used to legitimate the exclusion of disease from workers' compensation legislation and administration. First, it was commonly maintained that it was "difficult to establish whether a particular case of illness [was] due to strictly occupational causes or to a combination of occupational and non-occupational causes." Except in cases of specific poisons, such as phosphorus or lead, where acute symptoms could be linked to exposure on the job, most industrial diseases were not nearly as clear cut. Second, opponents charged that occupational diseases had "no particular moment of origin," often developing after gradual exposure to toxins. Hence, unlike an accident, which could be fixed in time and place, the etiology of diseases was much less clear. In light of the tremendous population and job mobility and the constant reality of layoffs, it was difficult to ascribe responsibility to a particular industry or company for a worker's disease. However, Bale argues that the fundamental reason that accidents were included rather than diseases was that workers were using the liability system to sue for damages and that this had created a "crisis" for capital and the legal system. In the process of developing the compensation system, the limits of social responsibility for work-related health problems were slowly worked out. It was not until workers began using the courts to claim liability awards for industrial diseases that state courts and legislators would be forced to grudgingly include industrially related diseases in the workers' compensation system.[21]

By the end of World War I, there were forty-two workers' compensation jurisdictions in the United States. Only four—California, Hawaii, Massachusetts, and the federal government—provided compensation for occupational diseases. In all other jurisdictions, occupational diseases were excluded from the operation of the compensation acts in one of three ways: by limiting the scope of the law to injuries caused by accidents; by adverse rulings by the courts and commissions; and by express provisions of the compensation acts. However, some diseases were covered if they could be linked to accidents or injuries; for example, if the disease was a result of a violent injury on the job or if exposure to a toxin could be traced to a particular time and place, courts might decide that it fell under the "accidental injury" rubric of the compensation laws. Also, if the disease was due to an exposure that was not commonly understood to be intrinsic to the job or if the employer had not taken minimal precautions to protect the work force from exposure, specific state boards were inclined to include some conditions.

In an article analyzing the state of occupational disease legislation in 1919,

---

[21] Bale, "Compensation Crisis," 469–70.

Carl Hookstadt, an official in the Bureau of Labor Statistics, noted the "paradox" of contemporary laws and regulations: "Our workmen's compensation laws have been enacted in the vague belief that industrial accidents were inevitable and constituted a permanent and integral part of our industrial life." He continued by noting that "these same reasons . . . are now used by the courts and commissions against compensation for occupational diseases."[22] Accidents were once understood to be unusual events whose occurrence was a result of negligence or fault on the part of employers or employees. Therefore, nineteenth-century restitution for injury was brought through the court system, where responsibility for fault was adjudicated. By the early decades of the century, however, underlying social assumptions regarding the nature of industrial accidents had subtly shifted. The premise underlying workers' compensation laws was that accidents were inevitable and inherent to the industrial process and were therefore inappropriate for the liability system, which was designed to decide the question of fault. The irony that Hookstadt described was that although occupational diseases also were inherent to the job, the lack of pressure on the state legislatures from workers' demands on the legal system allowed those who framed the workers' compensation systems to ignore disease.

The framers of the early occupational disease legislation were working from the industrial accident model. Occupational diseases were viewed as injuries that occurred in a particular place at a specific time. For example, when chlorine gases escaped from a vat in a chemical plant causing lung damage or scarring, the relationship between the exposure and the injury was clear. Similarly, a New York court ruled that a worker was entitled to compensation after he contracted anthrax from abrasions on his hands while unloading hides. Anthony Bale points out these situations were understood to be accidents—statistically predictable but "unexpected, unusual and extraordinary" regarding time, place, or victim. An occupational disease, on the other hand, was in the words of the New York court, the opposite—also statistically predictable but "expected, usual, and ordinary."[23] Neither chronic exposure to poisons that were part of the work process nor physical breakdown due to the "ordinary"—if harsh—routines of a job were adequate to justify inclusion in the compensation system. As C.-E.A. Winslow pointed out, the relationship be-

---

[22] Carl Hookstadt, "Compensation for Occupational Diseases in the United States and Foreign Countries," *Monthly Labor Review* 8 (April 1919): 200–05; See also John B. Andrews, "Compensation for Occupational Diseases," *The Survey* 30 (April 5, 1913): 15–19; "Compensation for Occupational Diseases under Workmen's Compensation Laws," *Monthly Labor Review* 3 (August 1916): 222–23. By 1921 Connecticut, New York, North Dakota, and Wisconsin also provided compensation for some occupational diseases. See Carl Hookstadt, "Cost of Occupational Disease under Workmen's Compensation Acts in the United States," *Monthly Labor Review* 12 (February 1921): 154–59.

[23] Quoted in Bale, "Compensation Crisis," 485.

tween cause and effect for accidents and acute illnesses was clear. "But the problems of lead poisoning, the problems of industrial tuberculosis, are vastly more complex and vastly more difficult."[24] Workers seeking redress for chronic diseases caused by long-term occupational exposures to toxins or dusts therefore, unlike their injured coworkers, continued to turn to the court system.

Throughout the 1920s, a few more states added occupational diseases to their compensation regulations. But most states continued to use the accident model for framing the limits of their compensation systems. Although the public health community and labor groups (as well as the burgeoning industrial hygiene profession) became more aware of the pervasiveness and "ordinariness" of occupational diseases for industrial workers, state compensation boards were slow to react.

The Allure of the Medical Expert

The heart of the problem facing the insurance companies, industry, labor, and government was how to define and compensate disability caused by occupational disease, specifically silicosis. Traditionally, workers' compensation systems specified a dollar amount for the type and severity of any particular accident. Loss of a limb, an eye, or a life were all given a price, and workers or their families could count on receiving a specific amount for a particular accident. These "scheduled" payments might differ in the several states, but the principle of concrete awards for predictable events was the basis of these systems.

Silicosis presented a host of new problems for the compensation system. Unlike acute conditions, it was extremely difficult to diagnose. Among experts, there was little agreement as to what effect silicosis had on the worker and what constituted disability. Throughout the thirties, there was substantial controversy over the course of the disease. Medical experts were unsure of how the disease progressed, whether disability and impairment were inevitable, and the length of time between exposure to silica and initial symptoms. In the face of these uncertainties, legislators, insurance company representatives, industry spokespeople, and labor were faced by the practical problem of developing legislation to defuse the financial and social crisis that had arisen. What constituted a compensable disease? If only disabling disease was to be compensated, then how was disability to be defined? Was x-ray evidence alone adequate for diagnosis? Was the prospect of disability in the future compensable today? Was it necessary to have demonstrable impairments? Who

[24] C.-E.A. Winslow, "Life Capital in Industry," in *Proceedings of the Tenth Annual New York State Industrial Safety Congress* (Albany: J. B. Lyon Co., 1927).

was to diagnose, evaluate, and decide on the degree of disability? All these issues needed to be addressed if silicosis was to be included in the workers' compensation systems and if these systems were to remain financially solvent.

The insurance, business, and most public health experts objected to the loose definitions of compensable disease that emerged from the numerous court decisions. Judges and juries were holding industry strictly accountable for bodily harm irrespective of its immediate impact on the ability of workers to work. "The present dilemma in which we find ourselves is [due] . . . to the fact that we apparently think of every case of pulmonary fibrosis as requiring compensation, whether disabled or able to work," wrote Roy Jones of the U.S. Public Health Service to the head of the National Founders Association in 1935.[25] Workers had been winning lawsuits simply for having silicosis defined by medical x-ray or opinion. This was similar to the principles that guided compensation for accidents, where physical disfigurement was generally sufficient. In 1920, one author noted that an employee "may become permanently partially disabled by the loss of some member of his body without suffering a loss in earning capacity." Despite the fact that the worker could continue at his or her job, "the majority of the states have provided in their laws for a schedule of such injuries."[26]

But insurance, industry, and public health experts sought to reorient the public conception of compensation so that workers would have to show that they were losing income and work because of the effects of disease. During the Depression, the old model of immediate compensation for accidental injury was dangerous. With millions of workers unemployed and a sea of potential silicosis claims, there was the actuarial potential for disaster. Insurance and industry spokespeople thus rejected the definition of disability that was based solely on a workers' stated inability to perform work. The "proof" of the existence of a disability was a worker's loss of income. Industry pressed, instead, for a system that depended on a physician's opinion regarding the worker's ability to perform his or her duties. It was the doctor who should decide who was capable of work, not the victim.[27]

Industry spokesmen sought to protect workers' compensation from the same problem that plagued the liability system. A representative of the foundry industry called for the "establishment of competent and impartial medical tribunals, free from political influences, to decide all medical questions involved in controverted cases." He complained that under the current compensation

[25] Roy Jones to E. O. Jones, December 10, 1935, National Archives, Record Group 100, 7-2-1-5-1.
[26] Martin C. Frinke, Jr., " 'Loss of Use' or the Impairment of Function," *Monthly Labor Review* 10 (August 1920): 121–30.
[27] See Max D. Kossoris and O. A. Freed, "Experience with Silicosis under Wisconsin Workmen's Compensation Act, 1920–1936," *Monthly Labor Review* 44 (May 1937): 1092, for a discussion of these two concepts.

system, "boards of laymen, after hearing the partisan opinions of physicians selected by the disputants, regardless of the weight of medical opinion" made the decisions in highly technical medical matters. If "difficult disease such as silicosis," were "brought under the compensation law," he maintained, "the results would be chaotic and probably ruinous."[28]

Insurance and industry leaders were more confident that a system based upon the medical profession would serve their own interests in limiting compensation claims for a number of reasons. Most physicians entering into occupational medicine were not coming from the traditions of reform and public health that had produced Alice Hamilton and C.-E.A. Winslow. Rather, the new occupational physicians were more likely to be employed by industry and concerned with the laboratory. This change in the structure of the profession was affecting not only the subjective opinions that guided the diagnosis of individual patients but also the very definition of industrial lung disease itself. The solution that was proposed was the appointment of a medical board that would be the final arbiter in silicosis and occupational disease cases. As early as 1925, the National Industrial Conference Board called for the establishment of a medical advisory panel, which would be appointed with the recommendation of the state medical society to determine objectively the outcome of accident and disease cases brought before the compensation system. They believed that such a process would "reduce the possibilities of political influence to a minimum and would give assurance that only properly qualified men would be considered."[29] By the 1930s, most others agreed. Anthony J. Lanza pressed for a "medical board to advise compensation officials both as to the diagnosis in disputed cases of silicosis and the extent of disability." He noted that the inclusion of such boards in workers' compensation legislation was "a recognition of . . . the desirability of removing this type of case from the sphere of ex parte medical testimony."[30] Lanza anticipated debates that would rage in the 1950s about expertise and which physicians and specialists had it.

It is commonly assumed that the legitimacy of professional opinion rests on professionals' ability to discern absolute truths from untruths. But the history of the development of medical panels indicates that it was the uncertainty of

[28] F. Robertson Jones, "Problems of Compensation for Occupational Diseases," Address Delivered at the National Convention of the National Founders Association, November 15, 1934, American Association for Labor Legislation Manuscripts, Occupational Disease Pamphlets, 1933–34, Industrial and Labor Relations Archives, Cornell University.

[29] "Uniform Medical Provisions for Workmen's Compensation Acts in the United States," Special Report No. 31 (New York: National Industrial Conference Board, Inc., 1925), 17. In New York State, a committee established through the State Department of Labor recommended that silicosis be incorporated into existing compensation legislation as early as 1926. See New York, Department of Labor, Bureau of Industrial Hygiene, *Bulletin, Silicosis in New York State, A Study of Fifteen Cases of Silicosis from the Standpoint of Compensation* (Albany, 1926).

[30] A. J. Lanza, "Health Problems in Mining," *Mining Congress Journal* 22 (November 1936): 26–27.

medical science that led to exclusion of laypeople and workers and the usurpation of the decisionmaking process by medical experts. The prestigious Committee on Pneumoconioses of the American Public Health Association declared their support for such a scheme in 1933: "Without some form of medical control, the management of compensation for a disease such as silicosis would be difficult." They maintained this position despite the lack of a medical consensus regarding either the mechanism by which silica dust affected lung tissue, the course of silicosis once it was diagnosed, or even the degree of disability associated with the various stages of the disease. The committee acknowledged that silicosis was "a disease in which the definition of disability is obscure." But they went on to urge that "medical advice is necessary to determine whether the worker's health is impaired to a degree which constitutes disability."[31]

The Changing Definition of Silicosis

This general change in the perspective of the field of industrial hygiene was even reflected in the changing definition of silicosis itself. In 1917, Lanza had pointed out that silicosis, whether early or late, characteristically inhibited breathing in its victims: "The first stage [was] characterized with slight or moderate dyspnea on exertion," even if they all "looked robust." Other investigators in the early 1920s recognized the insidious nature of silicosis. Dr. P. H. Hourigan, the medical director of an industrial concern in Buffalo, New York, described the paradox of silicosis. Noting that the first sign of the disease was dyspnea, Hourigan explained that "it comes on so gradually and insidiously, and the patient so unconsciously avoids efforts which increase this difficulty, that you marvel at the objective evidence of increasing difficulty of breathing developed before the person afflicted with silicosis recognizes the lessened capacity of his lungs."[32] Even in the conservative antilabor atmosphere of the mid-1920s, the insidious nature of silicosis raised a host of troublesome questions regarding critical aspects of the meaning of a diagnosis of silicosis. Hourigan wrote: "I am not prepared to say that [a worker] should not be compensated for that loss of physical well-being; that is a question which expert lawmakers must determine."[33] In primary silicosis, if you

[31] *Workmen's Compensation for Silicosis*, Report of the Committee on Pneumoconioses of the American Public Health Association (R. R. Sayers, A. J. Lanza, Adelaide Ross Smith, Emery R. Hayhurst) (New York: Association of Casualty and Surety Executives, 1933), 22, American Association for Labor Legislation Manuscripts, Occupational Disease Pamphlets, 1933–34, Industrial and Labor Relations Archives, Cornell University.

[32] P. H. Hourigan, "Silicosis: An Occupational Disease," in New York State Department of Labor, *Proceedings of the Eighth Annual New York State Industrial Conference*, December 2–4, 1924, 222.

[33] Hourigan, "Silicosis," 225.

searched for shortness of breath, even when the worker was unaware of it, you could find it.

By 1935, however, as the silicosis crisis intensified, the definition of early silicosis underwent subtle, but important, change. Now, primary silicosis was understood to be asymptomatic. R. R. Sayers of the Public Health Service gave one of the most authoritative summaries of prevailing medical opinion about the physical problems associated with silicosis, maintaining that primary silicosis was not characterized by shortness of breath. Such a change was extremely important for the developing debate over compensation. If early silicosis did not inhibit breathing, it was therefore not disabling. And if public health and medical experts agreed to this, then unemployed workers even with primary silicosis could not be compensated for industrial disease: "The term disability . . . may be defined as a decreased capacity to do the work required of the individual in the course of his usual occupation and/or an increased susceptibility to respiratory infection causing a loss of time from work which may reasonably be considered as primarily the result of the pulmonary fibrosis."[34] For Sayers, evidence of a person's having an occupational disease alone was not sufficient for compensation under the new system.[35] The prevailing professional opinion was that "disability in silicosis is seldom due to the silicosis itself."[36] In the years after the first onslaught of silicosis cases hit the courts, the definition of disability from silicosis became severely restricted: "In the past few years, however, opinions on the disability with simple silicosis have changed considerably. As one observed these individuals year after year he becomes impressed with the absence of complaints among those with even a moderately well-developed silicosis. . . ."[37] Employed

[34] R. R. Sayers, *Relationship of Asbestosis and Silicosis to Disability*, U.S. Department of Labor, Division of Labor Standards, *Bulletin No. 4* (Washington, D.C.: Government Printing Office, 1935), 71. See also C. O. Sappington, "Are All Dusts Hazardous?" *National Safety News* 25 (February 1932): 20, in which the director of the Division of Industrial Health of the Council declared that the first stage of silicosis is characterized by "some diminution of chest expansion and some shortness of breath on exertion."

[35] T. C. Waters, "Legislative Control and Compensation," in B. E. Kueckle, ed., *Third Symposium on Silicosis* (June 21–25, 1937), 245.

[36] A. J. Lanza, "Health Problems in Mining," *Mining Congress Journal* 22 (November 1936): 26. See also O. A. Sander, *A Practical Discussion of the Silicosis Problem*, U.S. Department of Labor, Division of Labor Standards, *Bulletin No. 10* (Washington, D.C.: Government Printing Office, 1936), 261: "As one observed these individuals year after year he becomes impressed with the absence of complaints among those with even a moderately well-developed silicosis. . . . It is emphysema which is the chief factor in a decreased function of the lungs."

[37] O. A. Sander, "A Practical Discussion of the Silicosis Problem," 261; "Occupational Disease—Disease, Silicosis—Disability," *Weekly Underwriter* 134 (February 22, 1936): 425. See also Committee of Five of Compensation Insurance Carriers, "Does Occupational Disease Require a Separate Form of Cover from Workmen's Compensation?" *Weekly Underwriter* 130 (January 20, 1934): 167: Even those who believed that silicosis in its early stages should be compensated noted that "such compensation should be limited well below compensation for

workers, fearful of losing their jobs during the Depression, hesitated to report their symptoms to industrial physicians. It was only the unemployed, with nothing to lose, who agitated for recognition of silicosis as a compensable disease.

In the midst of the Depression and in light of the growing crisis within the liability system, it was lack of work and the inability to earn a living as determined by medical experts that determined eligibility for compensation. This was in contrast to the formulation of the mid-1920s. At that time, Hourigan had explicitly recognized the complexity of the issue of decreased earning capacity. A worker not only suffered from an immediate decrease in earning capacity because of his or her disability but was threatened with a shortened life span as well. Hourigan raised the question of a worker's right to compensation for a shortened life, which placed not only the worker but his or her dependents at risk.

The Compensation Crisis in New York State

The situation in New York State perhaps best exemplifies the various forces at work in compensation controversies during the mid-1930s. Here, government officials and industry, insurance, and labor leaders all played important roles in shaping the compensation laws to include silicosis. In the process of modifying the state compensation act to include silicosis, compensation became so difficult to obtain and so limited that few workers found any redress through the system.

The crisis that led to the inclusion of silicosis in the compensation legislation was described by the state's Industrial Commissioner in early 1936. Elmer Andrews described how "certain industries in this State, particularly in the up-State areas, suddenly developed an intense interest in silicosis." In the early 1930s, workers in New York filed many suits under the common law for damages due to silicosis exposure. Despite the fact that since the inception of workers' compensation, industry had opposed any inclusion of silicosis or occupational disease in the legislation, Andrews pointed out, "immediately the attitude of twenty years was reversed." Andrews noted that "employers who had opposed inclusion of silicosis under the Workmen's Compensation Law came running to the State pleading for the inclusion of silicosis under the Workmen's Compensation Act so that they would be protected against the unlimited and terrifying common law damage suits which were being filed

---

disablement." See also R. Campbell Starr to Members of All Committees, National Silicosis Conference, January 23, 1937, National Archives, Record Group 100, 7-0-4(1), for Economic Subcommittee Concurrence in the view that compensation should only be paid "when the disease results in wage loss."

against them.''[38] In response to these suits, and to the growing financial crisis, the New York *Times* reported in March of 1934 that a bill sponsored by the foundry industry and their insurance representatives was introduced in the New York State legislature to add silicosis to the list of occupational diseases to become compensable under workers' compensation. Although the bill passed, Governor Herbert Lehman vetoed it, saying that he favored a blanket bill for all occupational diseases.[39] Within six months, the workers' compensation law was amended to include all occupational diseases, including silicosis, which prevented workers from going to the courts to sue companies and their insurers for liability.

Fearing that the amendment's passage would provoke a rash of claims under the workers' compensation laws, the insurance industry demanded that companies institute compulsory physical examinations and take medical histories at the worksite. The insurance industry worried about three problems: First, they feared that workers who had contracted silicosis in their previous employment would make claims against their current employers. Second, they were concerned that workers who had tuberculosis, emphysema, or other lung conditions would claim that their disability was due to silicosis rather than these nonoccupational diseases. Third, they wanted to weed out workers who had acquired silicosis in their current jobs in the hope that they would find other employment, move to other localities, or otherwise absolve the company of obligation to pay for future claims. The *Times* reported that the insurance industry went so far as to propose that employers be prohibited from participating in workers' compensation after September 1, 1935, the date that the new law took effect, unless all their employees had been screened.[40] At the same time, the insurance companies in New York announced that they were raising their rates for workers' compensation insurance, sometimes by as much as 400 percent, in anticipation of increased claims. Andrews described these rate changes: ''Insurance companies announced that they would charge employers in certain dusty industries four times the former compensation insurance rate and require cash deposits of as much as $600 per employee to cover accrued liability for employees who might have contracted the disease over the past fifteen or twenty years.''[41]

Within six months, all the major parties in New York State—labor, industry, insurance, and state government—had agreed that the new law was not

[38] News Release, New York State Department of Labor, March 31, 1936, Testimony of Elmer F. Andrews before New York State Senate Labor and Industries Committee, National Archives, Record Group 100, 7-2-1-5-1.

[39] *New York Times*, March 30, 1934, 7; *New York Times*, May 16, 1935, 8.

[40] *New York Times*, July 21, 1935, III, 7.

[41] News Release, New York State Department of Labor, March 31, 1936, Testimony of Elmer F. Andrews before New York State Senate Labor and Industries Committee, National Archives, Record Group 100, 7-2-1-5-1.

working. The employees were no better off, since the demands of the insurance industry to fire or not hire silicotic workers forced many plants to face "the threat of shutdowns which would put hundreds of skilled workers on the street and add many to the relief rolls." The demand for physical examination of workers was a special hardship: "This resulted in the elimination of many old and experienced workers not solely due to silicosis but for other possible physical defects that could be found."[42] In a less diplomatic moment, Andrews stated the reaction of insurance more succinctly: "They insisted that the working force be 'dry cleaned.' "[43] In summary, Andrews said, "faced with these rate increases, closed plants and unemployed workers, matters were in a critical condition."[44] In the short space of six months, the blanket coverage for occupational diseases provided for in the new compensation law had effectively alienated insurance carriers, industry, and labor alike. In addition, no one wanted to further disrupt the state's economy during the Depression.

In response to this crisis, the Crews-Shwartzwald bill was introduced on behalf of the foundry and insurance industries. This was even more limited in its scope than the earlier legislation, making it virtually impossible for workers to qualify for compensation. The bill provided that there should be no compensation for partial disability and that compensation for total disability should not exceed $3,000. Further, if disability or death should occur during the first calendar month during which the Act became effective, compensation should not exceed $500 and would increase only $50 every month thereafter. Compensation for silicosis was further restricted by a provision that where the last exposure occurred prior to September 1, 1935, no money was to be paid and that workers would have to resort to the courts. Although physical examinations were not banned by law, the new amendment sought to discourage them by declaring that physical examinations were contrary to the sense of the legislation.[45]

The issue of compensation forced organized labor to chose between workers' health and their jobs, and the New York State Federation of Labor sought to protect jobs.[46] At the legislative hearing, Industrial Commissioner Elmer Andrews acknowledged that the bill "is not an ideal one." But he defended it as "a compromise solution of an emergency situation and a difficult problem." The purposes of the bill were to keep employees at work by keeping

[42] "Hearings Held March 10th and March 11th in Senate and Assembly," *New York State Federation of Labor Bulletin*, March 23, 1936, 3–4.

[43] News Release, New York State Department of Labor, March 31, 1936, Testimony of Elmer F. Andrews before New York State Senate Labor and Industries Committee, National Archives, Record Group 100, 7-2-1-5-1.

[44] "Hearings Held March 10th and March 11th in Senate and Assembly," *New York State Federation of Labor Bulletin*, March 23, 1936, 3–4.

[45] Elmer F. Andrews, "Memorandum for Dr. Greenburg," April 13, 1936, National Archives, Record Group 174, Office of the Secretary, Folder: State Labor Department, New York, 1936.

[46] John Frey, quoted in *New York Times*, April 15, 1936, 6.

compensation rates low and plants open, to encourage dust prevention methods, and to discourage preemployment physicals. Both labor and industry appeared in support of the bill, with George Meany, the president of the New York State Federation of Labor defending the compromise as necessary, if not ideal. At the least, it provided some assurance that workers could continue to work at their trades.[47]

Others were not nearly as accepting of the need to compromise workers' health. Most notably, two of the leaders of labor reform efforts in the twentieth century, Secretary of Labor Frances Perkins and John B. Andrews, secretary of the American Association for Labor Legislation, both saw the Crews-Shwartzwald bill as a dangerous and destructive precedent in labor legislation. In late February 1936, John Andrews wrote to Verne Zimmer of the U.S. Department of Labor, enclosing a summary of his objections to the bill and asking Zimmer for his opinion. Shortly after, on March 4, 1936, during the hearings on the bill in Albany, Perkins herself responded to Andrews's letter with a detailed critique of the bill. She believed that the bill was a dramatic step backwards in occupational disease legislation. First, she pointed out that the bill placed a "definite limitation on workmen's compensation benefits payable for total disability and death." Second, she noted that there was a "drastic limitation on medical benefits," and third, she objected that the bill excluded "any liability whatsoever for partial disability regardless of extent or duration."

It was obviously particularly painful for Secretary Perkins to witness the "complete reversal" of the progressive features of New York's law, which was previously "among the most beneficial measures of its kind in the country." She had been an advocate of workers' rights since at least 1911, when she had witnessed firsthand the deaths of the young women and children employed in the Triangle Shirtwaist Company. She had worked for a number of philanthropic and state agencies, and in 1928 New York's Governor Al Smith had appointed her Industrial Commissioner of the State of New York, where she had later served under Governor Roosevelt. She complained that the provisions were inadequate for claimants and that the bill provided little or no protection for workers threatened with dismissal. There was no assurance "as to the retention of silicotic workers in industry through the abolition of medical examinations," she complained. In fact, the act's provision fixing liability on the last employer "seems to invite the continuance of pre-employment examinations as a protection against accrued liability." She was particularly disturbed by the section of the bill that prohibited the use of information on industrial conditions gathered through the offices of the Industrial Commissioner in compensation claims. This, she noted, completely undermined the chances

---

[47] "Hearings Held March 10th and March 11th in Senate and Assembly," *New York State Federation of Labor Bulletin*, March 23, 1936, 3–4.

for a claimant to achieve "a fair and equitable disposition of a pending compensation claim."

Her objections to this bill were so strong that she concluded her letter by asking for its complete rejection: "So restricted and meager are the benefits under this proposed amendment that it offers little to workers as a substitute for the common law remedy available previous to enactment of the all-inclusive occupational disease act effective last September." She concluded, "I would prefer to this weak palliative the frank elimination of silicosis from coverage until such time that suitable and acceptable compensation plan can be devised."[48] Despite her appeals to the governor and an intensive lobbying campaign by the American Association for Labor Legislation against the bill, it passed and was signed by the governor in June 1936.[49] The Industrial Commissioner of New York State summed up the position of state officials by acknowledging the weaknesses in the bill and asserting that the state had no other options without federal legislation. Appealing to the National Conference on Silicosis in mid-April, 1936, Elmer Andrews asked for their assistance "in bringing about, in the very near future, some measure of compensation coverage for silicosis in the principal industrial, mining and quarrying states. The almost total lack of such coverage is what has made necessary the appallingly low maximum compensation now proposed in the New York State bill."[50] The experience of the first three years following the bill's passage attests to its inadequacy. By the end of 1939, only seventy-nine workers had been compensated for silicosis claims, and they had received a total of $99,594.[51]

The difficulties in New York State were typical of the problem of reaching a satisfactory solution to the political, social, and economic issues raised by chronic industrial disease. In state after state across the country, inadequate regulations were grafted onto workers' compensation acts that stripped disabled workers of any meaningful financial protection and thus allowed the issue to fester.

The financial crisis could be addressed, however inadequately, through the

[48] Perkins to John B. Andrews, March 4, 1936, National Archives, Record Group 174, Folder: Secretary Frances Perkins, Labor Standards, January–April 1936, Box 59.

[49] See Press Release, "Workmen's Compensation Law Threatened," American Association for Labor Legislation, March 4, 1936, National Archives, Record Group 100, 7-0-4(1); John B. Andrews to Verne Zimmer, April 20, 1936, ibid.; Andrews to Fred Wilcox, February 25, 1936, National Archives, Record Group 174, Folder: Office of the Secretary, Labor Standards, January–April 1936; Perkins to Herbert H. Lehman, March 4, 1936, ibid.; "Anti-Silicosis Bills Signed by Lehman," New York Times, June 10, 1936.

[50] Elmer Andrews, "Memorandum to Dr. Greenburg," April 13, 1936, National Archives, Record Group 174, Folder: State Labor Department, New York, 1936.

[51] "Silicosis," Survey Midmonthly 76 (February 1940): n.p.; "Silicosis Pay Rise Signed by Lehman," New York Times, April 18, 1940, 18; "Silicosis Measure Is Signed By Dewey," New York Times, March 30, 1947, 4.

inclusion of silicosis in the various state compensation systems. But the political crisis remained as long as the issue was in the public arena. By the mid-1930s, silicosis was of interest to the medical and public health community, lawyers, labor unions, state government, and workers directly affected by the condition. But at this time, the issue became public in a much more direct and dramatic way.

Gauley Bridge

In the midst of the growing controversy over legal liability came the revelation that perhaps as many as 1,500 workers had been killed by exposure to silica dust while working on a tunnel project in Gauley Bridge, West Virginia. Newspapers and weeklies all over the country made silicosis a national scandal. In January 1936, *Newsweek* wrote of "tunnelling through an atmosphere of deadly dust" and *Literary Digest* titled its article "Village of the Living Dead."[52] Now, silicosis was no longer the preserve of a small group of scientists, physicians, engineers, and lawyers. It entered the popular lexicon.

The first hint of an industrial scandal appeared in a small, left-wing magazine. In January 1935, Albert Maltz, later to become a screenwriter who was blacklisted as one of the "Hollywood Ten," wrote a moving short story in the *New Masses*. It concerned a miner he picked up while driving through Gauley, West Virginia. In the story, Maltz described a man of about thirty-five years who was abandoning his family and going off to die. The hitchhiker dictated a letter to his wife explaining that he was unable to get work because no one would hire any miner who had worked in the tunnel:

> Hit it all comes from thet rock thet we all had to dril. Thet rock was silica and hit was most all of hit glass. The powder frum this glass has got into the lungs of all the men war worked in thet tunel thru their breathin. And this has given to all of us a sickness. The doctors writ it down for me. Hit is silicosis. Hit makes the lungs to git all scab like and then it stops the breathin.[53]

Martin Cherniack, in his book, *The Hawk's Nest Incident*, describes in detail the literary and epidemiological evidence that led to public awareness of what he calls "America's worst industrial disaster." In his book he tells the story of the black and white workers who died of acute silicosis and other respiratory diseases while constructing this tunnel for the Union Carbide Company.[54]

In January and February of 1936, the Committee on Labor of the House of

---

[52] "Tunneling through an Atmosphere of Deadly Dust," *Newsweek*, January 25, 1936, 33; "Village of the Living Dead," *Literary Digest*, January 25, 1936, 6.

[53] Albert Maltz, "Man on the Road," *The New Masses*, January 8, 1935.

[54] Martin Cherniack, *The Hawk's Nest Incident, America's Worst Industrial Disaster* (New Haven: Yale University Press, 1986).

Representatives convened in order to consider a joint resolution "to authorize the Secretary of Labor to appoint a board of inquiry to ascertain the facts relating to health conditions of workers" employed by a subsidiary of "the Union Carbide and Carbon Company." As the resolution read: "[O]ne hundred and sixty nine of said workers were buried in a field at Summersville, West Virginia, with cornstalks as their only gravestones and with no other means of identification."[55]

In the course of the hearings, witnesses testified that the workers had been placed at extraordinary risk while employed on the job. The 2,000 workers were mostly rural Southern blacks drawn to the job and away from their families farther south by the promise of steady pay during the Depression. They had been ordered to drill through a mountain that was composed of nearly pure silica, even then known as a substance that destroyed lung tissue, incapacitating and killing its victims. Workers were sent into the tunnel despite widespread knowledge of the long-term dangers of silica dust and the recognition that only strict safety precautions, such as wet drilling, proper ventilation, and masks could prevent massive exposure to silica dust. Workers complained that the company doctors told them they were suffering not from silicosis but from "tunnelitis," a fictitious condition meant to allay their fears.

The House Committee also heard testimony that company officials knew that they were systematically exposing workers to a disease that would eventually kill them. Company officials and engineers routinely wore masks when they entered the worksite. Furthermore, the company purposely bore through the site of the richest silica deposit so that silica rock and sand could be shipped to another subsidiary of Union Carbide to be used in manufacturing. Cherniack shows through a painstaking analysis of blueprints and engineering plans submitted to the state that the company altered the direction of their route through the tunnel in order to maximize the amount of silica that could be mined as a by-product.

The impact of the incident itself and the revelations brought forth during the hearings was widespread within the labor community. The *American Federationist*, the official organ of the American Federation of Labor, editorialized that in addition to the hundreds known to have died, hundreds more could expect the worst. In an article on the tragedy published in June, the *Federationist* maintained: "For more than twenty years labor leaders, government officials and independent experts have reported their findings on silicosis as the most widespread of occupational diseases in America, but it remained for

[55] U.S. Congress, House Subcommittee of the Committee on Labor, *An Investigation Relating to Health Conditions of Workers Employed in the Construction and Maintenance of Public Utilities*, 74th Cong., 2d sess., January 1936, reprinted in Jim Comstock, ed., *West Virginia Heritage*, vol. 7 (Richwood, W. Va.: West Virginia Heritage Foundation, 1972), 1–3.

the recent trail of death across a West Virginia countryside to startle the nation to doing something about it."[56]

In part, this disaster was exposed because management did not expect the symptoms of silicosis to appear so quickly. Usually, the symptoms of silica poisoning, like the symptoms of asbestosis, brown lung, and black lung, took years, if not decades, to appear. The long period between exposure and onset of symptoms would, therefore, obscure the company's role in its workers' deaths. At Gauley Bridge, however, the extreme exposure to which workers were subjected caused the development of symptoms almost immediately. Workers were dying on the job, causing the company to hire a local undertaker to dispose of bodies in the fields nearby. The fact that the workers were primarily poor, black migrants far away from their loved ones led management to believe that they could cover up the deaths. Families who inquired about the whereabouts of their husbands and sons were told that these men had "moved on." Despite testimony from workers, physicians, government officials, and company doctors that showed the company's total disregard for the health of the workers, management still maintained a stony silence, taking the position that any disease was caused by workers' carelessness.

Estimates of the number of affected workers varied greatly at the time. But Cherniack maintains that, conservatively, more than 700 men died of silicosis and an untold number were diseased and disabled. Of these thousands of victims of the disease, there were 538 suits for damages, and these workers settled

> for a sum of two hundred thousand dollars, only two-thirds of which actually accrued to them. In effect, the convergent acts or decisions of powerful corporate entities, state officials, and the courts had determined that less than four hundred dollars was the average worth of a tunnel worker's health or life.[57]

Although the compensation was intended to be tied to the severity of disability, in fact, the awards were based upon race. Single black laborers received the least, as low as $30, whereas the families of deceased whites received the most, as much as $1,600.[58]

The Argument over Standards

The general position of industry and the public health profession was that silicosis was not as bad as the press had made it sound. The disease could be controlled through appropriate medical and engineering innovations. But there

[56] Editorial, *American Federationist* 43 (March 1936): 245–46; "Silicosis Prevention," *American Federationist* 43 (June 1936): 596.

[57] Cherniack, *Hawk's Nest*, 73.

[58] Cherniack, *Hawk's Nest*, 67.

were two major problems with this position. First, it depended upon the achievement of standards of dust exposure that would actually prevent silicosis. Second, establishing these standards, in turn, depended upon developing technologies that could accurately measure dust levels in a variety of workplaces. In fact, however, the history of standards setting was a history of approximation, assumptions about what constituted a dangerous level of exposure, and primitive, if mechanically complex, technologies. The first problem was measuring the amount of dust in the air. During the 1920s, the Greenburg-Smith impinger and the midget impinger were introduced and used as a means of collecting dust samples for microscopic examinations. The impinger drew a sample of air through a liquid medium to trap the dust. A sample of the liquid was then placed under a microscope in order to count the number of particles of dust in the unit of air collected. This became the standard method for the next forty years.

From the very first, there were criticisms of the impinger method. It was recognized that there was little reliability in the results. Different results depended upon ever-changing conditions in the plant on any given day. Dust conditions were dependent upon whether or not sandblasters were in use, whether windows were open to increase ventilation during the summer months, and whether it was early in the workday or late in the afternoon. Samples taken by the same impinger in the same area of a plant and in the same time period would often produce very different results. Emery Hayhurst explained that another problem of counting dust was that "ultramicroscopic dust cannot well be counted" but that the "hazard is in direct relation to the fineness of the dust." Thus, the impinger method failed to find the most toxic dust particles.[59] Nor did this method provide the means to distinguish between "harmful" silica and other, "unharmful" dusts in the air. To establish the silica content of dust required complex, expensive chemical analyses, which were not generally used. Despite these and numerous other deficiencies in the impinger methods and the various assumptions about the relationships among dose, length of exposure to dusts, variations in size of particles, and length of time between exposure and onset, the impinger method became the basis for establishing dust exposure levels in the 1930s. In 1946, it would become the basis for the dust exposure standard established by the American Conference of Governmental Industrial Hygienists.[60]

[59] Emery R. Hayhurst, "Discussion of A. J. Lanza's Paper on 'Etiology of Silicosis,' " paper presented at Section on Preventive and Industrial Medicine and Public Health, Milwaukee Meeting, American Medical Association, June 14, 1933, Armed Forces Medical Museum, Otis Historical Archives, Vorwald Papers, Box 63.

[60] This discussion is based on Jack Oudiz, "Silica Dust Levels in U.S. Foundries" (M.S. thesis, University of Cincinnati, Department of Environmental Health, 1982); U.S. Department of Health, Education and Welfare, NIOSH, *Criteria for Recommended Standards, Occupational Exposure to Crystalline Silica* (1975); Leonard Greenburg and J. J. Bloomfield, "The Impinger

The major challenge to the impinger method came from those who argued that a better method for assessing the danger of silica was to measure the mass of material breathed by the work force rather than to depend upon a count of particles. They suggested developing a measure based upon the weight of dust in the air. In contrast to the counting method, which came up with a number for measuring the million parts per cubic foot (mppcf), the new standard should use the number of milligrams of dust in a cubic meter of air (mg/m3). This method depended upon the collection of dust by size-selective sampling techniques and itself had drawbacks rooted in the lack of knowledge about what size a particle had to be to constitute a hazard.

While many in the technical community were obsessed with finding methods for controlling the silicosis hazard, others believed that this emphasis would cloud the seriousness and pervasiveness of other conditions related to industrial exposures. There was a serious danger that focusing on silicosis would obscure the long-term hazards posed by other dusts in a wide variety of industries. The issue of silicosis could be used to either unmask or mask other industrial and chronic lung diseases. Daniel Harrington, the chief of the Health and Safety Branch of the Bureau of Mines, addressed the American Institute of Mining and Metallurgical Engineers in San Francisco, arguing forcefully that the real problem transcended the issue as then defined. He pointed out that silica was not the only dust threatening the health of workers and that the attention paid to silica obscured the many other mineral dusts that were undermining the health of American workers. Those who worked mining coal, shale, limestone, hematite (iron oxide) ore, and other ores were also at tremendous risk of developing disease. He feared that by focusing research only on silicosis, the public health community was losing an opportunity to understand and control other occupational dust hazards.[61]

Despite all the claims of progress made by industry and government, Harrington presented a savage critique of the "present-day 'racket' " that often accompanied the discovery of silicosis in a particular community. First, he called into question the statistics about the incidence of silicosis and other dust diseases, claiming that "many doctors apparently do not know how to diagnose the disease." He claimed that this was caused by the fact that "in the regions most afflicted a concerted effort usually has been made toward minimizing publicity. . . . Pussyfooting about dust disease not only in mining but in industry generally is now and has for many years been largely the rule and this more than any other influence has caused the present-day 'racket' in connection with dust disease." Harrington said that "there appears to have been

---

Dust Sampling Apparatus as Used by the United States Public Health Service," *Public Health Report* 47 (March 18, 1932): 654–75; D. G. Beadle, "The Shattering of Dust Particles in the Impinger," *Journal of Industrial Hygiene and Toxicology* 21 (April 1939): 109–20.

[61] Daniel Harrington, *Silicosis as Affecting Mining Workmen and Operations*, U.S. Bureau of Mines Information Circular 6867 (January 1936, mimeo).

a concerted effort to hide the facts in most instances and to take as few measures as possible toward elimination of the diseases and the conditions causing them." He blamed the mine owners and labor equally for ignoring the pressing problem of dust, saying that neither wanted to face up to the real problem and its implication. The miners refused to allow themselves to be examined and opposed the use of wet drills. The owners ignored the existence of dust disease and considered new or safer equipment "to be impractical or . . . the dream of the theorist."

He noted that the doctor and pathologist might be useful in diagnosing disease or the cause of death, but that these professionals had little to add in the way of prevention. Despite volumes written on the dust diseases by the medical profession, he maintained, there was still a "vast amount of uncertainty in the medical ranks as to the disease, its diagnosis, remedies, or almost any other strictly medical phase of the subject." "In other words," he concluded,

> while the engineers and mine and industrial operating officials have either ignored or dodged the issue . . . the medical people, pathologists, and others . . . have given practically no definite data as to causation of the disease or of its treatment. . . . As far as preventing the disease is concerned, relatively few of the most prominent dust experts ever saw the inside of a mine, hence any so-called advice they may give as to dust-disease preventive measures for mining should be (and usually is) essentially worthless.[62]

Neither experts, officials, nor the public had the slightest grasp of the true extent of the silicosis hazard in particular and the dust problem in general.

The New Deal and Growing Federal Involvement

By the mid-1930s, as Harrington indicated, the professionals still had a relatively limited understanding of the disease, but the social and political crises that it had highlighted continued to intensify. The New Deal in its first few years had focused on the immediate economic crisis of the Depression, but after 1935, the Roosevelt administration turned its attention to the long-term social crises caused by the extreme dependence of the industrial work force. Congress passed the National Labor Relations Act and the Social Security Act and even began serious discussions about national health insurance. The silicosis issue was a "natural" for the newly revived Department of Labor under Frances Perkins because it was a national problem that was causing dependence, disability, ill-health, and economic disorder among elderly, retired,

---

[62] Harrington, *Silicosis as Affecting Mining Workmen*. See also, for an earlier statement of Harrington's views, "Mine Ventilation and Its Relation to Safety and Efficiency," *The American Zinc and Lead Journal* 10 (September 1920): 6–8.

unemployed, and disabled workers, the very groups that Perkins had targeted in the social security legislation.

Hence, after the tragedy at Gauley Bridge,[63] Secretary of Labor Perkins suggested that the department sponsor a conference that would bring together representatives of government, labor, and industry to help resolve the silicosis crisis.[64] The importance of a national approach that would give workers a voice had been driven home to her by the experience in New York State, where the state initiative to reform the compensation system had virtually disenfranchised silicotic workers. The Department of Labor recognized from the first that the success of any program to control the dust hazard could not depend upon national legislative action and regulatory authority. Only eight months earlier, the National Industrial Recovery Act, which had given the federal government wide authority to regulate hours, wages, and working conditions for millions of workers, had been declared unconstitutional. New legislation faced massive industry opposition. Although Congress had passed the National Labor Relations Act (1935), which guaranteed labor's right to organize, even the strongest advocates of legislative and regulatory remedies in the Department of Labor did not believe that it would be possible to pass federal legislation to address the silicosis problem.

The Department of Labor could call a conference but could ensure the participation of business only by making the meeting as nonthreatening as possible. Verne A. Zimmer, the director of the Division of Labor Standards, who had begun his career as a factory inspector and served with Perkins in the New York State Department of Labor, recognized that no legislative remedies were possible and that any reform would come through industry's voluntary acceptance of standards. Trade groups feared that the New Deal administration of Frances Perkins would blame business for the silicosis crisis and attempt to use the conference as a means of pressing for a voluntary accord that would impose restrictions on business. Thus, from the very outset, Zimmer found that he had to stack the conference disproportionately with management representation if he was to gain what he considered industry's vital support. In a memo to Secretary Perkins immediately following the first planning session for the April 1936 conference, Zimmer stated his disappointment that the committee of silicosis experts had pressed him to include more industry representation and less input from labor at the next planning meeting.

The Steering Committee, made up of representatives of the Air Hygiene Foundation, the National Safety Council, the American Standards Association, the Casualty and Surety Underwriters, the U.S. Public Health Service,

---

[63] R. P. Blake to Zimmer, January 20, 1936, National Archives, Record Group 100, 7-2-1-5-1: Department of Labor officials were closely monitoring the congressional subcommittee hearings. They did not believe that they could do much in regard to Gauley Bridge since "the work has been completed and no correctional measures can be applied."

[64] Zimmer to the Secretary, February 6, 1936, National Archives, Record Group 100, 7-0-4(1).

the American Foundrymen's Association, the Union Carbon and Carbide Company, the United Mine Workers of America, the American Federation of Labor, and another representative of the Division of Labor Standards, pressed Zimmer, saying that it "would be necessary to break down the reluctance on the part of employers . . . in other words, to allay suspicion of an ulterior motive." Significantly, of the twenty-six new planning committee members invited to the following meeting, fifteen represented various affected industries and only three represented labor.[65]

At this meeting, which was held on February 26, 1936, Zimmer urged Secretary Perkins to address the group and to allay business fears. "The main purpose of calling in the employer associations," Zimmer reminded Perkins, "is to break down any possible resistance against a movement inaugurated by the Labor Department."[66] The planning conference, which was held in February, heard speaker after speaker attest to the good intentions and good works of the various industries.[67] Despite the limitations in its organization, Perkins and Zimmer hoped that an honest and open discussion of silicosis could lead to policies that would meet the needs of workers and pull together all the various contending groups to resolve this social, political, and public health crisis.[68] Implicit in the conference's goal was a tension between individual administrators' dedication to workers and the larger belief in consensus as a tool of corporate liberalism.

[65] Zimmer to Secretary Perkins, February 19, 1936, National Archives, Record Group 100, 7-0-4(1). Zimmer related that the representative of the American Federation of Labor, John Frey, objected to Zimmer's suggestion that John L. Lewis of the United Mine Workers be part of the planning group. This was due to ongoing struggles within the American Federation of Labor regarding the organizing drives undertaken by the Committee on Industrial Organization.

[66] Zimmer to Secretary Perkins, February 25, 1936, National Archives, Record Group 100, 7-0-4(1).

[67] "Digest of Proceedings at Conference on Silicosis and Similar Dust Diseases," February 26, 1936, National Archives, Record Group 100, 7-0-4(1). The industry representatives included the American Foundrymen's Association, the American Mining Congress, the Grinding Wheel Manufacturers Association, the National Crushed Stone Association, the National Sand and Gravel Association, the U.S. Potters Association, and even the Union Carbon and Carbide Company, recently deeply implicated in the Gauley Bridge disaster.

[68] Even with industry's disproportionate representation on the planning committee, some conservative interests were still suspicious of the Department of Labor's ultimate objective for the conference. Some saw the involvement of labor, management, technical, and medical personnel, no matter what the proportions, as a potential disaster, with little more respectability than a political mass meeting. "In all probability," an editorial in the *Engineering News-Record* proclaimed, "hopeless confusion would be the result [of a silicosis conference with so many groups included] . . . . The conference would be a modern Tower of Babel, for the several groups do not speak the same language or understand each other's viewpoints." The editorial went on to directly attack Frances Perkins herself for her misconceived approach to such an important problem: "Mass meetings are excellent for safety education and propaganda," but silicosis "is far too complex, too involved and too little understood to be suited to mass-meeting methods." "A Tower of Babel," *Engineering News-Record*, 116 (March 5, 1936), 360. From the engineer's perspective, only technical experts were really competent to address the issue.

In the early years of the Depression, the crisis over silicosis seemed to mirror the crisis in American society in general. In the midst of increasing labor and management discord and in social and economic conditions that no one truly understood, the problem of disease, disability, and death seemed to be spiraling out of control. In these early days, the issue of chronic industrial disease, specifically silicosis, was subject to a broad examination in the professional as well as the popular press and the courts. For the first time, an issue that was formerly the preserve of a narrow band of experts gained the attention of labor, management groups, insurance executives, and finally government officials. The early efforts at defusing the crisis through amending workers' compensation laws met with only partial success because of the complex local politics of labor and management in any given state. Without national legislative standards and without a uniform approach, such efforts sometimes created more turmoil rather than easing tensions. The Department of Labor therefore stepped in to help create a national consensus that would respect labor's point of view and integrate labor into the decisionmaking process that would define the parameters of the silicosis issue.

IV

"THOSE THAT ARE COMPETENT TO SPEAK"

> During the past few years so many conflicting statements have
> been made about the subject of silicosis that many persons have
> become confused. They do not know what to believe or what to
> do. Alarmed workers have filed claims against their employers,
> sometimes unjustly. Apprehensive employers and insurance
> carriers in some cases have adopted employment and
> underwriting policies that have reacted unfavorably against
> themselves and the workers. A few incompetent attorneys and
> physicians, particularly in court cases, have further complicated
> the situation, so that today a condition exists that fully deserves
> thoughtful consideration and some definite declarations by those
> that are competent to speak.
> (*National Silicosis Conference, Summary of Reports*, 1937)

WHILE Verne A. Zimmer and Frances Perkins sought to use the 1936 National Conference on Silicosis to ensure open discussion and debate,[1] the business and public health communities sought to restrict and redirect the conference. They saw the meeting as an opportunity to defuse the political crisis by reestablishing the preeminence of professional opinion in the arena of occupational disease. The conference's program and participants were representative—including business, labor, and professional groups. But Zimmer and Perkins did not appreciate the ability of a recently organized industry-sponsored group, the Air Hygiene Foundation (later renamed the Industrial Hygiene Foundation) to create a powerful new force that would undermine the Department of Labor's objectives of openness and labor-management consensus.[2]

The Formation of the Air Hygiene Foundation

On December 1, 1934, as the insurance crisis deepened, and before the public disclosure of the Gauley Bridge tragedy, some business executives in the dusty

---

[1] U.S. Department of Labor, Division of Labor Standards, "Designated Special Committees, Personnel and Duties, National Silicosis Conference Committee," April 14, 1936, National Archives, Record Group 174, Folder: National Silicosis Conference Committee, Chief Clerk's Files, 167/3314.

[2] H. B. Meller to E. R. Weidlein, October 9, 1934, Carnegie-Mellon Archives, courtesy of Joel Tarr.

trades asked Dr. E. R. Weidlein, the director of the Mellon Institute of Industrial Research in Pittsburgh, to help them. Organized in 1913 with funds from steel magnates and bankers Andrew W. Mellon and Richard B. Mellon, the institute "sponsored field and laboratory research on its premises and also functioned as an umbrella for organizations directly involved in the politics of industrial and environmental health."[3] Even though its work was funded by industry, the institute had a good deal of credibility with the general public because of its early attention to air pollution in Pittsburgh.

On January 15, 1935, a day before the congressional hearings on Gauley Bridge began, over 200 industry executives met at the University Club in Pittsburgh for a closed-door meeting called a "Symposium on Dust Problems." The executives elected a temporary organizing committee to establish a permanent organization to plan a coordinated industry-wide research and evaluation program on dust and its impact on workers' health. The committee, composed of representatives from seven industries including foundries, iron, steel and iron ore, and asbestos, proposed that a new association, tentatively called the Industrial Dust Institute, be established in association with the Mellon Institute.[4] The organizers hoped that they could enlist fifty companies to contribute $500 each for an initial budget of $25,000.[5]

The organization was formed in the image of the National Civic Federation (NCF), the Progressive Era group that joined business, labor, and social reformers around a corporate liberal agenda. Although it was not nearly as broad based as the NCF, the Air Hygiene Foundation also saw its responsibilities in the broadest possible terms. It was not short-term profit that defined its mission. Rather, it saw long-term business success as closely linked to public attitudes toward business itself. It sought to combine the success of the trade associations that flourished in the 1920s with the ideology of corporate liberalism. From the vantage point of its organizers, the silicosis crisis was symptomatic of a broader crisis for American capitalism, and business needed to address both if was to survive and eventually prosper. The Air Hygiene Foundation believed "that the employer's no. 1 job today is not to sell his products but to sell the system that makes those products possible." It saw itself as "a

[3] William Graebner, "Hegemony through Science: Information Engineering and Lead Toxicology, 1925–1965," in Rosner and Markowitz, eds., *Dying for Work* 145.

[4] Roger A. Hitchens, "A Brief Outline of the Events Leading up to and Occurring at the 'Symposium on Dust Problems' held in Pittsburgh, Pa., January 15, 1935," in W. G. Hazard to Dr. L. R. Thompson, March 21, 1935, National Archives, Record Group 90, "State Boards of Health" (0875–96–49, Pittsburgh, Pa.)

[5] Roger A. Hitchens, "A Brief Outline of the Discussion and Action Taken by the Temporary Organization Committee at a Special Meeting Held at the Duquense Club, Pittsburgh, Pa., on Friday, February 1, 1935," in W. G. Hazard to Dr. L. R. Thompson, March 21, 1935, National Archives, Record Group 90, "State Boards of Health" (0875-96-49, Pittsburgh, Pa.) See also Rachel Scott, *Muscle and Blood* (New York: E. P. Dutton and Co., 1974), 176–177, for an account of the origins of the Air Hygiene Foundation.

collective effort by employers in behalf of employee health" and therefore as a "clear cut illustration of [the] 'assumption of greater social responsibility,' as advocated by progressive leaders of business."[6] Such activities could serve as "anti-toxin for the agitation against private enterprise."[7] The foundation was a voluntaristic, industry-sponsored alternative to the threat of federal action: "Either employers will deal intelligently with industrial health, through collective cooperation—and the Foundation is the only existing agency where they can do that—or they can continue their present disorganized course and await government inspection and enforcement of factory health standards."[8]

The organizers assumed that such an organization could have a major impact on how the silicosis issue was perceived and acted upon. In the early years of the Depression, industry had been in a defensive position, responding to a myriad of forces over which it had no control. Through unified action, the dusty trades had an opportunity to protect their own interests as well as to give structure to the silicosis debate.

The issue of silicosis was being defined at the time of the Air Hygiene Foundation's initial meetings in terms that were extremely threatening to a business community already on the political defensive. In the midst of the Depression, silicosis was frequently framed as a labor and management problem, not solely as a health issue. Industry recognized that it had to find a way of defusing the political conflict that such a model could promote and provide a viable, apolitical alternative. They wanted to return the discussion of silicosis to the realm of science and medicine, where experts from the Public Health Service, industry, and other academic and research entities could reassert the dominance of industry-sponsored professionals over politicians and labor unions. Roger A. Hitchens, the chairman of the temporary organizing committee, complained that "there is now no one place where there is available *all* information on *all* phases of the problem; and no *concerted* planning is being done either as to the present or future as to *all* many different phases."[9] And the director of the Mellon Institute of Industrial Research argued that it was in the interests of industry to collect research studies as well as to initiate and direct research efforts: "It is necessary that there be some organization representing industries for the reason that no program of research investigation could be carried on without assurance of continuity and financial support."[10]

[6] John F. McMahon to Dr. E. W. Tillotson, January 17, 1939, Carnegie-Mellon Archives, courtesy of Joel Tarr.

[7] McMahon to Weidlein, January 16, 1939, Carnegie-Mellon Archives, courtesy of Joel Tarr.

[8] John F. McMahon to Dr. Hamer, March 5, 1941, Carnegie-Mellon Archives, courtesy of Joel Tarr.

[9] Roger A. Hitchens, "The Industrial Dust Problem," in W. G. Hazard to Dr. L. R. Thompson, March 21, 1935, National Archives, Record Group 90, "State Boards of Health" (0875-96-49, Pittsburgh, Pa.)

[10] E. R. Weidlein, "Plan for Study of Dust Problems," in W. G. Hazard to Dr. L. R. Thomp-

The organization of industry behind a research effort was especially important in addressing chronic diseases, where it might be necessary to follow the long-term development of symptoms in humans and animal subjects. Hitchens argued that by organizing a research institute, it was possible to avoid the charge that the organization was a "special interest" that was pursuing a narrow agenda. The organization, he said, "must have a broad outlook, a sympathetic understanding of the problem, and wide contacts with all cooperating agencies; and it must have the confidence of the industries, and of the physicians, engineers and all institutions, groups or individuals who might cooperate to advantage."

Industry could achieve major benefits by providing the funding for such an organization. The new organization could determine which specialists "may not be properly qualified and whose results might, therefore, not be entirely acceptable . . . ; to be in position to make reasonable grants to qualified individuals and agencies to study special problems or phases of problems." Weidlein suggested that industry could retain some control over the dissemination of information, if it were to support a permanent research organization. On a more practical level, such research could be "important from both medical and legal standpoints in the preparation of court cases" and assist "in the preparation of safety codes and fair laws."[11]

Weidlein outlined a five-point program by which industry could band together to both control their own members' behavior and to set the agenda for the nation as a whole. In the medical phase of the effort, Weidlein proposed to collect all existing information on dust diseases, to focus attention on areas that demanded more research and finally to secure the cooperation of the American Medical Association "in setting up authoritative and approved standards of diagnosis and correction." In what he called the "preventive" area, he maintained that the organization should assume the role of establishing "authoritative and approved standards." By voluntarily establishing standards and pressuring industry to live up to them, companies would be able to erect a "defense against personal injury suits." In the legal arena, the organization could serve as a legal clearinghouse and advise businesses facing liability suits; in the legislative arena, the organization could help "secure the enactment of state laws, of a uniform character, which, when complied with, will fairly and properly protect the interest of industry and those engaged in industry and of enlisting the cooperation of the federal government in that direction." Finally, the new organization would publicize what measures "are being and should be taken in the direction of protecting both human life and property." The sum of all this activity would be that industries most affected

son, March 21, 1935, National Archives, Record Group 90, "State Boards of Health" (0875-96-49, Pittsburgh, Pa.)

[11] Weidlein, "Plan for Study."

by the silicosis debate could collectively shape a research agenda, legal frame-work, and legislative program compatible with their interests. Faced with a crisis of overwhelming proportions, the affected industries were hardly defen-sive. Rather, they acted to gain control over dust research and public policy.[12]

They succeeded beyond their wildest expectations. At the end of 1935, the Air Hygiene Foundation of America, Inc., was established with 20 companies and industry groups; by the time of its first annual meeting on April 1, 1937, it had 168 members. Nearly every company and trade association with a "sil-icosis problem" had signed on, including Union Carbide, Harbison-Walker Refractories, the American Mining Congress, the American Zinc Institute, the Barre Granite Association, the Foundry Supply Manufacturers' Association, the National Industrial Sand Association, the Tri-State Zinc and Lead Ore Pro-ducers Association, the U.S. Potters Association, and the Lead Industries As-sociation, among many others. The foundation established immediate legiti-macy in the fields of medicine, law, and engineering by attracting to its various working committees nearly all of the top names in the silicosis research and engineering communities: A. J. Lanza, R. R. Sayers, Dan Harrington, Leroy U. Gardner, R. R. Jones, O. A. Sander, and Philip Drinker. It established research links with Harvard, the Saranac Laboratory, and the University of Pennsylvania, as well as the Mellon Institute itself. In the midst of the De-pression, with limited funds available and the federal government incapable of embarking on a major research effort, the Air Hygiene Foundation and the public health researchers associated with it emerged as major forces shaping occupational lung research and the technical debate about silicosis in the United States for the next two decades.[13]

The foundation began with the assumption that "basic knowledge [was] essential in seeking the cause and prevention of silicosis." By studying the "mechanism by which silica exerts its effect upon the body" and establishing "how silica injures the tissue" the foundation scientists believed that they could then define more closely the means of prevention and cure. Was silica a "poison"? Was it an "irritant"? Were all silicates injurious or only free sil-ica? Were anthraco-silicosis and bituminosis distinct conditions or merely a subset of silicosis? How much silica was necessary to create symptoms? And, how long an exposure time was necessary? Were there materials that could alleviate symptoms or cure the disease? What was the relationship between silicosis and tuberculosis? Particularly, why was the silicotic individual more

---

[12] Weidlein, "Plan for Study."

[13] *History of Industrial Hygiene Foundation* (Pittsburgh, Pa.: Mellon Institute, 1956), 2–3; Air Hygiene Foundation of America, *Proceedings of Annual Meeting and Research Program* (Pitts-burgh, Pa., April 1, 1937), 12–14. For examples of the aggressive public relations campaign that the foundation waged both within industry and in the popular press, see Air Hygiene Foundation, "Progress Reports," Mellon Institute of Industrial Research, Carnegie Mellon University Ar-chives, Papers of the Mellon Institute.

susceptible to tuberculosis? How could one scientifically diagnose disease? How could the x-ray be used systematically to diagnose disease? All these questions were basic to their medical agenda.[14]

The research program of the Air Hygiene Foundation reflected, in part, the agenda of industry. But it also reflected the faith and optimism of the scientific community. Even in the midst of the social chaos of the Depression, many scientists and physicians held a marked faith in the potential of medical research to answer some of the most complex issues of human disease without, they hoped, having to confront the social issues surrounding and intertwined with the definitions of disease. The decline of tuberculosis and infectious diseases was seen as the victory of laboratory science, and there was little reason to suspect that silicosis and the other lung diseases could not be conquered as well. Careful research, delineation of the mechanisms that caused symptoms, and identification of cures or palliatives for the afflicted, along with proper engineering and preventive measures, were as useful in dust research as they were in research into controlling bacterial infections. The medical research agenda of the Air Hygiene Foundation was born of the amalgam of industrial need and scientific optimism.

The National Silicosis Conferences

The Air Hygiene Foundation approached the Labor Department's National Conference on Silicosis warily. This was not the kind of forum that industry was comfortable in. This was a political conference where debate was to be encouraged; it was an open public meeting rather than a closed technical discussion among experts. In this setting, organized labor had the opportunity to lay out its position on the silicosis issue with the same authority and legitimacy accorded to business and public health officials. But the real work of the conference was done by four committees that were dominated by Air Hygiene Foundation members and other experts, who developed a consensus that would define the silicosis issue in the coming years and even decades. This consensus held that technologically feasible engineering and medical standards could be developed to prevent silicosis from shortening a person's worklife. The impact of silicosis was to be measured by its effect on a worker's ability to earn a living, not upon his or her own sense of well-being or the quality of his or her life after retirement. Although the conference addressed questions about the definition and prevalence of the condition, the proceedings

[14] Air Hygiene Foundation of America, *Proceedings of Annual Meeting and Research Program* (Pittsburgh, Pa., April 1, 1937), 3–7. See also John F. McMahon, "Progress Report for Week Ended July 22, 1939," Mellon Institute of Industrial Research, Carnegie Mellon University Archives, Papers of the Mellon Institute, Industrial Fellowship 259-5, for an example of the types of basic research that the foundation supported.

and conference reports were primarily concerned with the implications of clinical, legal, and engineering decisions on industry liability through the compensation system. Industry and its allied experts hoped that the workers' compensation system could contain the silicosis crisis. Labor and its allies in the federal Department of Labor sought to move public policy away from business-dominated voluntary reform and toward legislative and political efforts.

The conference convened in Washington on April 14, 1936. Of the people present, half were "representatives of employers in the dusty trades," a quarter were public officials, 10 percent represented insurance companies, and 5 percent represented labor.[15] Among the most prominent members were R. R. Sayers of the U.S. Public Health Service, A. J. Lanza of the Metropolitan Life Insurance Company, L. U. Gardner, director of Saranac Laboratories, C. H. Watson, president of the National Safety Council, Cyril Ainsworth of the American Standards Association, J. J. Bloomfield of the U.S. Public Health Service, and E. O. Jones of the American Foundrymen's Association. Also present was John Frey, representing the American Federation of Labor.

Despite the apparent diversity of the program participants, the Air Hygiene Foundation tied together many of the key participants. Of the three major papers read at the Conference, two were by foundation members. A. C. Hirth, the chair of the legal committee of the foundation, presented a paper on the viewpoint of management to the conference. Dr. R. R. Sayers of the U.S. Public Health Service doubled as a member of the foundation's "medical committee." He delivered the address on the "engineering and medical aspects" of the silicosis hazard. In addition, the foundation was heavily represented in the four working committees that were set up to carry out the work of the conference:

> Five trustees, three committee chairmen and six members of committees of Air Hygiene Foundation are members of one or other of Mr. Zimmer's committees; Three of them are chairmen . . . . It is plain that the Foundation is being extended an opportunity to collaborate fully, to aid especially in giving the views and attitude of the industries.[16]

The conference was important in framing the generic positions of labor and management regarding the causes, the consequences, and the means of addressing the problem of silicosis. Management argued that silicosis was a preventable condition that was already well under control and that ventilation engineering had already eliminated the problem for future generations of workers. They maintained that respirators, positive pressure, wet drilling, and suction exhaust systems had lowered dust levels in granite, mining, and foun-

[15] "National Silicosis Conference," *American Labor Legislation Review* 26 (1936): 60.

[16] H. B. Meller, "Silicosis: Program of United States Department of Labor, and Interest and Cooperation of Air Hygiene Foundation," [1936], Carnegie-Mellon Archives. We are indebted to Joel Tarr for providing us with this document.

dries to "acceptable limits." Management emphasized the screening of workers before and during employment to eliminate those workers who showed signs of tuberculosis or previous or current exposure to silica dust.[17] For industry spokespeople, silicosis was a disease of the past that had gained notoriety because "shyster" lawyers and "quack" doctors interested in the fees they could extract from lawsuits inflamed the passion of a work force seeking to alleviate dependence brought on by the Depression.

In a major address to the conference by Alfred Hirth, a corporate lawyer working for Owens-Illinois Glass Company, these major themes were laid out. Hirth first emphasized the goodwill of industry as illustrated by its cooperation with the Public Health Service and the Bureau of Mines. He argued that mechanical means of dust control had been pursued for many years and that "the existence of a dust hazard is already on its way out." Linking dust control to the physical examination of workers, Hirth maintained that industry could establish "safe" dust levels: "Whether or not the hazard has in fact been removed will be finally demonstrated by the fact that the lungs of workmen are not being affected and this can only be determined by an x-ray examination." Industry was convinced that small amounts of silica would cause only small amounts of silica dust to be retained in the lungs. This minimal exposure was expected not to be disabling and not to adversely affect a person during his or her worklife.[18]

Hirth sought to establish a medical definition of silicosis that would not adversely affect industry. He suggested that silicosis was a problem only at the point that workers were incapable of working, not when they had evidence of silica dust in their lungs: "The question of disability seems to be ignored

[17] The public health emphasis on prevention dovetailed neatly with management's interpretation of the existing evidence regarding the true source of tuberculosis. If silica dust was a danger only for a select group of susceptible workers weakened by exposure to tuberculosis in the home environment, then a reasonable method for reducing risk both to the worker and to the company was to screen all workers for signs of tuberculosis infection before employment. If all at-risk workers could be eliminated from the work force, then neither the worker nor the company would be harmed. Furthermore, periodic medical examinations of employees and the transfer or termination of susceptible ones would protect the rest of the work force from infection. It was often maintained that the reason that tuberculosis was still a scourge for many groups of industrial workers was not that the workplace was unhealthy, but because industry refused to screen incoming workers properly. See "Tuberculosis as an Industrial Health Problem," *Monthly Labor Review* 22 (April 1926): 880–82. See also "New Jersey Health Service for Industry," *American Journal of Public Health* 17 (August 1927): 868–69; "The Greatest Toll of Tuberculosis is from Men in Industry," *American Journal of Public Health* 17 (July 1927): 759; "Industries and Tuberculosis," *American Journal of Public Health* 17 (April 1927): 410.

[18] It is important to remember that during the 1930s most men died during or shortly after their productive years. The average life expectancy for a twenty-year-old male entering the work force in 1930 was another forty-six years, meaning that some workers now could expect to live into retirement. Industry's formulation ignored workers who developed disabilities or disease after they left the workplace.

entirely, whereas it is really the meat of the question. . . ." For Hirth, the x-ray exam was a misleading diagnostic tool, for only workers with symptoms that inhibited their functioning on the job were truly diseased. He held that all workers were healthy whether or not they had fibrosis if their work was not impaired. "Ignorance and sensational journalism" had produced "the popular belief . . . that to inhale silica is to have Silicosis." Disability and impairment were the problems: "If we talk more about disability and less about silicosis, we would be more accurately expressing our ideas." Why, he asked, was everyone talking about silicosis? It was because of the "shyster lawyer and quack doctor, who have been with the United States always, but whom we hope we may someday exterminate."[19] He maintained that their influence had been so pervasive that "the great majority of cases which have come to my attention have been without merit. . . . The silicotic is rare as compared to the legion of men who have been driven from their jobs by shysters."[20] The compensation crisis shaped Hirth's view of disease.

The labor representative, John Frey of the American Federation of Labor, argued that silicosis was a problem for workers even before they became disabled. Workers should not come in contact with any silica because any silica in the lungs was pathological. Frey maintained that silicosis was not a disease of the past limited to only a handful of employees who labored years ago in primitive worksites. Rather, it was a potentially devastating affliction that threatened hundreds of thousands, perhaps millions, of workers and their families in a host of contemporary industries. In contrast to Hirth's analysis, which charged that public concern with silicosis had been artificially created by unsavory professionals and the economic conditions of the Depression, Frey saw the "rapidly increasing public interest" as a rational response to "the knowledge that silicosis is frequently fatal." He maintained that Hirth's emphasis on disability and impairment led management to rely on preemployment physicals and periodic screening as a means of denying employment or firing diseased workers. Such workers "have been discharged to learn immediately after that other employers, for that reason were unwilling to place them on the payroll. They have been barred from the opportunity of earning a livelihood." The real issue was not to eliminate diseased workers from the workplace but to "eliminate the silica from the air, and prevent additional infections."[21]

Unlike industry spokespeople, who sought to reduce the problem of silicosis

[19] Note the anti-Semitism implied by the use of *shyster* and the call for extermination, which echoed the views of Nazis and anti-Semites during the 1930s.

[20] "Proceedings of National Conference on Silicosis and Similar Dust Diseases," April 14, 1936, National Archives, Record Group 100, 7-0-4(1), 4–5. See also Hirth, "Silicosis as an Employer Problem," in Hirth to Zimmer, April 6, 1936, *ibid*.

[21] "Proceedings of National Conference on Silicosis and Similar Dust Diseases," April 14, 1936, National Archives, Record Group 100, 7-0-4(1), 6–7.

to an engineering and cost-benefit issue that balanced the health of the work force against the cost to industry, Frey based his argument upon the older public health reformers' analysis, which emphasized protecting communities rather than individuals. "Silicosis is an industrial disease which can be eliminated as effectively as typhoid germs can be removed from the city's drinking water," he began in his analysis of the issue. He noted, "When pollution of drinking water leads to typhus and typhoid, the citizens are not removed from their homes by the authorities." The cost of protecting the work force was a public obligation. Industry argued that the feasibility of cleaning the air people breathed was frequently determined by the cost of the available technology. But Frey argued that health should not be limited by what industry or public health officials thought was economically feasible. Just as modern city administrations had decided that the very high cost of purifying the water supply was justified by the improvements in health of the population, so too the cost of purifying the work environment was justified by the need to protect all workers from risk of contracting a preventable condition.[22]

The contrasting views of labor and management reflected the enormous political and economic stake that these two groups had in the definition of the silicosis hazard. If silicosis was defined in terms of one's inability to work it was possible to address the disease through the compensation system. If, on the other hand, it was defined as a long-term threat to the health and well-being of active and retired older workers, then the costs to industry through liability suits or preventive engineering measures could be enormous.

The meeting did not attempt to reconcile these points of view, a fact that greatly pleased the leaders of the Air Hygiene Foundation. It told its members that Zimmer and the conference organizers should "be highly commended upon the absence of any factors that might have caused controversy on the floor, and so would at least have distracted attention from the purpose."[23] Rather, the conference left the resolution of the issues to members of the four committees that held real power. The four committees, made up of fifty men and women, examined (1) "[t]he prevention of silicosis through medical control"; (2) "the prevention of silicosis through engineering control"; (3) "the economic, legal and insurance phases of the silicosis problem"; and (4) "the regulatory and administrative phases of the silicosis problem." The committees met a number of times, but left the drafting of most of their report to smaller groups of experts, usually those known for their experience with silicosis.[24]

The final reports were presented at the Second National Silicosis Confer-

[22] "Proceedings of National Conference on Silicosis . . . ," 8.

[23] H. B. Meller, "Silicosis: Program of United States Department of Labor, and Interest and Cooperation of Air Hygiene Foundation," [1936], Carnegie-Mellon Archives, provided to us by Joel Tarr.

[24] "Washington Moves to Check Silicosis," *New York Times*, May 3, 1936, 17.

ence held on February 3, 1937, and reflected the business and public health perspectives. First, the conferees wanted to reassure the public concerning the overall danger. Silicosis, it was argued, was not as serious a problem as had been feared. The vast majority of workers were not at risk. Rather, it was a threat in only a few select and scattered industries. Second, the conference participants sought to reassure both the public and industry that the problem could be addressed through existing regulatory and insurance mechanisms and did not require national legislation to control silicosis or a drastic reorganization of the system of compensation. Third, the conferees agreed that there were relatively straightforward technical solutions, such as wet drilling, ventilation, and respirators. It was agreed that these techniques could be applied to the few seriously affected industries and that their adoption could eliminate the silicosis hazard. The report emphasized that reduction in levels of exposure, without total elimination of contact, would be sufficient to control the problem. No fundamental alteration of industrial production would be required by the mining, foundry, stonecutting, and other industries. In light of the severe economic disruptions brought on by the depression, the conferees sought to allay fear and emphasize that work could go on as usual. On this issue, management and labor had essentially the same goal: to reduce the hazard without undercutting the industries that created scarce jobs.

The final report adopted industry's position that silica was a disease of the past that had largely been defused by voluntary action. It estimated that 500,000 workers were exposed to silica dust in American industries on the basis of a 1934 estimate by Anthony J. Lanza and Robert J. Vane. Despite the fact that Lanza and Vane themselves called their numbers a "very rough, but obviously conservative estimate" based upon data that "leave much to be desired,"[25] the report converted these numbers into a nationally accepted index of the severity of the silicosis problem.

Seeking to allay the public's sense of crisis, the report concluded, "From a purely statistical point of view . . . the problem of silicosis is not as serious or general as some other industrial problems, such as lead poisoning or industrial accidents."[26] Of the half a million workers who were exposed to silica dust, the report estimated that 100,000 had silicosis but that fewer than 5,000 "suffered any work disablement at this time."[27] It legitimated industry's position

[25] A. J. Lanza and Robert J. Vane, "The Prevalence of Silicosis in the General Population and Its Effects upon the Incidence of Tuberculosis," *American Review of Tuberculosis* 29 (January 1934): 10–11.

[26] U.S. Department of Labor, Division of Labor Standards, *National Silicosis Conference, Summary of Reports, Bulletin No. 13* (Washington, D.C.: Government Printing Office, 1937), 2.

[27] A.J. Lanza and Robert J. Vane, "The Prevalence of Silicosis in the General Population and Its Effects upon the Incidence of Tuberculosis," *American Review of Tuberculosis* 29 (January 1934): 8–16. It should be noted that this study was very clear in stating that the data available for determining the prevalence of silicosis were very inadequate and that the study's estimates were very conservative. The study took little account of job mobility, turnover, or retirement in its

that disability rather than disease was the real problem and that this "problem is not particularly serious."[28] In this formulation, persons who became disabled near or after retirement, and perhaps died from complications of the disease, were not counted in these tallies.

The Engineering Committee endorsed the idea that dust control methods had to keep down the costs to industry of any technological improvements in ventilation: "To be put into practice these methods must be economically feasible so that industries both large and small may utilize them in the solution of their dust problem." The engineering group noted that safer substances were generally unavailable to most industries or, if available, were too costly, and therefore "the solution of the problem depends upon reduction of the concentration of the dust to safe limits." The engineering group began with the assumption that workers would always be exposed to some silica dust.[29]

The Committee on the Prevention of Silicosis through Medical Control shared this cost-conscious, voluntaristic philosophy. They endorsed the prevalent notion that standards could be adopted in every industry that would reduce or eliminate the silicosis hazard.[30] What were these standards based on? Those who developed the standards recognized that they were designed not only to protect the workers and to provide governments with a basis for protective legislation, but also to "protect industrial concerns from racketeering in liability cases."[31] In large part, the standards were developed retrospectively and as an enormous political compromise that traded on workers' health. "Safe" levels were determined by studies that correlated degree of dustiness with length of time on the job and the presence of disease. In the 1930s, everyone recognized that the excessive dust level that existed in the plants up to that point had produced fibrosis in a large number of workers. Engineers found that they could reduce dust levels to 5 million particles per cubic foot and that over the course of the five to ten years researchers followed

estimates. Despite these caveats, the conservative numbers it quoted regarding the prevalence of silicosis were used over and over again by industry spokespeople, who emphasized how few workers were really at risk.

[28] U.S. Department of Labor, *National Silicosis Conference Summary*, 3.

[29] U.S. Department of Labor, Division of Labor Standards, *National Silicosis Conference, Report on Engineering Control*, Bulletin No. 21, Part 2 (Washington, D.C.: Government Printing Office, 1938), 1.

[30] U.S. Department of Labor, Division of Labor Standards, *National Silicosis Conference, Report on Medical Control*, Bulletin No. 21, Part 1 (Washington, D.C.: Government Printing Office, 1938), 34. See also H. S. Cumming, Surgeon General, to Hugh Booth, February 8, 1935, National Archives, Record Group 90, General Files: "In the case of granite dust . . . a tentative figure of 10 million particles per cubic foot of air was suggested, and for anthracite coal . . . 50 million particles of dust per cubic foot was found associated with practically no deleterious effects."

[31] Cyril Ainsworth, "Committee of Experts Starts Work to Find Danger Limits of Industrial Dusts, Gases," *Industrial Standardization and Commercialization Monthly* 7 (June 1936): 147. Ainsworth was the engineer in charge of safety work for the American Standards Association.

foundry workers, miners, and potters, workers did not get sick. They assumed that this was sufficient time to reveal latent disease. Therefore, this was assumed to be a "safe" level and thus was made the standard.

The standard was not the result of a conspiracy by the business community to poison workers. Rather, it resulted from the desire by public health professionals and business alike to develop "objective criteria" to be able to eliminate the silicosis hazard. But some worried that in its enthusiasm to objectify a political issue, the technical community had become obsessed with measurement for its own sake. By 1935, public health officials had adopted a "standard" of 10 million particles pure cubic foot of air in granite and other industries where the silica content of rock was 35 percent.[32] This standard was widely accepted as indicating a safe work environment, but was never rigorously evaluated. In 1930, the American Public Health Association's Committee on Silicosis (composed of R. R. Sayers, A. J. Lanza, and Emery R. Hayhurst)[33] pointed out that such a standard "was not found to prevent the occurrence of silicosis." Rather it only protected workers in the dusty trades from contracting tuberculosis as well as silicosis. The committee also made clear that the standard was developed in part because it "could be reached by the use of economically practicable ventilating devices."[34]

Dan Harrington, of the Bureau of Mines, was one of the few experts to say that the emperor had no clothes. He argued that "to state what is that dangerous quantity or what is a safe limit is difficult—in fact, it is impossible—with our present facilities and knowledge." He called the various maximum dust limits established in South Africa, Europe, and the United States "arbitrary" and noted that measurement techniques were crude at best. Different technicians hardly ever attained similar readings of dust concentrations, with results often varying by factors of four or more.[35] Despite these criticisms, the conference perpetuated the idea that the recommendations were based upon neutral science, not social convenience and economic feasibility.

The two remaining committees, the Committee on the Economic, Legal, and Insurance Phases and the Committee on Regulatory and Administrative Phases, both adopted the optimistic assessments of the engineering and medical groups[36] but believed that their mandate was to find means by which to

[32] H. S. Cumming, Surgeon General, to Hugh Booth, February 8, 1935, National Archives, Record Group 90 (Public Health Service), General Files.

[33] These three public health officials were involved in numerous industrial hygiene activities. Hayhurst was particularly active in the collusion that resulted in the establishment of tetraethyl lead as an accepted gasoline additive. See David Rosner and Gerald Markowitz, "A 'Gift of God'? The Public Health Controversy over Leaded Gasoline during the 1920s," *American Journal of Public Health* 75 (April 1985): 344–52.

[34] "Effect of Dust on the Lungs," *American Journal of Public Health* 20 (April 1930): 372.

[35] Daniel Harrington, *Silicosis as Affecting Mining Workmen and Operations*, U.S. Bureau of Mines Information Circular 6867 (January 1936, mimeo).

[36] U.S. Department of Labor, Division of Labor Standards, *National Silicosis Conference, Re-*

compensate past and existing victims. This reflected the view of labor and business alike that the crisis was caused by the widespread firing of workers who were diagnosed as silicotic. But this attention to the compensation system also reflected the business view that silicosis was not a real problem until it caused disability and that silicosis was only of marginal importance in disabling workers. They defined disability as "a decrease in capacity to do the work required of an individual in the course of his usual occupation." They also believed that pure and simple silicosis rarely was the cause of a worker's inability to work.

In adopting this definition, the committees were driven by business's need to limit the potential burden of a compensation system that incorporated silicosis. Just a few years earlier R. R. Sayers had recognized that even simple silicosis predisposed its victims to infectious pulmonary diseases, most notably tuberculosis and pneumonia. And infectious illnesses caused by the action of silica on the lungs constituted part of the disability that silicotics suffered. But at the conference, the committee that was chaired by Sayers refused to ascribe to industrial conditions the widely prevalent disease of tuberculosis. The committee went out of its way to separate out the issue of silicosis from the larger issue of the relationship between occupationally induced diseases and bacterial disease. It obscured the industrial origins of chronic conditions by arguing that disability did not result from a single factor; rather, "more often several otherwise unrelated systemic conditions may contribute towards disability."[37] Tuberculosis in the silicotic worker had changed from an occupational disease to an "unrelated systemic condition." Where tuberculosis coexisted with silicosis, industry did not want to bear the responsibility for the worker's poverty, personal hygiene, and poor living conditions.

The conference committees sought to ensure that whatever specific regulations were adopted by state compensation boards, the final decisions about who should get compensation would be in the hands of medical experts rather than the political appointees on the boards. Three of the four committees established by the conference endorsed the proposal that business had been pushing since the 1920s that final authority in disease claims should reside in a medical board. In spite of the medical uncertainty and conflict engendered by this uncertainty, one committee noted that "it becomes necessary to search for impartial, objective, quantitative measures by means of which the subjective complaints may be evaluated." The medical board, removed from the politics of workplace struggle and the real-life pressures of unemployment during the

---

port on Economic, Legal, and Insurance Phases, Bulletin No. 21, Part 3 (Washington, D.C.: Government Printing Office, 1938), 1.

[37] U.S. Department of Labor, Division of Labor Standards, National Silicosis Conference, Report on Medical Control, Bulletin No. 21, Part 1 (Washington, D.C.: Government Printing Office, 1938), 60–61.

Depression, would be the arbiter of workers' complaints.[38] This position echoed a long-standing belief of those associated with industry that the medical profession would serve industry better than would lay juries: "Neither lawyers nor laymen are in the position to pass upon medical questions nor to determine the existence of occupational disease in industry nor the disabling effect thereof. The determination of such injuries must be taken from lay juries and from commissions incompetent to determine such medical questions."[39]

This recommendation was in direct contrast to the original intent of the Department of Labor administrators, who had hoped that the conference would lead to a broadening of input into the decisionmaking process rather than a narrowing of authority. Martin Durkin, an official from the Illinois Department of Labor who would later serve briefly as secretary of labor under Eisenhower, objected to the medical board proposal. "No body of men has reached such a state of perfection," he wrote, "that they should be set apart and become a super–fact finding body, whose opinions are not to be questioned by cross-examination to determine if they are correct in the conclusions on 'doubtful medical points.' "[40] He pointed out that "medicine is not an exact science, and doctors, even experts, have been mistaken." He objected to the substitution of the uncertain science of medicine for the judgement of courts and juries of citizens: "It is fallacious to argue that because industrial commissions' findings of fact are final that courts cannot set them aside if there is any evidence to sustain them, that medical boards, composed of experts, should be the final arbiters of disputed medical questions." He wondered why the committee was so convinced that medical expertise should be supreme. "Why all this sanctity?" he asked. "Are these [medical] men so immune from error that their opinion (and that is all they can give) cannot be tested or disputed? Such a procedure violates every known idea of American justice and denies a person the right to a trial of the important issue." He suggested that "if there is to be a medical advisory board, such a board should be appointed by the compensation administrators, and that the findings of the board or of the impartial examiners should be subject to examination and cross-examination by any of the parties at interest."[41] From Durkin's perspective, the

[38] U.S. Department of Labor, Division of Labor Standards, *National Silicosis Conference, Report on Medical Control, Bulletin No. 21, Part 1* (Washington, D.C.: Government Printing Office, 1938), 62–63; U.S. Department of Labor, Division of Labor Standards, *National Silicosis Conference, Report on Regulatory and Administrative Phases, Bulletin No. 21, Part 4* (Washington, D.C.: Government Printing Office, 1938), 3.

[39] Theodore C. Waters, "What the Employer Should Know about Silicosis," *Stone* 57 (November 1936): 405.

[40] U.S. Department of Labor, Division of Labor Standards, *National Silicosis Conference, Report on Regulatory and Administrative Phases, Bulletin No. 21, Part 4* (Washington, D.C.: Government Printing Office, 1938), 6.

[41] U.S. Department of Labor, Division of Labor Standards, *National Silicosis Conference, Re-*

conference's willingness to grant medical personnel broad authority was part of a broader effort to take the silicosis issue out of the broader political arena and undercut workers' impact on its definition.

Durkin was responding to what he perceived to be an attempt to diminish the importance of labor in the compensation system. The effort to restrict labor's influence was paralleled by an effort to restrict the very definition of compensable diseases. The problem for industry and the insurance carriers was the danger that too broad a definition of occupational disease would stimulate claims from workers in a broad range of industries. But too narrow a definition would exclude so many diseases that workers would be forced back into the liability system, which would do nothing to resolve the crisis that had given rise to all this activity. What is interesting is that this problem for industry and insurance became a problem for the medical and public health profession as well. Ludwig Teleky, an internationally renowned authority, noted in 1941 that there were two competing methods for covering occupational disease that affected the definitions of what constituted an occupational disease. The first method, blanket coverage, was all-inclusive, encompassing all diseases associated with employment. From this vantage point, an occupational disease was one that was contracted as a result of work conditions, which could include infectious diseases, such as pneumonia. The second definition was much narrower. It included only those diseases "peculiar to a certain occupation," and these would have to be clearly and definitively enumerated in a schedule in the workers' compensation laws. In this case, pneumonia, a disease that was not specifically associated with a particular industry, would not be compensated, even if working conditions in a particular plant predisposed workers to this illness.[42]

Not surprisingly, insurance carriers and industry representatives pushed very hard for the schedule and opposed blanket coverage. The Association of Casualty and Surety Executives proposed that each state develop "a schedule of the diseases to be deemed 'occupational diseases' " peculiar to that state in the opinion of medical authorities. Such diseases would have to "be traced to origins in 'trade risks,'—i.e. risks, not of ordinary life, but created by special practices or processes in industrial occupations."[43] Henry Sayer argued that "general and vague language will lend itself to the inclusion of any and every

port on Regulatory and Administrative Phases, Bulletin No. 21, Part 4 (Washington, D.C.: Government Printing Office, 1938), 6–7.

[42] Ludwig Teleky, "The Compensation of Occupational Diseases," *Journal of Industrial Hygiene and Toxicology* 23 (October 1941): 357–58.

[43] *Perils in Measures for Compensation for Occupational Diseases* (New York: Association of Casualty and Surety Executives, February 28, 1935), American Association for Labor Legislation Manuscripts, Pamphlets, Occupational Diseases, 1935–1936, Industrial and Labor Relations Archives, Cornell University. See also Lewis A. Mills, "Occupational Disease Situation in Hands of a Body of Experts," *Eastern Underwriter* 36 (December 6, 1935): 86–87.

sort of illness and disease to which human flesh is heir.'' He concluded, ironically, with the derisive comment that such absurd notions could lead to the inclusion of seemingly ''natural'' diseases, such as tuberculosis, pneumonia, and cancer, as occupational diseases: ''We surely do not think of colds, pneumonia, tuberculosis, . . . and cancer as occupational diseases.''[44]

His second objection to blanket coverage was that it could edge over into a welfare system. Any worker who died from any illness would ''become a liability of the industry by which he was employed. This is literally health and life insurance for workers at the expense of the employer.'' He maintained that where industry was directly responsible for a worker's ill-health, the industry should pay. But ''no such obligation should be placed on industry'' for the general ill-health of the society.[45]

F. Robertson Jones, general manager of the Association of Casualty and Surety Executives, summarized the fear that workers' compensation would become a tool of reformers seeking to shift the costs of social welfare benefits for unemployment to their industry: ''The chief trouble today is that we have confused compensation with relief. If we can keep these two ideas separate and can restrict the tendency to turn the compensation system into a universal pension system having no particular relation to employment, we shall have accomplished something.''[46] Theodore C. Waters, a lawyer who represented industry in the various liability suits, also warned that ''occupational disease compensation should not be permitted to become health insurance.'' Compensation should be strictly limited to diseases that were specific to particular industries. He specifically attacked labor advocates who favored blanket coverage: ''In my judgement the 'all-inclusive' occupational disease acts tend inevitably to health insurance and enable the Department charged with the adminsitration thereof to award compensation to all the human ills that may occur to employees in the course of their employment.''[47]

[44] Henry D. Sayer, *Occupational Diseases—Real and Supposed*, n.d., American Association for Labor Legislation Manuscripts, Pamphlets, Occupational Diseases, n.d., Industrial and Labor Relations Archives, Cornell University.

[45] Others in the insurance industry also worried about the danger that blanket coverage for occupational diseases could quickly evolve into an industry-supported health insurance system rather than a compensation system. See, for example, ''Tendencies in Workmen's Compensation,'' *Weekly Underwriter* 131 (August 1934): 289–90: ''The tendency to liberalize the construction and application of occupational disease provision to such an extent that the laws become in effect broad compulsory health insurance has also created a number of problems.'' See also Henry D. Sayer, *Occupational Diseases—Real and Supposed*, n.d., American Association for Labor Legislation Manuscripts, Pamphlets, Occupational Diseases, n.d., Industrial and Labor Relations Archives, Cornell University.

[46] F. Robertson Jones, ''Problems of Compensation for Occupational Diseases,'' November 15, 1934, American Association for Labor Legislation Manuscripts, Pamphlets, Industrial and Labor Relations Archives, Cornell University.

[47] Theodore C. Waters, ''What the Employer Should Know about Silicosis,'' *Stone* 57 (November 1936): 404–05.

Organized labor dissented strongly from the general position of insurance carriers and industry. First, some labor representatives objected to organizing compensation for occupational disease through private insurance carriers in the individual states. Second, labor representatives objected to the use of physical exams as a means of screening workers before and during employment. Third, they rejected the notion that schedules were the only reasonable means of organizing coverage. Fourth, they rejected the idea that compensation should supersede in importance factory inspection and regulation of the workplace. Finally, they proposed a system of federal grants-in-aid that would establish national standards for compensation and federal regulation of occupational disease hazards.

Robert J. Watt of the Massachusetts Federation of Labor made the most pointed critique in a dissent from the report of the Economic, Legal and Insurance Committee of the National Silicosis Conference. He began by stating that the federation "cannot concur with respect to several features of the report which deal particularly with the protection of" workers exposed to silica dust. His strongest objection was the compensation system's reliance on private insurance carriers: "We are convinced that an adequate solution to the silicosis problem cannot be reached as long as the incentive of private profits is the governing factor in the scheme of compensation insurance which is provided." He maintained that insurance carriers' obsession with the problem of accrued liability derived from their own immoral decisions in the past to avoid addressing the problem of silicosis at the workplace. Accrued liability, from his point of view, was a direct result of the carriers' and industry's decision to avoid the problem in the past. Because of this history, Watt proposed that silicosis and other occupational diseases could only "be adequately insured through exclusive state workmen's compensation funds in the various jurisdictions."[48] Further, he pointed out the extreme inefficiency of the private system of insurance, claiming that "only 30 cents out of the premium dollar" ever found its way into the pockets of injured and diseased workers. The rest, he claimed, went for lawyers' fees, doctors' bills, and charges for administration by the companies. The existing compensation system, he said, discriminated against elderly workers, as well as injured and diseased workers.[49] Watt's position reflected that of the American Federation of Labor and the recommendations of the Third National Conference on Labor Legislation in 1936, held under the auspices of the Secretary of Labor.[50]

[48] Robert J. Watt, "Draft of Report Supplementing Report of the Economic, Legal and Insurance Committee—National Silicosis Conference," February 2, 1937, National Archives, Record Group 100, 7-0-4(1).

[49] Watt, "Draft."

[50] Watt, "Draft"; Joseph A. Padway, General Counsel, American Federation of Labor, "What We Expect under Workmen's Compensation and What We Are Getting," U.S. Department of

Watt also pointed out the injustice of using the medical profession to screen workers for employment. He acknowledged the importance of preemployment and periodic physicals as a tool in diagnosing silicosis and any subsequent infections. But, he stated, organized labor was "unalterably opposed to a provision for such examinations unless and until the profit motive in compensation insurance is eliminated . . . and until the worker and his dependents are adequately taken care of through hospitalization, rehabilitation, re-eduction, etc."[51] In the absence of a comprehensive national social and health insurance program, workers' compensation should provide blanket coverage for the disease and disabilities created by the industrial workplace. The American Federation of Labor had gone on record earlier in support of such a blanket provision. They argued that "a disease may grow out of the employment and be caused by it, and yet not be 'characteristic' of it, or 'peculiar' to it." The schedule method of payment limited workers' access under the workers' compensation law and prevented them from gaining restitution for legitimate injuries to their health and well-being. The schedules would "not include any new disease until long after its discovery and after considerable harm has been done to the worker."[52]

In the end, labor's dissent from the committee's reports went unnoticed and unappreciated. The business and public health approach had prevailed. To a very great extent, the conference resolved the major issues of the day by adopting recommendations that ignored the enormous gaps in scientific and technical knowledge and the tremendous differences in perspective among the different communities affected by the silicosis issue. Perhaps most important, the conference gave its imprimatur to the idea that there was no silicosis crisis, that the danger of silicosis had been overstated and was restricted to a relatively small number of workers in a few industries. The conference also affirmed that it was possible to establish standards for dust exposure that could eliminate the hazard in the future. They did not reach total agreement about the precise compensation mechanisms to be adopted by individual states. But the conference participants did agree that such legislation should be left in the hands of the states. With appropriate constraints on the generosity of the compensation system, that system could calm the highly charged atmosphere in which silicosis was being debated. Overall, the conference reasserted the primacy of the professional, the technician, and the expert and the ability of industry and public health officials together to solve the political and technical problem of silicosis. Given the makeup of the conference, with the extraordinary influence of business and conservative public health experts, it is not surprising that it produced such a skewed set of recommendations. The con-

Labor, Division of Labor Standards, *Bulletin No. 36* (Washington, D.C.: Government Printing Office, 1939), 24.

[51] Watt, "Draft."

[52] Padway, "What We Expect," 31.

ference chairman, Verne A. Zimmer, tried to make the best of a bad situation but took pains to underline his opinion that the reports should not be seen as the final word regarding silicosis and its prevention. Specifically, he pointed out that the reports generally reflected the opinions of the technical experts and did not give equal weight to the opinions of management, labor, and the public. He was particularly concerned about the general absence of labor in the formulation of the final document: ''We wish to stress the need for giving careful consideration to labor's views, which in many fundamental respects are at variance with those expressed in the committee reports.''[53] One year after the second conference, the Department of Labor published its own assessment of the silicosis issue, succinctly summarizing its objections to the public health model: ''[P]revention is mainly the responsibility of management''; and ''respirators are no substitute for silica-free air.''[54]

Zimmer's dissent was also based on his knowledge that the industry's rhetoric of reform and voluntarism did not match its actions. One case that attracted national attention was exposed just months before the final reports were made public. In September 1936, 1,400 foundry workers in the Caterpillar Tractor Company plant in Peoria, Illinois, were given complete physical examinations, including chest x-rays, to determine the extent of silicosis among the company's employees. Two months later, 179 of these men were laid off and told that they had silicosis. The company laid responsibility for this injustice on its insurance company, which ''had refused to carry the risk on these men.'' Ten days later, the new Illinois Occupational Disease Act became effective. It provided compensation for silicotics, with the last employer liable under the act. But these workers were not eligible because they had been fired previous to the date on which the act took effect. This was viewed by labor as a cynical attempt to circumvent the law and a callous disregard for the workers' needs. In light of the miserable conditions in the plant, labor saw this as another indication of the willingness of management to avoid responsibility even for the most grievous insults to workers' health. *The Nation* magazine denounced the company: ''The brazenness of the Caterpillar Company is perhaps unique in the long story of industrial murder.'' Labor reported that ''silica dust in the Caterpillar foundry was so thick that the men operating hand trucks collided in the main gang-way.''[55]

The U.S. Department of Labor was also constantly receiving letters complaining of continued abuse of workers' rights and health. One letter detailed

[53] Verne A. Zimmer, Foreword, U.S. Department of Labor, Division of Labor Standards, *National Silicosis Conference, Report on Regulatory and Administrative Phases, Bulletin No. 21, Part 4* (Washington D.C.: Government Printing Office, 1938), viii.

[54] U.S. Department of Labor, Division of Labor Standards, *The Cause and Prevention of Silicosis*, Industrial Health and Safety Series No. 9 (Washington, D.C.: Government Printing Office, 1938).

[55] Milton S. Mayer, ''Slow Death in Illinois,'' *The Nation* 144 (April 17, 1937): 432–34.

the history of neglect and racism of Harbison Walker Refractories Company, a company that had ostensibly accepted the recommendations of the conference. Edwin W. Kenworthy, an instructor at the extension division of Indiana University in East Chicago, revealed in a letter to Perkins that the company had a serious silicosis problem that it sought to cover up. It systematically fired silicotic workers or transferred them to departments free of dust. In accord with the recommendations of the National Silicosis Conference, the company had used postemployment physical examinations and transfers to less dusty work environments. But they used the examinations and transfers as tools to obscure the relationship between original exposure to silica dust and later deaths: "Three years ago the company had x-rays taken of all the men in the plant. Not one man was informed of his condition by the company, though subsequently many men were discharged, or sent south with no, or small compensation, until they died." Kenworthy concluded that the "plant is a death mill, and a constant hazard to the health of the employees."[56]

The department was impressed by his letter and encouraged Kenworthy to conduct a fuller study of the plant and its workers. In April 1940, Kenworthy sent his study to the department, further documenting the deplorable conditions in this plant. He described the irony of the safety propaganda that the plant managers distributed and the terrible reality of working conditions. Over the entrance to the plant was a sign: "WE WANT TO PROVIDE A SAFE PLACE FOR EVERYONE EMPLOYED IN THIS PLANT. REPORT ANY DANGEROUS CONDITIONS TO YOUR FOREMAN." Further, the plant manager maintained that the factory had "the best and most modern equipment known to science." This "modern" equipment consisted of "tying rags and paper over the holes in the leaky, second-hand dust conduits, and speeding up the rpm of an overworked 15 inch fan that was used to clear some 400,000 cubic feet of dust-laden air." In November 1939, Local 12120 of the United Mine Workers called a strike that had three major demands: a five cent an hour pay increase, vacations with pay, and adequate machinery to exhaust the dust.[57] After three months, the workers won the first two demands and an agreement to set up "a 6-man employer-employee safety committee" made up of half union and half company officials. The agreement also provided for "the installation of mechanical equip-

[56] Edwin W. Kenworthy to Secretary Perkins, December 1, 1939, quoted in Gerald Markowitz and David Rosner, eds., *"Slaves of the Depression"* (Ithaca: Cornell University Press, 1987), 128–33.

[57] Edwin W. Kenworthy to Zimmer, April 1, 1940, National Archives Record Group 100, 7-1-5-1. Kenworthy believed that the strike had been successful in forcing the company to reform. However, the union representatives a month and a half later believed that the company was reneging on its agreement, with the help of the state and federal agencies. See Gilbert Soltwedel to Zimmer, May 28, 1940, *ibid*. For other expressions of union concern with the continuing problem of silicosis, see, for example, Steel Workers Organizing Committee to Zimmer, October 31, 1940, *ibid*; New Hampshire State Federation to Perkins, November 13, 1936, National Archives Record Group 100, 7-2-1-5-1.

ment to lessen the dust hazard.'' The United Auto Workers remarked on the significance of this agreement and called for the inclusion of similar health and safety provisions in ''all UAW-CIO contracts where silicosis or other occupational health hazards exist.''[58]

Labor distrusted not only business but also public health officials, whose ostensible claim to scientific objectivity and neutrality cloaked their probusiness sympathies. Present and former officials in the Public Health Service and the Bureau of Mines, for example, moved easily between their public service in the U.S. government and their private roles as employees and consultants to giant corporations and industrial trade associations. R. R. Sayers, R. R. Jones, W. P. Yant, and Daniel Harrington, for example, were on the board of trustees and various committees of the Air Hygiene Foundation. A. J. Lanza, who once worked for the Public Health Service was now employed by Metropolitan Life Insurance Company, the major industrial insurer. Other experts who played a prominent public health role, such as Leroy U. Gardner, O. A. Sander, and even Philip Drinker, saw nothing unusual or problematic in serving as paid industrial consultants. New Deal administrators and representatives of the labor movement felt that the new disciplines of industrial hygiene and medicine were often used as tools of management against the interests of labor. Throughout the 1920s, companies had used physical examinations to discriminate against workers and had appropriated industrial physicians as ''company'' doctors whose salary was paid by industry and whose loyalty was to those who paid them. If the Public Health Service was an advocate for industry, the Department of Labor, Clara Beyer declared, ''should be a service agency for labor.''[59]

Labor also felt threatened because the claim of the rising profession of industrial hygiene to scientific objectivity and legitimacy provided the rationale for shifting moneys and programs for industrial hygiene work from state labor departments to state health departments. The Social Security Act of 1935 provided for the allocation of money to state health departments to establish industrial hygiene units. Until that time, most state government safety and health programs were organized through departments of labor rather than health departments. Dominated by the Air Hygiene Foundation and Public Health Service officials, the National Silicosis Conference strongly supported this shift of power to public health authorities. The conference report called for the expansion of authority for bureaus of occupational hygiene in state public

[58] ''Strike Against Silicosis,'' *United Auto Worker*, March 20, 1940, 4; ''Silicosis,'' *Survey Mid-Monthly* 76 (April 1940): n.p.

[59] Clara Beyer, Memorandum, ''The Division of Labor Standards: Its Functions and Organization,'' November 1934, National Archives, Record Group 100, 1934–1937, 1-1, Box 24. See also David Rosner and Gerald Markowitz, ''Federal Occupational Safety and Health Policies during the New Deal,'' *Journal of Social History* 18 (Spring 1985): 364–81.

health departments and for the limitation to an advisory role of bureaus of inspection in state departments of labor.[60]

Organized labor took particular exception to the conference's call for power to be vested in state departments of health: "We are of the definite opinion that industrial hygiene units, by whatever name, must be located in that agency of the State government which is concerned primarily and intimately with the administration of labor laws . . . rather than in such department as has only to do with general matters of public health," remarked Robert J. Watt, the president of the Massachusetts Federation of Labor, in a dissent to the final report. He continued by explaining his reasons for rejecting the majority report's support for state departments of health:

> It is only through a tie-up of the industrial hygiene activities with specific inspection and enforcement powers, coupled with the statistics gathering function, that satisfactory administration can be obtained. The gap which exists between medical theory and the practical protection of the worker cannot be bridged by any agency other than that which is regularly concerned with the welfare of workers as such.[61]

Others agreed with the basic tenets of labor's objections to the report. John Andrews, the long-time head of the American Association for Labor Legislation, pointed out the highly political nature of the silicosis problem. Complaining specifically about the Public Health Service approach, Andrews wrote, "[A]lways in this country there has been money for more and more study; never has there been similar encouragement for legislative action." He continued: "[T]he responsible public authorities as well as those who are directly in charge of our industries should never again be permitted to forget those who have for our common comfort and financial profit given their lives prosaically amid death dealing dusts."[62]

The business community emerged from the conference emboldened. The Air Hygiene Foundation continued its slow, steady attempt to capture professional opinion and urge its members to clean up their plants. But the National Safety Council took a more short-sighted, crassly opportunistic approach.[63] Immediately following the conference, the council prepared a report that used

---

[60] U.S. Department of Labor, Division of Labor Standards, *National Silicosis Conference, Summary of Reports, Bulletin No. 13* (Washington, D.C.: Government Printing Office, 1938), 8; Gerald Markowitz and David Rosner, "More Than Economism: The Politics of Workers' Safety and Health, 1932–1947," *Milbank Quarterly* 64 (Fall 1986): 331–54.

[61] Watt, "Draft."

[62] John B. Andrews, "The Tragedy of Silicosis," *American Labor Legislation Review* 26 (1936): 4–5. See also Leonard Greenburg, "Dangerous Dust," *Survey Graphic* 25 (December 1936): 664–68.

[63] "First Draft Proposed Pamphlet Silicosis," in W. Dean Keefer, Director, Industrial Division, National Safety Council, to Health Advisory Committee, March 22, 1937, C.-E.A. Winslow Manuscripts, Box 89, Folder 1459, Yale University Library.

the conclusions of the National Silicosis Conference to trivialize the silicosis hazard. It circulated a draft to a number of readers, including C.-E.A. Winslow, who it hoped would provide his imprimatur for its analysis. It suggested that silicosis was declining as an industrial health problem and was not as important as other industrial health problems, such as lead poisoning and industrial accidents.

Winslow, who only a few years before had removed his name from a study sponsored by the council, once again vented his rage at the "number of very doubtful statements in the report." He told the council that he believed that the problem of silicosis was "very much more serious and very much more general than that of lead poisoning, and probably as serious as that of industrial accidents." He further took issue with the report's misuse of Lanza's and Vane's original estimates of the number of people affected by silica dust, maintaining that those estimates were "extremely low and misleading about the number of workers who were disabled with both silicosis and tuberculosis." He also "seriously questioned" the draft's assertion that for "the 105,000 workers who have silicosis, but no disability and no tuberculosis, the problem is not particularly serious." The report recommended that the standard of 5 million particles per cubic foot of air be accepted as safe. But the report went even further than that. The National Safety Council maintained that this standard might be much too stringent: "If the result [of air sampling] is more than 5 million, one cannot say with assurance that the conditions are unsafe." Winslow called this interpretation "misleading." He also complained that the draft's emphasis on wet methods as a means of eliminating the dust hazard did not make it clear that such methods were "entirely inadequate to produce the effect desired."

Finally, Winslow objected to the description of air-purifying respirators as being "suitable for protection against silica dust." Experience had shown, he wrote, "that there are no such types of respirators that are efficient."[64] There was widespread acknowledgement at the time that respirators could be efficient if they were worn for the entire workday. However, this was rarely the case. As one Works Progress Administration study summarized, "[F]ew if any workmen can stand such masks on their faces throughout a day." Because the masks were tight fitting, they caused perspiration and irritation and often were quickly clogged with dust:

> Mr. Average Workman may stand the mask for an hour, then off it comes, "just for a little while" and the deadly dust resumes its attack. The periods of mask wearing become shorter and shorter. Tomorrow, next week, next year, is a long time away; why worry about five, ten or fifteen years?[65]

[64] C.-E.A. Winslow to W. Dean Keefer, May 10, 1937, C.-E.A. Winslow Manuscripts, Box 88, Folder 1431.

[65] WPA Silicosis Project, September 1936, Pamphlet File, Industrial and Labor Relations Archives, Cornell University.

Winslow concluded by bluntly stating, "The report throughout has the effect of whitewashing a very serious industrial menace."[66] The National Safety Council responded to Winslow's critique by saying that they had merely summarized the National Silicosis Conference findings.[67]

The Air Hygiene Foundation adopted a more sophisticated approach. In addition to publicizing concrete efforts to end the hazard, the foundation undertook an extensive research program that would become the basis for national voluntary standards in the field of occupational safety and health. In the years after the National Silicosis Conference, the foundation saw its role as "a partnership of industry and science for the advancement of industrial hygiene." The leaders recognized that fundamental research was "hard to 'sell,' " but they warned that "if industry doesn't do it then government must. . . . Viewed broadly, the support of Air Hygiene Foundation by industry is an investment in the American system of business and the preservation of that system."[68] It was through the Air Hygiene Foundation, their university-affiliated industrial hygiene departments, and the public health and medical researchers affiliated with them that nearly all research was carried out. It was the Air Hygiene Foundation that would henceforth seek to define "who was competent to speak" about silicosis and occupational disease.

Labor left the conference with a different political agenda. The American Federation of Labor rejected the Air Hygiene Foundation's basic premise, which called for voluntary adoption of standards for industrial hygiene. Rather, the federation followed the model of the National Labor Relations Act and called for an expanded federal role in workplace regulation that would complement the compensation mechanism. Rather than breaking off compensation from workplace regulation, inspection, and control, it called for an integrated approach coordinated by the federal Department of Labor rather than state or federal health authorities: "We feel it is only through application of the federal aid principle to this problem that the situation can be adequately

---

[66] C.-E.A. Winslow to W. Dean Keefer, May 10, 1937, C.-E.A. Winslow Manuscripts, Box 88, Folder 1431. See also Watt, "Draft," in which Robert J. Watt of the Massachusetts Federation of Labor called the estimates used by the committee too conservative and pointed out that even if the number of workers was accurate, the true number of people affected by the social impact of silicosis was at least 2 million. He maintained that the families of silicotics also had to be included in any estimate of the social cost of this disease.

[67] Keefer to Winslow, May 13, 1937, Winslow Manuscripts, Box 88, Folder 1431. Other industry-supported groups also quickly adopted the conference findings and the optimistic assessments contained therein: "The [Air Hygiene] Foundation is composed of approximately a thousand companies and has adopted a program almost identical with that of the Department of Labor as revealed by its committee set-up. . . . [With the adoption of various mechanical devices] the existence of a dust hazard is already on its way out." Alfred C. Hirth, Air Hygiene Foundation of America, 1936, National Archives, Record Group 174, Folder: Conferences, National (Silicosis and Similar Dust Diseases, April 14, 1936), Office of the Secretary.

[68] John F. McMahon, "Confidential Memorandum to Dr. Weidlein and Dr. Hamer," April 5, 1940, Carnegie-Mellon Archives, courtesy of Joel Tarr.

met.'' Watt suggested that such legislation "would provide minimum standards to which a state must subscribe before becoming eligible for participation in the disbursement of federal funds on a dollar for dollar basis.'' He continued by stating that the Massachusetts Federation of Labor supported the Department of Labor's claim that "industrial hygiene units . . . [should be] located in that agency of the State government which is concerned primarily and intimately with the administration of labor laws and those rules and regulations dealing with the welfare of the workers.'' It opposed the Social Security Act change that had placed the control of industrial hygiene units "in such department as has only to do with general matters of public health.'' Workers' compensation had to be part of a larger program of regulation and compensation organized through labor departments.[69]

Labor's suggestion was acted upon within two years by Verne Zimmer. In early 1939, at the suggestion of Senator James E. Murray of Montana, Zimmer drafted a bill to address the problems raised by the silicosis crisis.[70] Despite the general agreement among the health professionals that the silicosis crisis had largely passed, and the general mood within the country favoring inclusion of silicosis either by blanket or schedule coverage in state workers' compensation laws, both labor and Department of Labor officials believed that further action was necessary. In a memo to Secretary of Labor Perkins, Zimmer identified two major purposes in drafting the legislation. First, the bill was aimed at providing financial assistance to the states, through the Secretary of Labor, for control of silicosis in industry. Also, the bill sought to provide funds to the states' compensation system specifically in order to "give full benefits to claimants for silicosis.''[71]

Senate Bill 2256 was introduced on April 27, 1939. It authorized annual appropriations to states with compensation and silicosis prevention plans that had been approved by the U.S. secretary of labor. Such plans had to include "compulsory workmen's compensation coverage'' for "disabled workers or their dependents'' in case of death resulting from "dust diseases or other diseases . . . aggravated by dust diseases.'' State plans also had to prohibit "the waiver of disability or death benefits by workers'' and prohibit "discrimination'' against employees who had previously been exposed to silica or other dusts but who had not yet become disabled. State compensation plans had to provide "safeguards . . . to insure the prompt payment of the full amount of such benefits.'' The bill also established standards for each state's dust pre-

[69] Watt, "Draft.'' See also Robert J. Watt, "Labor's Viewpoint on Occupational Disease Prevention,'' November 15, 1939, in John F. McMahon to Florence Bradley, February 7, 1940, Metropolitan Life Insurance Company Library (Air Hygiene Foundation).

[70] Verne Zimmer to The Secretary, June 7, 1939, National Archives, Record Group 174, Office of the Secretary, Bills, Miscellaneous, 1939, in which Zimmer noted that the "bill was drafted by Mr. Rhetts of the Solicitor's Office and myself in response to a request by Senator Murray.''

[71] V. A. Zimmer to The Secretary, June 7, 1939, National Archives, Record Group 174, Office of the Secretary, Bills, Misc., 1939.

vention plan.[72] This was the first attempt at establishing federal regulation of safety and health conditions since passage of the Walsh-Healey Act of 1936.[73]

The next year, Senator Murray introduced another bill whose objectives were essentially the same as those of Senate Bill 2256. Its purpose was "the prevention of industrial conditions hazardous to the health of employees." Specifically, Senate Bill 3461 of 1940 proposed to provide for the administration of state industrial hygiene departments through state departments of labor and to set minimum standards for such departments to receive federal grants-in-aid. As in the previous bill, each agency "upon the request of the agency charged with the administration of the State workmen's compensation act, [would] aid in the adjudication of compensation claims for disability or death due to occupational diseases."[74] In hearings before a subcommittee of the Committee on Education and Labor, different opinions were aired by representatives of labor, management, the public health community, and the Department of Labor regarding the possible impact of this proposal on state and federal roles in protecting workers at the worksite. For representatives of the public health community, the significance of the bill rested in its provision that industrial hygiene matters would be administered through the labor departments of various states rather than through the state health departments.[75]

Labor representatives rallied behind the Department of Labor's effort to regain administrative control but also emphasized the importance of the Murray bill for establishing national standards for controlling occupational disease and workers' compensation laws. At the hearings on the bill, representatives of the American Federation of Labor, the Tri-State Survey Committee, and the American Association for Labor Legislation stressed the need for more vigorous enforcement of industrial hygiene codes, the need to involve workers and unions in addressing occupational disease problems, and the inequitable treatment of workers under state compensation laws.[76] But the CIO representative gave the most detailed and impassioned defense of the bill.

[72] U.S. Congress, S. 2256, 76th Cong., 1st sess., April 27, 1939.

[73] Theodore C. Waters, an attorney and public health official in Baltimore, Maryland, expressed the opposition of the public health community to a bill that placed so much power in the hands of Department of Labor officials. His objections mirrored the ongoing debates regarding the limits of public health reform and labor advocacy for workplace reform. See Waters, "A Critical Review of Occupational Disease Legislation," *Mining Congress Journal* 25 (December 1939): 34–36.

[74] U.S. Congress, S. 3461, 76th Cong., 3d sess., February 29, 1940.

[75] For fuller discussions of the ongoing battles between the Public Health Service and Department of Labor over industrial hygiene see David Rosner and Gerald Markowitz, "Research or Advocacy: Federal Occupational Safety and Health Policies during the New Deal," in Rosner and Markowitz, eds., *Dying for Work*, 83–102.

[76] See the testimony of Paul Scharranberg, the legislative representative of the American Federation of Labor, the testimony of Elizabeth Wade White of the Tri-State Survey Committee, and the letter of the American Association for Labor Legislation in U.S. Congress, Senate, *Hearings before a Subcommittee of the Committee on Education and Labor on S. 3461*, 76th Cong., 3d sess., May 13, 14, 16, 1940, 59–61, 62–64, 117.

Dr. Walter N. Polakov, a director of the United Mine Workers of America, explained the importance of health to American workers. Having studied the problem of silicosis and anthraco-silicosis over a number of years, Polakov explained that "health for wage earners is not merely freedom from pain and disease; it is an essential requirement for earning a livelihood, maintaining a home, and caring for children."[77] Polakov said that the Murray bill was the best way to "control and prevent industrial conditions hazardous to employees." He noted that there was a direct relationship between increasing disability and poverty among American workers. Workers who earned $1,000 or less a year were more than twice as likely to be disabled than those who earned $5,000 or more per year. Unlike representatives of management and industry, who used the term *disability* to describe the physical shortcomings of individual workers, Polakov saw disablement from a very different perspective. He pointed out that if disability was defined by one's ability to find work, then all those workers who had been excluded from employment because of a suspicious chest x-ray or other medical finding were, technically, disabled. He also sought to broaden the definition of disability to include "any organic or functional disorder the source of which may be traced to harmful working conditions or environment." He argued that simply to make up a list of occupational diseases was inadequate since it would not

> include the occupational hazards resulting from the tempo of the work and from the nervous strain of maintaining continuous sustained attention, correct perception, and prompt reaction in the environs of general nervous tension in the work and great responsibility in modern mass production, where a slight mistake in touching the wrong button may kill a number of people to say nothing about damage, of course.

The control of these hazards should not be the responsibility of medical and insurance personnel.[78]

Industry representatives took a very different position regarding the Murray bill. Theodore C. Waters, a member of the Air Hygiene Foundation's legal committee and the chairman of the Maryland Occupational Diseases Commission, explained to the foundation's annual meeting in November 1939 his objections to the bill. These included his belief that the control of industrial conditions should properly be left to the states rather than the federal government. J. Dewey Dorsett, the manager of the Casualty Department of the Association of Casualty and Surety Executives, reaffirmed Waters' analysis even engaging in verse to emphasize his point:

> Hush little state or commonwealth
> Hush little state industrial commission

[77] *Hearings . . . S. 3461*, 65.
[78] *Hearings . . . S. 3461*, 65–70.

Hush little state health and industrial hygiene division, don't you cry;
The central government will take you over by and by.

While he respected the work that the federal Department of Labor had done on silicosis, he preferred to keep the major responsibility for silicosis prevention with the federal Public Health Service and the state health departments: "Labor departments properly possess police powers. We look upon the inspectors of our labor departments as policemen enforcing the labor laws. Somehow we believe it would be difficult under such circumstances for the scientist with an open mind to search for the truth." He summarized the feelings of industry by saying that "there is not a man in this room who believes for one minute that industrial health can be better cared for by a labor department rather than by the health department."[79]

The National Silicosis Conference had not resolved the silicosis issue. Rather, it had spurred the contending groups to organize nationally. The Air Hygiene Foundation had pulled together research scientists, public health officials, and business leaders into a common organization that over the coming years would have a decisive influence in shaping the silicosis issue and industrial health in general; in the short term, the Department of Labor had mobilized the national union leadership to rally behind a new federal initiative. But in the context of the Depression and the oncoming mobilization for war, only the united support of the Roosevelt administration could have gotten the bill through Congress. In the closing months of the New Deal, the attention of the White House turned away from domestic legislation and toward preparation for war. With the Public Health Service opposed to the bill because it would strip it of its authority with respect to industrial disease, the White House, never fully behind the bill, provided little political support.

This effort at establishing federal regulation of safety and health failed. But it pointed to the dramatically conflicting interpretations of the meaning of industrial disease to laborers and professionals. For the work force, industrial disease was a threat insofar as it disabled or destroyed the ability of workers to enjoy their lives and support their families. In the absence of a social security system that adequately provided for workers and their families during times of unemployment and economic downturns, disease took on an added significance. For professionals, however, disease was almost an abstraction, not rooted in the physical or social realities of workers' day-to-day existence. Rather, disease was to be defined by the laboratory, the expert, and the needs of the industrial economy. For business, especially during the Depression, it

[79] Air Hygiene Foundation of America, *Fourth Fall Meeting of Members* (Pittsburgh, Pa., November 14–15, 1939), 10–16. The Air Hygiene Foundation continued to follow closely the attempt by the Department of Labor to regain control of industrial hygiene. See Memorandum by Theodore C. Waters, General Counsel, Air Hygiene Foundation, February 28, 1941, in John F. McMahon to Dr. Hamer, March 5, 1941, Carnegie-Mellon Archives, courtesy of Joel Tarr.

was unacceptable that the compensation system should be liberalized to the point where it would function as a substitute for an inadequate or nonexistent welfare program. It was here that business and the scientific community found common ground: Both wanted to distinguish health and disease from socially and economically created forms of dependence. The experience with silicosis set the stage for what would become an ongoing debate about the nature of work-related disability in twentieth-century America. This was the core issue that had festered in the Tri-State region of Missouri, Oklahoma, and Kansas, where silicosis was first identified as a major industrial disease. In the context of the Depression, the Tri-State would once again bring silicosis, dependence, and death to the attention of professionals, labor, and the public alike.

V

"STREET OF WALKING DEATH": SILICOSIS IN

THE TRI-STATE

> Would it be possible for the U.S. department of labor to make a
> health and hygiene survey of the tri-state area of Missouri,
> Oklahoma and Kansas in order to focus national attention upon
> this district and secure federal legislation to compel the
> companies to install ventilation systems and safety devices. The
> average life of a miner in this district is from 7 to 10 [working]
> years. Many die in 2 or 3 years. The health hazard here is
> silicosis, caused by breathing particles of silica dust caused by
> drilling and breaking by dynamite the ore bearing rock containing
> lead and zinc. Silicosis is the most dreaded industrial disease
> known to medical science . . . . Please give this matter your
> immediate attention and let me hear from you. It is a matter of
> life and death to the thousands of workers in this district.
> *(E. Cassell, Secretary, Cherokee County Central Labor Body, to*
> *Frances Perkins 1938)*

FOR A FEW MONTHS in 1940 national attention was focused on the
Tri-State region of Missouri, Kansas, and Oklahoma, a 4,000 square
mile expanse of prairie and farm country. At that time, federal labor
and public health officials, along with representatives of private organizations,
descended on the area to investigate, discuss, and address a major health ca-
tastrophe. In the midst of all the tragedies that marked the Great Depression,
this rural, remote backwater came to symbolize for many the plight of the third
of the nation "ill-housed, ill-clad, ill-nourished." The popular press and radio
revealed that "the tri-state" was "America's plague spot" and that over the
past few decades thousands of zinc and lead miners and their families had died
from silicosis and tuberculosis created by horrid working and living conditions.[1]

This chapter examines how the changing interests, definitions, and politics
of occupational health were played out against a background of prolonged
labor struggle in the largest lead- and zinc-mining area in the country: the Tri-
State region of Missouri, Kansas, and Oklahoma. We will discuss the chang-

---

[1] "America's Plague Spot," *New Republic* 102 (January 1, 1940): 7.

ing conditions of work that led to the widespread prevalence of silicosis, which the federal government asserted "typifie[d] the whole occupational disease problem."[2] The story of the Tri-State's experience with silicosis illustrates the complex nature of the social negotiation over industrial disease. It also illustrates the local political and social base that set the stage for federal New Deal reform.

The history of the Tri-State is also a special case: Extraordinarily harsh working conditions led a radical labor union to do battle for over thirty years with an especially repressive industry. In the course of this prolonged conflict, an isolated rural area became the focus of federal study and intervention and ultimately widespread popular attention as well. The Public Health Service was the first governmental agency to study and document the deteriorating health conditions of the community. But following the National Silicosis Conference, the U.S. Department of Labor saw this local conflict as an opportunity to remove silicosis and industrial hygiene from the exclusive preserve of professionals and business groups in the Air Hygiene Foundation and the Public Health Service. To a large extent they succeeded, if only in the short run. In this more limited arena, labor, reformers, and New Dealers played a significant role in shaping the definition of silicosis.

The story of the Tri-State labor struggle is more than a recounting of an important labor dispute. It is also the story of the role of chronic industrial disease as a source of labor conflict. We will outline how speedups and the degradation of work discussed by David Montgomery and other labor historians resulted in the disintegration of the health of hard rock miners and their families in the Tri-State area. During the Depression, workers' health emerged as a politically charged issue. In the course of debating responsibility for the industrial health disaster that plagued the region, labor, management, government, and physicians pushed their competing and often conflicting models of chronic occupational disease. This conflict would continue to influence national consciousness and legislation about the relationship between disease and industrial society.

The Social and Economic Origins of a Health Crisis

The plight of the people of the Tri-State region coincided with the country's emergence as the world's leading industrial power at the turn of the twentieth century. The growth of the auto, steel, and petrochemical industries, particularly, spurred the expansion of metal mining with zinc production growing

[2] "Silicosis (Some Pertinent Facts about This Occupational Disease for Use by the Secretary at Joplin, Missouri)," April 26, 1940, National Archives, Record Group 174, Office of the Secretary, Joplin, Mo.

over 800 percent and lead production growing almost 400 percent between 1880 and 1905.[3] In the succeeding decades before the Depression, zinc and lead production would more than double.[4] Zinc was used in the production of everything from steel and brass alloys to pharmaceuticals and cosmetics. Similarly, lead was essential in batteries, paints, solders, inks, tires, munitions, gasoline, and hardware for plumbing and construction, to name a few.[5]

The Tri-State region was the world's major source of lead and zinc during these boom years. In the first two decades of the twentieth century it emerged as the "greatest zinc producing field in the world," and during the early 1920s accounted for over two-thirds of domestic production of zinc and one-third of the domestic consumption of lead.[6] Along with this new status came new diseases that spurred conflicts between labor and management, federal and state officials, and others.

In the mid-nineteenth century, the sparsely populated agricultural community of southwestern Missouri became the center of mining operations for the area. The population began to grow in the midst of open prairie and rolling hills as many small mines were established to extract the high-grade ore from the outcroppings of flint and quartz just below the surface. Similarly, during the 1890s the value of zinc and lead produced tripled as new mines and mining communities were established in Webb City, Carterville, Porto Rico, Prosperity, and Oronogo.[7] By the turn of the century, Joplin, Missouri, had become the heart of the region's mining industry.

The geological structure of the region helped establish a pattern of small mines and mills scattered over the area. The deposits of lead and zinc were widely dispersed and often very close to the surface. Unlike zinc and lead deposits in other areas of the country, where greater mechanization was necessary in order to reach deeper deposits, the geological configuration of the region "enabled men with little or no capital to become mine operators."[8] In much of the region, it was common practice for two-man crews to lease small parcels of land from the area's landowners in return for royalties based on anticipated profits. If a significant strike was made, the prospector would hire on others from the region. In some cases, the original leaseholder would sub-

[3] U.S. Bureau of the Census, *Historical Statistics of the United States, Colonial Times to 1957* (Washington, D.C.: Government Printing Office, 1960), 369.

[4] Between 1905 and 1929, zinc production rose from 204,000 short tons to 724,000 short tons. Lead production during the same period rose from 388,000 to over 650,000 short tons. See *ibid.*

[5] "The Story of the Tri-State Mining District" (Joplin, Mo.: privately published souvenir booklet, 1931), 31, 35.

[6] "Story of Tri-State Mining District," 7.

[7] C. E. Verne, "Zinc's Record Breaking Year," *American Zinc and Lead Journal* 2 (June 1916): 4. Our discussion of the geological structure of the community and technical means of early mining is drawn primarily from Arrel M. Gibson, *Wilderness Bonanza, The Tri-State District of Missouri, Kansas and Oklahoma* (Norman: University of Oklahoma Press, 1972).

[8] Gibson, *Wilderness Bonanza*, 68.

lease most or all of his land to other teams of prospectors.[9] From the very first, the character of the industry in the area surrounding Joplin, Missouri, was highly competitive and also inefficient. Hundreds of mines owned by scores of different producers dotted the landscape. In addition, scores of mills were begun close to each mine to process and refine their ore, as most of the leases required that milling operations had to be carried out on the parcel of land where the mine was located.[10] In good years, when the price of zinc and lead was high, these small enterprises could survive and even prosper. But during periodic recessions and drops in the world price for these metals, these same producers faced tremendous pressure, with many operators going out of business. Like many small, independent farmers, with whom they sometimes compared themselves, the mine operators were buffeted by economic forces that they could not control. Mining in this environment of pyramiding royalties, undercapitalized producers, and decentralized control was characterized by a tremendous intensity of the pace of work for the laborer.

Beginning in the early twentieth century, larger and better capitalized companies began operations. By 1915, the center of the industry shifted from Joplin to richer deposits around the newly developed community of Picher, Oklahoma.[11] Spurred by the skyrocketing demand for lead and zinc created by the outbreak of war in Europe, new mining companies developed that were more in step with the corporatization of the American economy. The new companies employed more modern machinery and mining techniques.[12] While during the 1920s there were still 100 companies and 187 mines in the region, the process of consolidation and centralization accelerated.[13] By 1939, the top three companies—Eagle-Picher, Commerce, and Federal—were producing and processing more ore than that of all the other companies combined.[14]

From very early in the century, mine owners recognized that the highly competitive nature of their industry undermined their long-term stability and solvency. With little or no control over the outside markets, the only way that

[9] "Story of Tri-State Mining District," 16.

[10] This system of redundant mills was linked to the royalty system that existed between landowner and mine operator. To guarantee accurate measurement of the ore, it was essential to establish another check on how much was produced.

[11] O. S. Picher, "Picher, Oklahoma's Rich New Mining Camp," *American Zinc and Lead Journal* 1 (October 1915): 10–11. The leasing system continued because most of the land was part of the Quapaw Indian Reservation. The mineral rights to this land were leased from the Quapaws by the mining companies. During the Harding administration, the Department of Interior aided the companies in securing favorable terms for the leases at the expense of the Quapaws. See Gibson, *Wilderness Bonanza*, 156–57.

[12] The newer mines were deeper and richer and therefore were more amenable to mechanization.

[13] Julian D. Conover, "Zinc Mining in the Tri-State District," *American Zinc, Lead and Copper Journal* 20 (June 1928): 1–2.

[14] *A Preliminary Report on Living, Working and Health Conditions in the Tri-State Area* (New York: The Tri-State Survey Committee, 1939), 44.

individual mines could survive was by producing ore in greater and greater quantities. This practice of overproduction, in turn, led to further reductions in price of the ore and even greater pressure on individual owners to overproduce. Because of the Sherman and the Clayton Anti-Trust acts, the owners could not openly collude to control production and regulate prices. But in 1915, two attempts were made to "influence" the free market. The first was a call to establish a system of warehouses, similar again to the grain elevators in the Midwest, that could be used for storing the ore during slack periods of low demand. If storage facilities were developed, it was hoped, individual mines would be less inclined to dump their ore. During periods of high demand, the stored ore could then be sold at inflated prices.[15] Although an effective warehousing system was never established, the mine owners were successful in organizing the Tri-State Zinc and Lead Ore Producers Association, which sought to exchange information and coordinate the actions of the various owners. In 1928, the secretary of the association claimed that there had been "a much more intelligent conduct of output than would otherwise have been possible, resulting in general prosperity for the mining industry and for the district."[16]

In practice, the association could have only limited impact on the price of the region's ore. It could not totally control its own member's output because of the competitive nature of the industry. But, more important, the national metal-mining industry was undergoing structural changes that undermined the producers' efforts. During the second and third decade of the century, lead and zinc mining expanded in the West. Between 1919 and 1939, the Tri-State region accounted for about 50 percent of the total mines in the nation. But, during this period the value of its ore continually declined. In 1919, the value of all zinc and lead shipments in the nation was $75.5 million, of which the states of Kansas, Missouri, and Oklahoma accounted for 61 percent. By 1929, and throughout the 1930s, these three states accounted for only 45 percent of the total value (by 1954, the ore they produced represented only 28 percent of the value of the nation's lead and zinc ore).[17] The boom times for the Tri-State region occurred between 1915 and 1926, when the production of zinc and lead almost tripled. But beginning in 1926, the prices of the ores declined, and production in the region began falling. The Tri-State Producers' Association attributed this decline to the 40 percent increase in zinc production in the West: "The effect of increased recovery of western zinc upon the Tri-State district

[15] J. A. Potter, "Joplin District's Great Need," *American Zinc and Lead Journal* 1 (September 1915): 3.

[16] Julian D. Conover, "Zinc Mining in the Tri-State District," *American Zinc, Lead and Copper Journal* 20 (June 1928): 2.

[17] U.S. Bureau of the Census, *1954 Census of Mineral Industries*, vol. 1, *Summary and Industry Statistics*, United States (Washington, D.C.: Government Printing Office, 1955), 10 E-8.

is already evident in a lessened demand upon this district.''[18] The decline of the Tri-State region was reflected in the dramatic drop in employment in the mines of the three states. In the decade following World War I, over 11,000 miners were employed. But by 1939, fewer than 6,600 and by 1954, only 4,000 miners were employed.[19]

The miners and the families that were affected by the decline of metal mining were unlike those in the coalfields of the East or even those of the West. Most significantly, the metal miners in Butte, Montana, or Couer d'Alene, Idaho, were often single men, often first-generation American. The miners of the Tri-State were generally descendants of Scotch-Irish and English pioneers who migrated with their families from the nearby Ozark Mountains of Tennessee or from the farming communities of Arkansas and Missouri. Public health officials described these people as "intelligent, independent, and industrious; as a rule they marry young, and large families are frequent.''[20] They came to the boomtowns of the Tri-State in search of steady work and the possibility of establishing their own mines. In the early years, laborers often migrated back and forth between the mines and their family farms not too far away. Others built small homes on land owned or leased by the mining companies, where they maintained small gardens and kept some animals that could sustain them during slack times. By the early years of the century, miners would construct shacks, usually surrounded by mountainous heaps of residue ores and millings, commonly called chat piles. The shacks lacked sanitation, pure water, and toilet facilities and were considered substandard and inadequate even for that time period. "In general, the housing is of poor quality, and often wretched," noted a report of the Bureau of Mines in 1915.[21]

Working Conditions in the Mines

In order to understand the extraordinary impact of silicosis and tuberculosis in the region, it is necessary to briefly review the harsh conditions under which miners labored. In the early period before 1900, the two-man teams who established the first mines usually used few or no power-driven tools in the mining process: "Their mining tools included a double-pointed pick, a square-point scoop shovel for loading the ore can, and a light, round-pointed shovel for digging." With the aid of a horse or windlass to help in hoisting the ore

[18] Conover, "Zinc Mining in the Tri-State District," 3.

[19] Census, *1954 Census of Mineral Industries*, vol. 1, 10 E-8.

[20] A. J. Lanza and Edwin Higgins, eds., *Pulmonary Disease among Miners in the Joplin District, Missouri, and Its Relation to Rock Dust in the Mines; A Preliminary Report*, U.S. Bureau of Mines, Technical Paper No. 105 (Washington, D.C.: Government Printing Office, 1915), 8.

[21] Lanza and Higgins, *Pulmonary Disease*, 40; *Preliminary Report on Living, Working and Health Conditions in the Tri-State Mining Area*, 12–27.

cans from below the surface, two men could effectively excavate the ore. One worker below ground dug the ore and loaded it into the can, while the other waited above to dump the ore.[22]

While these relatively primitive methods worked effectively in shallow mines with limited ore content, the exploitation of deeper and more extensive deposits demanded the introduction of more highly mechanized, capital-intensive techniques. After 1900, and particularly after the development of the Oklahoma fields, steam- and air-powered drills were introduced, which, with the use of dynamite, created shafts and underground chambers hundreds of feet below the surface. The mines varied in size and depth but had certain common characteristics. Generally, they were large chambers, about 18 feet high, supported by massive pillars carved out of the surrounding rock and spaced approximately 40 to 100 feet apart. Miners created these caverns by drilling and blasting the rock and shoveling the broken rock and ore onto trams, which were hauled to one or more vertical shafts. There they were hoisted to the surface by steam- or electrically powered elevators. Above the ground, structures were built on supports high above the surface to house the motors that lifted the ore. A series of chutes and trams was used to distribute the ore, slag, and stone to huge piles surrounding the mine shaft and buildings.[23]

Underground, different groups of miners performed highly specialized tasks. Drillers, blasters, haulers, powdermen, and others faced daily perils from accidents due to mine collapses and explosions. But among those in greatest danger were the shovelers, who were responsible for breaking up rock and loading it into giant cans that would be hauled to the surface. Making up the vast bulk of the work force, these men were the heart of the mining operation. The cans held between 1,000 and 1,650 pounds of rock and ore, and each physically fit shoveler filled between sixty and ninety cans in an eight-hour shift. While David Montgomery notes that common laborers for nearly three centuries had generally lifted between 3,200 and 3,800 pounds a day,[24] a healthy shoveler in the Tri-State mines would load about two or three times

---

[22] See Gibson, *Wilderness Bonanza*, ch. 5, 67–78.

[23] Our discussion of the mining process in the Tri-State region is based upon a series of reports and technical papers written by the staffs of the U.S. Bureau of Mines and Public Health Service. See, for example, Edwin Higgins, "The Mines of the Joplin District," in Lanza and Higgins, *Pulmonary Disease*, 13–33; Edwin Higgins, "Mining Operations as Related to Production of Siliceous Dust," in Edwin Higgins, A. J. Lanza, F. B. Laney, and George S. Rice, eds., *Siliceous Dust in Relation to Pulmonary Disease among Miners in the Joplin District*, U.S. Bureau of Mines, *Bulletin No. 132* (Washington, D.C.: Government Printing Office, 1917), 3–17; Clarence A. Wright, *Mining and Treatment of Lead and Zinc Ores in the Joplin District; A Preliminary Report*, U.S. Bureau of Mines Technical Paper No. 41 (Washington, D.C.: Government Printing Office, 1913), 11–32.

[24] David Montgomery, *The Fall of the House of Labor* (New York and Cambridge: Cambridge University Press, 1987), 58.

that amount, between 75,000 to 100,000 pounds of rock a day. "One can hardly realize the severity of this work without seeing it," said a public health official in 1915.[25]

The intensity of the work was a product of the piecework system of payment that was in use in the Tri-State mines. Unlike other categories of workers, who were generally paid a set amount per shift, shovelers were paid five to eight cents per can of ore. Each worker loaded his own cans and frequently had to push it to the elevator and back again. At the surface, each can was identified by marking on its side and credited to the shoveler below. Because of the piecework system, shovelers could make between $3 and $5 per day, in contrast to the machine drillers, who usually made a wage of between $2.50 and $3 per day.

The Effect on Health

The effect of the work environment and the piecework system was disastrous to the health of the shovelers. Even before the machine drill created a severe dust hazard in the mines, shovelers, many of whom began work when they were teenagers, were subjected to the dangers associated with physical breakdown and injury. They could expect to work for only a few years at the relatively high pay. The mine owners argued that the piece rate system was essential to raising the productivity of the miners and guaranteeing the profitability of their business. But it was clear to health officials that "such piecework when unrestrained except by the individual strength and willingness of the miner, is probably responsible for the physical breakdown of many men."[26]

Beginning in the second decade of the century, these employees were also subjected to life-threatening diseases associated with the introduction of the new technologies. In contrast to other mining areas of the country, miners in the Joplin area were at greater risk of dying from disease than from accidents. "Disease causes far more deaths and far more disability among the miners in the Joplin district than do accidents, and the disease is clearly defined and evident to all," noted the federal investigators who came to Joplin in 1915.[27]

[25] A. J. Lanza, "Sanitation at the Mines and Other Considerations," in Lanza and Higgins, *Pulmonary Disease*, 38.

[26] Lanza, "Sanitation at the Mines," 38.

[27] Lanza and Higgins, *Pulmonary Disease*, 40. See also George S. Rice, "Historical Review of Silicosis," in Higgins et al., *Siliceous Dust in Relation*, 96. See also Alan Derickson, " 'To Be His Own Benefactor': The Founding of the Couer d'Alene Miners' Union Hospital, 1891," in David Rosner and Gerald Markowitz, eds., *Dying for Work: Workers' Safety and Health in Twentieth Century America* (Bloomington: Indiana University Press, 1987), 5. In *Workers' Health, Workers' Democracy* (Ithaca: Cornell University Press, 1988) Derickson develops this theme in relation to the metal miners of the West. While the methods of production differed substantially from those of the Tri-State region, the effect of the introduction of power drilling

The use of power drills and high-intensity explosives created both dangerous safety conditions and an extremely dusty atmosphere. Especially because most of the ore was imbedded in flint, which had a silica content of over 95 percent, workers were, for the first time, exposed to large amounts of this potent industrial poison. In the years after the introduction of power tools and dynamite blasting, it became apparent that miners and their families in the Tri-State region and elsewhere were developing debilitating and life-threatening lung conditions at a high rate. By the teens, public health officials were noting the extraordinary incidence of lung disease among workers and their families: "It seems to be the general opinion in Jasper County [where Joplin was located] that lung diseases became more prevalent after the beginning of active mining in the sheet ground, in the early eighties, and that the flint dust from drilling and other mine operations is largely responsible for this condition."[28] In more recent years, however, the problem had intensified. One owner told the Bureau of Mines that he had employed 750 men between 1907 and 1914. He reported that "only about 50 of these were still living, and all the others except not more than a dozen were said to have died from tuberculosis."[29] Officials of the Bureau of Mines and Public Health Service noted that the increased incidence of tuberculosis was directly tied to the growing exposure of workers to silica dust.

The changing work conditions and the increasing prevalence of lung diseases spurred organizing drives in the Tri-State area. As ownership of the mines passed from entrepreneurs working in small teams to corporations, such as the Eagle-Picher Lead Company, labor relations deteriorated in the region. The Western Federation of Miners in affiliation with the Industrial Workers of the World organized a local in Joplin in 1906. By 1910, the union had achieved a membership of over 600, despite high labor turnover and out-migration of significant numbers of miners and their families. In that year, the union went on strike to protest the working conditions and poor pay.[30] Although the strike was broken, five years later, an independent, grass roots union, the American Metal Miners' Union, conducted another bitter but unsuccessful strike over health and safety conditions. With little external support and operating within a community that was totally controlled by the mine owners, this union lost the strike and soon collapsed.[31]

---

and dynamite was equally disastrous to the health of the work force. See also William J. Cassidy, "The Tri-State Zinc Lead Mining Region: Growth, Problems and Prospects" (unpublished Ph.D. diss., University of Pittsburgh, 1955), Ch. 4.

[28] Lanza and Higgins, *Pulmonary Disease*, 9.

[29] Lanza and Higgins, *Pulmonary Disease*, 10.

[30] Gibson, *Wilderness Bonanza*, 227–229.

[31] Alan Derickson, "Federal Intervention in the Joplin Silicosis Epidemic, 1911–1916," *Bulletin of the History of Medicine* 62 (Summer 1988): 243. This article is the most sophisticated and comprehensive account of the evolution of federal and public health involvement in the Tri-State region during the Progressive Era.

The Western Federation of Miners, however, continued organizing in the area. It charged that the growing corporatization of the mining industry and the increasing number of absentee owners had created a piece rate system that amounted to a speedup and further undermined the health of the operatives. The use of "modern machinery to apply to the deeper and harder ledges has brought in the era of extensive operations, the absentee owner, and the hired manager," argued an author in the Western Federation of Miners' *Journal* in 1915.[32] (In 1916, the WFM changed its name to the International Union of Mine, Mill and Smelter Workers.)[33]

It was in the context of this labor strife that the U.S. Public Health Service had been originally brought into the area and for the first time did a community study of this industrial condition. During the 1920s, in response to the 1915 report of the Bureau of Mines and the continuing labor agitation, some of the larger mine owners introduced wet drilling techniques, which led the industry to believe that "in two or three more years" silicosis would "be a thing of the past in the southwest Missouri district."[34] The various interests of the Public Health Service and Bureau of Mines in evaluating the technological means of limiting exposure to dust along with the industry's interest in self-protection led the federal government, the mining companies, and Metropolitan Life to organize a clinic to determine the extent of silicosis among the Tri-State miners. The study evaluated 7,722 miners and prospective employees in the Picher area between July 1, 1927, and June 30, 1928. Contrary to the hopes of the industry, however, silicosis was found to remain a major problem.[35]

[32] "Consumption among Joplin Lead Miners," *Miners' Magazine*, December 2, 1915, 1. As early as 1900, *Miners' Magazine* linked union organizing efforts to the disastrous health conditions in the mines and smelters of the region. See *Miners' Magazine*, May 1900, 17–20. This was the first volume of the Western Federation of Miners' journal, and it gave extensive coverage to the underlying health and safety rationale for the eight-hour movement. The state of Missouri passed legislation in the wake of the strike to control dust and disease among the population of the region. But this was largely inadequate especially in light of the declining importance of the Missouri mines and the rising significance of the Oklahoma fields. See "Gaining on Tuberculosis in Missouri," *Survey*, May 22, 1915, 1.

[33] Briefly described in William Cassidy to Don Grafton, July 28, 1947, in Tri-State File, Tamiment Library.

[34] "Consumption is Ravaging Miners," *Miners' Magazine*, March 2, 1916, 3. See also "Miners' Consumption," *ibid.*; H. I. Young, "Need of Proper Mine Sanitation," *American Zinc and Lead Journal* 5 (November 1917): 9–10.

[35] In 1927–1928, there were approximately 7,000 miners employed in the entire Tri-State region (Cassidy to Grafton, July 28, 1947, 82). It is impossible to estimate the percentage of these workers who ultimately were evaluated by the clinic. But given that the clinic concentrated on the mines in Picher, it is clear that a very high percentage of those examined were prospective employees, rather than longtime miners of Picher. This suggests two points: First, the percentage of silicotics reported in the Public Health Service study may have been an underestimate of the true prevalence of this condition. Many of the miners evaluated may never before have been exposed. Second, the study may have reflected the prevalence of silicosis in the entire Tri-State area, rather than conditions in the Picher mines. Many of the job applicants may have been exposed in the

Overall, 21.3 percent were diagnosed as having silicosis in some stage. Furthermore, 38 percent of those who worked at the face of the mine as shovelers, shovelers' helpers, drill helpers, machinemen, trackmen, roof trimmers, and powdermen were afflicted. As in the previous study, the relationship between the length of employment and silicosis remained. Although less than 6 percent of the miners employed less than two years had silicosis, those who had been employed eleven years experienced a 44 percent disease rate, while 62 percent of those who had been on the job for nineteen years or more had this disease. Workers who began to work in their late teens or early twenties could expect to have contracted silicosis by the time they were forty.[36]

The Industry Response

Despite all the attention given to the Tri-State region, improvements in health status remained relatively limited. In part, this was due to resistance on the part of mine owners to any change in traditional practices. But in part it was because neither the Public Health Service nor the Bureau of Mines had the statutory authority to enter the mines, much less to mandate reforms. In order to conduct their studies they therefore had to win the confidence of mine owners. Rather than publicly condemn the unhealthy conditions, the agencies sought to privately educate and cajole owners to make necessary reforms. Also, they allowed mine owners and the insurance company to administer and control the Picher Clinic for their own purposes. While management and government claimed that the clinic was part of a program "to improve the working

---

older mines of the region. A final point relates to the number of miners with advanced stages of silicosis who may have been fired or "encouraged to leave" before the formal study began. The study was conducted in 1927–1928, but the clinic had been in operation since 1924. While the company claimed that no workers who were discovered to have silicosis would be laid off, we may surmise that workers were encouraged to leave once silicosis was discovered. In the government report, the authors wrote that "the prognosis in early silicosis is good if the patient can be removed from his dusty occupation and be placed in the open but with advance of the disease the prognosis becomes less favorable." Despite the inaccuracy of this analysis of the progress of the disease, it could have led many workers either to quit or to be transferred away from the dusty environment. See R. R. Sayers, F. V. Meriwether, A. J. Lanza, and W. W. Adams, *Silicosis and Tuberculosis among Miners of the Tri-State District of Oklahoma, Kansas and Missouri—I. For the Year Ended June 30, 1928*, U.S. Bureau of Mines Technical Paper No. 545 (Washington, D.C.: Government Printing Office, 1933), 25. See also M. D. Harbaugh, "The Tri-State Zinc and Lead Mining District in 1935," *Mining Congress Journal* 22 (February 1936), 30–31; Sayers et al., *Silicosis and Tuberculosis*, 1.

[36] Sayers et al., *Silicosis and Tuberculosis*, 4, 5, 12, 14. See also R. R. Sayers, Emery Hayhurst, Anthony Lanza, "Status of Silicosis," *American Journal of Public Health* 19 (June 1929): 635–40. Although the government, industry, and insurance companies continued to study the area until 1933, none of the later data were published.

conditions in the district,'' the workers claimed that the producers used the clinic to diagnose diseased miners and fire them.[37]

The introduction of wet drilling techniques, in which water was constantly applied to the rock as it was drilled, could certainly reduce the amount of finely ground dust that became air borne and therefore dangerous to the work force. But these technical improvements were limited to the newer, more modern mines. The dozens of older mines were unaffected. In the following decade, as the economy collapsed, employers fired sick and disabled workers, and silicosis again emerged as a critical organizing issue that galvanized the community. A representative of the Tri-State Zinc and Lead Ore Producers' Association outlined their program: ''Necessarily, men who were found to be in such condition that they were a hazard to themselves and their associates, were taken out of employment in the mines.'' The producers' response to the growing health crisis in the area was to fire diseased workers identified in the clinic organized by management, the insurance company, and government.[38]

Labor Conflict over Silicosis

During the Depression, conflict over deteriorating health conditions reached a climax as employment in the Tri-State mines plummeted from over 7,000 in 1929 to 1,331 in 1932. During these years, the International Union of Mine Mill and Smelter Workers (IUMMSW) began a concerted organizing effort that stressed the health hazards posed by silicosis and tuberculosis as well as inadequate wages, speedups, and other harsh working conditions.[39] Assisted by Section 7(a) of the National Industrial Recovery Act (NIRA), IUMMSW representatives unionized ''nearly everyone in the [Tri-State] district.'' In addition to organizing the miners, the IUMMSW set about developing a union of retail clerks, public relief workers, and smelter and lead plant workers in Galena and Joplin.[40] Together with traditional demands for higher wages and shorter hours, the union organizers promised that a successful union drive would result in ''the elimination of the examining bureau or clinic, so that physical examinations would no longer be necessary and many unemployed men would be able to get jobs.''[41] The union charged that the clinic was not

[37] M. D. Harbaugh, ''Labor Relations in the Tri-State Mining District,'' *Mining Congress Journal* 22 (June 1936): 20–21.

[38] *Ibid.*

[39] Press Committee, District No. 4, International Union of Mine, Mill and Smelter Workers, Joplin, Missouri, to James Robinson, May 15, 1935, National Archives, Record Group 100, 7-0-6-13. At that time the IUMMSW was affiliated with the American Federation of Labor. In 1935 it was one of the unions to form the Committee on Industrial Organization, soon to break away as the Congress of Industrial Organizations (CIO).

[40] Harbaugh, ''Labor Relations,'' 22.

[41] Harbaugh, ''Labor Relations,'' 22.

for the benefit of diseased workers but, rather, for the benefit of management. Management used it to diagnose, identify, and fire diseased workers so that efficiency would increase and so that the true prevalence of disease among workers and their families would be masked. Because most federal surveys studied only employed workers, they mistakenly assumed that conditions in the area's mines had improved. In a letter from James Robinson, the secretary-treasurer of the union headquarters in Salt Lake City, to Frances Perkins, Robinson noted that a census study that examined miners, whether they were working or not, found 205 cases of silicosis in 544 homes in the city of Picher. He charged that "the mining companies in this district make no effort to alleviate this condition."[42] The union appealed to the widespread understanding among miners and their families that silicosis was a pervasive and devastating reality in the Tri-State region. Despite the denials of management, the union continually pointed out the high disease rates among workers and the lack of attention to this problem by management or state inspectors.

The International was well-suited to organize an area like the Tri-State because of its own historical commitment to industrial unionism and mass organizing. Growing out of a radical and syndicalist heritage, the Mine, Mill and Smelter Workers sought to organize the larger community to counteract the mine owners' control of the economic and political life of the region. The problems of the work force transcended the workplace, reaching into the home and community. The mines created dependence and disease. Silicosis and tuberculosis were part of the same problem that destroyed miners' health and their ability to earn a living and support their families. A successful organizing drive would improve working conditions and stop the destruction of family life, health, and the very social order of the community. The miners were well aware of the social costs of this industrial disease. Writing to Eleanor Roosevelt, the secretary of one union local offered to send the First Lady "plenty of factual and documentary evidence that men are dieing [sic] like flies and that 8 out of every 10 women in this district are widows, 75 percent of the children orphans." The union claimed that the mine owners were willing to spend money "to buy tear gas, munitions, and to hire thugs and gunmen to terrorize union men and women" rather than to install "air cleaning devices" to combat silicosis.[43]

While the union argued that it was impossible to separate the issues of work and community, the Producers' Association maintained that these issues were unrelated and refused to bargain with a union that represented "a host of un-

[42] James Robinson to Frances Perkins, May 23, 1935, National Archives, Record Group 100, 7-0-6-13, quoted in Gerald Markowitz and David Rosner, eds., "Slaves of the Depression," Workers' Letters about Life on the Job (Ithaca: Cornell University Press, 1987), 134–35.

[43] E. C., Secretary, Cherokee County Central Labor Body, to "Respect Madam" [Roosevelt], September 4, 1938, in Markowitz and Rosner, "Slaves of the Depression," 140.

employed and relief workers.''[44] Faced by the intransigence of the mine owners, the union called a strike in May 1935 against all of the producers, but with particular attention to the Eagle Picher Lead Company, the area's largest producer.[45] The union found itself faced with a lockout by the company and the establishment of a company union, which quickly negotiated a contract that brought about 2,000 workers back into the mines.[46]

The owners' near-total control over the region forced the International to broaden its struggle by seeking national attention.[47] They appealed to the recently organized National Labor Relations Board (NLRB) to gain recognition as the bargaining agent for workers in the area. After the National Labor Relations Act (NLRA) was passed in 1935, the International filed an unfair practices suit with the NLRB against the Eagle-Picher Company. Management obtained an injunction preventing the NLRB's hearings, which was not struck down until after the Supreme Court upheld the constitutionality of the NLRA in 1937. The hearings began on November 29, 1937, and ended on April 29, 1938, during which time scores of witnesses testified to the vicious union-busting tactics employed by the mine owners to destroy the International. In a decision rendered on October 27, 1939, the NLRB "confirmed most of the complaints of discrimination and denial of rights protected by the federal law.''[48]

Despite the fact that the union was "fighting . . . in our strike to have pure air pumped down to the miners," it did not raise the issue of health and disease during the hearings.[49] The union was constrained by the narrow requirements for determining unfair labor practices under the NLRA, which forced the International to ignore or deny the pervasiveness of disease and disability in the Tri-State region. The union had to prove that the companies discriminated

[44] Harbaugh, "Labor Relations," 23.

[45] Robinson to Perkins, May 23, 1935, in Markowitz and Rosner, *"Slaves of the Depression,"* 134–35. See George G. Suggs, Jr., *Union Busting in the Tri-State, The Oklahoma, Kansas, and Missouri Metal Workers' Strike of 1935* (Norman: University of Oklahoma Press, 1986), for a detailed discussion of the formation and organizing efforts of the International Mine, Mill and Smelter Workers' Union.

[46] Harbaugh, "Labor Relations," 24.

[47] See Tony McTeer, President, Tri-State Miners' Union, No. 15, International Union of Mine, Mill and Smelter Workers, to Senate Committee on Education and Labor, March 24, 1936, in U.S. *Hearing before a Subcommittee of the Committee on Education and Labor, United States Senate*, 74th Cong., 2d sess., April 1–2, 1936, 89–90.

[48] Suggs, *Union Busting in the Tri-State*, 194–96. Suggs describes the day-to-day struggle of workers and management in the Tri-State in great detail.

[49] Ted Shasteen, President, Treece Local No. 111, Mine, Mill and Smelter Workers, Treece, Kansas, to President Roosevelt, December 10, 1936, National Archives, Record Group 100, 0-2-0-1. Treece, Kansas, was noted for its extremely diseased population. A local newspaper captioned a picture of its main street " 'The Street of Walking Death' because of the prevalence of silicosis in the community." See "Madam Perkins Comes to Missouri," *St. Louis Post Dispatch*, April 28, 1940, National Archives, Record Group 100, 7–0–4(3).

against its members, not that work conditions were horrendous.[50] Management's strategy, however, was to show that a wide range of factors went into the decision to hire or fire workers. Disease or disability was, for management, one of these factors. By showing that workers were diseased, the owners could claim that union-busting was not their aim and the union's suit was frivolous.[51]

The union's attempt to broaden its base of support led it to forge alliances both with the New Deal administration and with the political left. During the 1936 election, the union attacked Roosevelt's Republican opponent, Alf Landon, then the governor of Kansas, who had ordered the Kansas National Guard into the Tri-State area in June, 1935.[52] In a demonstration at a Landon rally in New York, Young Communist League members carried a mock coffin with the inscription "here lies the body of one of the victims of the dreaded mine disease of Kansas—silicosis. This and thousands of other lives would have been saved if Landon had compelled the mine owners to take elementary safety measures to stop the spread of silicosis." The New York *Times* commented that this "Communist-arranged 'coffin act' stole the show" as the demonstrators "attracted a crowd of 1,000."[53]

James Robinson, the secretary-treasurer of the International in Salt Lake City, wrote to Frances Perkins, inviting her to see the effects of silicosis firsthand. "You would have to visit the community to realize the poverty, squalor and disease existing there," he wrote to Secretary Perkins in May of 1935. "According to the report of the census enumerator for the City of Picher, Oklahoma, in a visit to 544 homes he found 205 cases of Silicosis. . . . The mining companies in this district make no effort to alleviate this condition with the result as indicated by the census enumerator."[54]

The union's concern about silicosis occurred at the same time that Gauley Bridge and the National Silicosis Conference were in the public eye. Over the course of the next two years, the labor movement pressed for the federal government to undertake an independent investigation of the health conditions in

[50] See "Official Report of Proceedings before the National Labor Relations Board, Case No. C-73, Eagle-Picher Mining and Smelting Co. etc. (Typescript), Joplin, Mo.," National Archives, Record Group 25, National Labor Relations Board, Transcripts and Exhibits, 1935–1948, Box 616, 3413–3420; 3378–3379; 3583–3588; 4042–4046; 4474–4478; 4576–4579, for examples of the use of the health and illness issue.

[51] "In the Matter of Eagle-Picher Mining and Smelting Company . . . and International Union of Mine, Mill and Smelter Workers . . . , Case No. C-73," in *Decisions and Orders of the National Labor Relations Board*, vol. 16 (Washington, D.C.: Government Printing Office, 1940), 727–871.

[52] Suggs, *Union Busting in the Tri-State*, 86–87.

[53] *New York Times*, September 26, 1936, 6. It should be noted that Landon, the former governor of Kansas, lost his home state in the 1936 election.

[54] James Robinson to Frances Perkins, May 23, 1935, National Archives, Record Group 100, 7-0-6-13, quoted in Markowitz and Rosner, *"Slaves of the Depression,"* 134–35.

the Tri-State district. They specifically wanted the "U.S. Department of Labor to make a health and hygiene survey . . . to focus attention upon this district and secure federal legislation to compel the companies to install ventilating systems and safety devices." Calling such a survey "a matter of life and death to the thousands of workers in this district," labor denounced the fact that there were "absolutely no facilities for taking care of the thousands of miners who had contracted this dreaded disease."[55] Ed Cassell, the secretary of the Cherokee Central Labor Body of Columbus, Kansas, spoke of the fear under which miners in the Tri-State area lived:

> If the mine operators who control our school districts, our Republican sheriff, our newspapers knew I was writing a letter of this type to you [Eleanor Roosevelt] they would do like they have in the past, have me thrown in jail on framed up charges of which I always have come clear, so don't give this letter any publicity under any circumstances.[56]

By the late 1930s, silicosis had transcended the domain of professionals, management, insurance, and labor. The groundwork had been laid for liberal and left-wing political groups to transform silicosis from a health problem into a symbol of the effects of unrestrained corporate greed. Just as the Memorial Day Massacre at Republic Steel's South Chicago mill represented industry's resistance to industrial unionism and the Scottsboro case represented lynch justice in the South, so silicosis in the Tri-State represented corporate greed causing the slow death of working-class communities. The major propaganda effort on behalf of the workers was spearheaded by the National Committee for People's Rights, a left-wing organization based in New York, whose leadership included such well-known radicals as Rockwell Kent. In the fall of 1939, it issued a report publicizing the living, working, and health conditions of the Tri-State region.[57] The report began by charging that the area "represented a denial of the basic rights of decent living to a whole community, and therefore had to be considered as a matter of concern to the nation itself." It described the substandard housing and noted that living conditions had not improved since the Public Health Service had first surveyed them twenty-five years earlier. It reminded readers that this poor housing contributed to the area's extremely high tuberculosis rate and that the health problems in the area were exacerbated by the absence of proper sanitation. While commending the

[55] Ed Cassell to Madam Perkins, August 21, 1938, National Archives, Record Group 100, 7-0-6-13, in Markowitz and Rosner, "*Slaves of the Depression*," 138–39.

[56] Ed Cassell to Eleanor Roosevelt, September 4, 1938, National Archives, Record Group 100, 7-0-6-13, in Markowitz and Rosner, "*Slaves of the Depression*," 139–40. During the strike, the sheriff deputized the members of the company union, who proceeded to attack strikers, injuring many.

[57] Gifford A. Cochran to Frances Perkins, May 26, 1938, National Archives, Record Group 100, 7-0-6-13.

owners of the mines for initiating some improvement in controlling the dust hazard, the report pointed toward the inadequacy of these efforts.[58]

The report also illustrated the ways in which the organization of work in the Tri-State mines affected workers' health. Because miners were paid a piece rate, any attempt to take time for health or safety matters cost the miner rather than the owners. In many mines, the shovelers were responsible for wetting down the slag heaps in order to cut down on silica dust but they rarely took the time to do this:

> Failure of the shovellers to wet down muck piles may not necessarily imply an ignorance on their part of the hazard involved. The working hours of these men are limited by regulations, and they receive their pay on a piece work basis. The shoveller's weekly pay check is large or small on the basis of how many ore cans he has been able to load on each of his shifts. Naturally, such men have an incentive which amounts to an absolute pressure to work at top speed shovelling the ore. . . . Under these circumstances, delegating the responsibility for wetting down the muck to the shovelers is tantamount to asking them to finance the mine dust control program. If the shovelers knowingly slight a responsibility which they could meet only at a sacrifice of earning capacity, the failure is an understandable manifestation of human frailty.[59]

The national media picked up on the report and as *Time* magazine, in an article titled "Zinc Stink," noted, silicosis was not only an occupational disease but "a public health menace" as well. *The New Republic*, in an article titled "American Plague Spot," suggested that the report should be "compulsory reading for all those who, under the pressure of news of wholesale misery abroad, have forgotten that we have our share of it at home." It went on to say that successful implementation of its recommendations depended upon "educating the employers to their responsibility toward something besides profits. . . . Their best energies seem so far to have been aimed at crippling the miners' attempts to better their lot through organization."[60] Even *Business Week* devoted a major article to what they called "a sizzling report detailing desperate living conditions among the miners there."[61] Walter Winchell announced on his radio program that the National Committee for Peoples' Rights "would release a scandalous expose of living and working conditions in the Tri-State mining district."[62]

---

[58] Tri-State Survey Committee, "A Preliminary Report on Living, Working and Health Conditions in the Tri-State Mining Area (Missouri, Oklahoma and Kansas)," 1939, National Archives, Record Group 174, Office of the Secretary, Joplin, Missouri.

[59] Tri-State Survey Committee, "Preliminary Report," 63–65.

[60] "Zinc Stink," *Time* 34 (December 4, 1939): 30; "American Plague Spot," *New Republic* 102 (January 1, 1940): 7. See also "Silicosis Program in Four States Scored," *New York Times*, November 27, 1939, 19; "Silicosis," *Survey* 76 (February 1940), 74–75.

[61] "Silicosis: Tri-State Dust Storm," *Business Week*, December 9, 1939, 51–52.

[62] Evan Just, "Living and Working Conditions in the Tri-State Mining District," *Mining Congress Journal* 25 (November 1939): 44.

The Tri-State was also the subject of other media attention. In conjunction with the report, Sheldon Dick went to the region to take photographs but was so moved by what he saw that he decided to make a movie. He produced a 16½-minute documentary with professional actors, including Will Geer, who did the narration.[63] In 1939, W. W. Norton and Company published a novel by L. S. Davidson called *South of Joplin*. The story, by a former schoolteacher in the area, told of the miners' struggle and about harsh life in the district during the years of the strike.[64] The next year, a novel about the Gauley Bridge disaster began by alluding to the people who came "out of Joplin, Missouri, and Picher, Oklahoma, searching their way toward the rocky irregular state" of West Virginia, where they would once again experience the tragedy of silicosis.[65]

The mine owners reacted strongly to the publicity generated by the report of the National Committee for People's Rights. Their first response was to garner support from the Public Health Service officials who had helped them in the 1920s. In a telegram to R. R. Sayers of the Public Health Service, the Tri-State Zinc and Lead Ore Producers Association attacked the report. "A group reported to be communistic has been attempting to publicize local living, working and health conditions in the hope of creating a national scandal," began the telegram. The producers said they were writing to the Public Health Service because of its long familiarity with conditions in the Tri-State region and that the agency was "aware that our mine operators practice modern methods of dust control but that silicosis is a hangover from past conditions, not a result of present day operations, and that surface dust conditions are not dangerous also, that the consequences of silicosis are commonly overstated." In an attempt to counter the unfavorable national publicity, the producers sought to enlist the Service in a counteroffensive. They urged that the Public Health Service "enter this district again and bring your investigations up-to-date. We promise you full cooperation on the part of the members of this organization."[66]

At the same time, the producers dispatched their secretary and spokesperson, Evan Just, to Washington to confer with Verne Zimmer. In a summary of the meeting, Zimmer suggested that Just had come to see him in order to secure an investigation that would be "a white wash" of the producers' culpability for the problems of the area. But as the conversation progressed, Zimmer found that Just's true agenda was to keep the Department of Labor from intervening in any way. To the suggestion that the Department of Labor con-

[63] "Men and Dust," [1939] a description, National Archives, Record Group 100, 7-0-6-13.

[64] L. S. Davidson, *South of Joplin* (New York: W. W. Norton and Company, 1939).

[65] Hubert Skidmore, *Hawk's Nest*, reprinted in *West Virginia Heritage*, vol. 4 (Richwood, W. Va.: West Virginia Heritage Foundation, n.d.).

[66] Tri-State Zinc and Lead Ore Producers Association to Dr. R. R. Sayers, October 16, 1939, National Archives, Record Group 443, Records Relating to NIH Divisions.

duct a survey of the health and living conditions in the area, Just "rather hesitantly suggested that it would perhaps be more desirable if we did not come into the picture inasmuch as 'the employers in this section feel that the Labor Department is radical and definitely prejudiced.' " Just feared "that any investigation would be in the nature of a star chamber proceeding." The producers preferred that federal involvement come through the Public Health Service, which had a long and sympathetic relationship with the mine owners.[67] Zimmer understood that management had more faith in the Public Health Service than in the Department of Labor. But, he pointed out, "it was equally true that Labor had more confidence in the Department of Labor . . . [because] the previous investigations [by the Public Health Service] resulted in no permanent improvements in the area from the standpoint of the worker."[68] The Department of Labor's entrance into the Tri-State area highlighted two fundamentally different federal approaches to occupational safety and health issues in general.

By 1939 the national publicity surrounding the plight of Tri-State workers and their families had focused attention on the failure of the Public Health Service approach to industrial hygiene. Unlike other labor disputes, which were wholly within one state, the problems of the Tri-State demanded federal coordination, at least. Further, the outbreak of war in Europe and the potential involvement of the United States lent even more urgency to the need for a settlement. It was in this context that the Department of Labor was able to supersede the Public Health Service as the major federal agency in the region. Immediately following Zimmer's meeting with Just, Zimmer wrote to Frances Perkins suggesting that the department call a conference of all the interested parties in the Tri-State. By doing this, the department was directly challenging the Public Health Service's long-standing cooperative and low-key approach to the problems of the area. Zimmer argued that the old Public Health Service approach had failed and that the problems of the Tri-State could not be addressed by owners, professionals, and government representatives alone. Despite strong opposition from management, Zimmer "strongly urge[d] that we not abandon the idea of a conference in the Tri-State Mining Area."[69] Despite

[67] In a telegram to R. R. Sayers of the U.S. Public Health Service, the Tri-State Zinc and Lead-Ore Producers Association attacked the report: "In view of the gross misrepresentation which subversive agencies are now making concerning living and working conditions here, we urge your Service to enter this district again." In an attempt to counter the unfavorable national publicity, the producers urged that the Public Health Service conduct a new health survey. See Tri-State Zinc and Lead Ore Producers Association to Dr. R. R. Sayers, October 16, 1939, National Archives, Record Group 443, Records Relating to NIH Divisions.

[68] Verne Zimmer to Secretary Perkins, October 25, 1939, National Archives, Record Group 100, 7-0-6-13.

[69] Zimmer to Secretary Perkins, "Meeting in the Tri-State Mining Area," March 2, 1940, National Archives, Record Group 100, 7-0-4-(3). See also Perkins to Tony McTeer, March 28, 1940, National Archives, Record Group 100, 7-0-4-(3).

the view of public health advocates and management that silicosis was a medical and public health problem, he maintained that it was also "a labor problem" and this aspect had previously been neglected. In addition it was a federal rather than a local issue because "the problem crosses state lines and . . . any remedial program involves unified effort by the states along with some help from the Federal Government." Silicosis in the area would get worse because of the "increasing activity due to war conditions" and it was necessary to focus national attention on the area to stimulate action, rather than study.[70]

In light of the new national significance of the Tri-State struggle, Zimmer hoped that federal power and publicity could be used to counter the enormous influence of mine owners at the state and local level. Over the past several years, he had been frustrated by the Oklahoma Department of Labor's inability to act on behalf of the miners. The state labor commissioner had acknowledged that "there always has been a serious condition in that section of our State." But he confided to Zimmer that he was helpless to initiate action because of opposition from management.[71] Another official confessed that he had avoided enforcing safety and health regulations in the Picher district for fear of destroying the mining economy of the area.[72] Knowledge of these events reinforced Zimmer's resolve to push Perkins to call a conference in the area in order to place pressure on owners and state officials alike to initiate reforms. She ultimately did so, and, in contrast to the National Silicosis Conference, the Department of Labor structured the meeting to give the representatives of the International Union of Mine, Mill and Smelter Workers a prominent role.

The Conference

In April 1940 the conference convened in Joplin, Missouri, and for a few weeks national attention was focused on the Tri-State region. This two-day conference was the culmination of forty years of debate over silicosis, tuberculosis, and responsibility for disease in the Tri-State region. It was the labor strife that had forced government, management, union officials, and others to attend and it was the relationship of health and disease to this broader struggle that dominated the conference. The debates among representatives of labor,

[70] Zimmer to Secretary Perkins, "Meeting in the Tri-State Mining Area," March 2, 1940. See also Perkins to Tony McTeer, March 28, 1940.

[71] W. A. Pat Murphy to Zimmer, June 3, 1935, National Archives, Record Group 100, 7-0-6-13.

[72] Tri-State Conference, "Proceedings," April 23, 1940, National Archives, Record Group 100, 7-0-4(3), 32; Zimmer to Secretary Perkins, "Tri-State Conference," April 8, 1940, National Archives, Record Group 100, 7-0-4-(3).

management, industrial hygienists, and government officials brought into high relief the health problems of the Tri-State region and the question of who should bear the responsibility for risk.

The position papers and proceedings of the conference revealed the intense politics that shaped the ostensibly objective and scientific debates over disease and public health. In the course of arguing over who should pay for the costs in life and limb of unsafe and unhealthy working conditions, a much more fundamental debate emerged over the very notion of disease itself. The mine owners promoted the view that industrialization had made the traditional dichotomy between the healthy and diseased meaningless. The common understanding of medicine and public health had not kept pace with the revolutionary changes of the new industrial society that exposed millions of people to industrially created dusts and chemicals. In modern societies dependent upon coal, gasoline, and other new forms of energy, dust in the working and living environment was no longer exceptional. The inhalation of some dust was a normal everyday occurrence for people living in industrial communities and the growing urban centers. Under these modern conditions, health and disease were part of one continuum, not two dichotomous categories. It was not the presence of dust in workers' lungs that was pathological; only the existence of "excessive" amounts that limited a person's activity could be considered pathological. Management argued that the boundaries between normal and abnormal, the healthy and diseased, had to be redrawn to accommodate the new industrial realities.

Labor representatives and their advocates in the Department of Labor argued from a more traditional model of health and disease. The presence of dust and chemicals in the environment, however prevalent, could not be considered normal. In humans, they produced physiological changes that were part of a disease process. Such changes in working and living conditions indicated a fundamental imbalance between humans and their environment. Especially in the case of industrial disease, such imbalances were not natural but the product of choices made by the community. Disease was the result of conscious social decisions, and it was the role of social workers, public health, labor officials, and management to control and regulate the environment to protect the public.

Management and labor could have such radically different interpretations of the origins and nature of silicosis because of the host of new problems that chronic industrial disease posed for the medical and public health community. Unlike accidents, the cause and effect of such disease were rarely clear cut. Except in cases of acute poisonings or death, chronic disease might or might not show symptoms at a particular time. Often, symptoms would appear years, even decades, after exposure to toxins. Some workers were affected by relatively limited exposures to toxic materials, while others were far more tolerant. Some workers might show physiological changes without exhibiting physical symptoms. Others might not have any physiological change, yet find themselves losing strength. In the case of silicosis, the diagnosis of the disease did not preclude conflicting opinions regarding its importance in the life of a worker. Some believed that mild silicosis rarely interfered with the worker's ability to earn a living and hence the condition was of little significance. Others saw the issue differently, believing that physical limitations, whether affecting work or not, were unacceptable and should be redressed. In the face of such medical uncertainty, the political agendas of both management and labor became especially critical.

The position of industry was laid out by Evan Just, the secretary of the Tri-State Zinc and Lead Ore Producers Association, who defended industry's activities on behalf of workers' health and safety. He attacked those who publicized the wretched living conditions in the area and criticized those who characterized silicosis "as a horrible, deadly disease" caused by "heartlessly negligent" employers. Industry had sought to alleviate the worst of the conditions over the years, but "such a process is inevitably slow and requires persistent painstaking efforts on the part of a great many people." He claimed that the U.S. Public Health Service had certified the safety of the mines by showing that dust levels were significantly below the accepted standard of 5 million particles per cubic foot established in 1937 at the National Silicosis Conference.[73]

Just defined silicosis as resulting from the "inhalation of excessive amounts of silica dust over a long period of time." But he held that the inhalation of silica per se was not dangerous. The body could defend itself from minute silica particles by producing tissue around the dust particles, creating a benign "condition known as fibrosis," and "almost every adult person has some." Silicosis was, according to Just, merely a more advanced case of a normal fibrotic condition, and "the effect is simply to reduce lung capacity by the substitution of non-functional tissue for functional tissue." He minimized the problems associated with silicosis by claiming that "because the body is normally equipped with considerably more lung capacity than it needs, silicosis per se does not result in noticeable disability. Only in very advanced cases is any impairment of functions noticeable and this exists in shortness of breath in exercising."[74] Just claimed that the large number of silicotics in the area were "a residue, a hangover, of a condition which dates back years . . . a residue in the community which we believe is not being created today."[75]

[73] Evan Just, "Dust Prevention in Tri-State Mines," in Just to Zimmer, December 6, 1939, National Archives, Record Group 100, 7-0-6-13. Just's private position closely paralleled his public writings. See Evan Just, "Living and Working Conditions in the Tri-State Mining District," *Mining Congress Journal* 25 (November 1939): 44–45.

[74] Evan Just, "Dust Prevention," in Just to Zimmer, December 6, 1939, National Archives, Record Group 100, 7-0-6-13.

[75] Evan Just, in Tri-State Conference, "Proceedings," April 23, 1940, National Archives, Record Group 100, 7-0-4(3), 13–19.

In his speech, Just had maintained that the focus of the conference was wrong. The real problem of the area was tuberculosis, an infectious disease caused by poor living conditions, not silicosis, the industrial scourge. Further, the widespread prevalence of tuberculosis was the product of the free choice workers and their families made about how to spend their wages. "The wages paid in our industry are certainly adequate to support decent living," but "many people who can afford better homes, prefer to live in small, unpainted two or three room shacks and spend their surplus funds on automobiles and radios," he asserted. To the charge of union representatives and labor advocates that the mining companies could improve the housing stock available, Just responded that "it has never been customary here to provide living quarters or commissaries for employees or otherwise to exercise any control over their mode of life." To the charge that health statistics were terrible in the region, Just claimed that the health status of residents of the area "compare[d] favorably with the average." Just maintained that the whole issue of living and health conditions in the Tri-State region was outside the province of management and government activity. It was the workers' life-style that was the root cause of the health crisis, and only they could change it.[76] Dr. Jesse Douglas of the local management-supported Webb City Sanitarium reiterated the producers' position that tuberculosis was the real problem in the area. Douglas maintained that the problems of the area had little to do with the mines and everything to do with the long history of tuberculosis infestation of the area. He held that "the American stock has carried along with it tuberculosis. The district had been well seeded with the tuberculin bacilli; has been seeded for years and years and has been kept on being seeded and the germ is being seeded today, without sufficient effort to control it."

Officials in the Department of Labor and union representatives presented opposing arguments underscoring their differences with management's medi-

[76] Just, in Tri-State Conference, "Proceedings," April 23, 1940, 13–19. In other forums, Just went even further, claiming that the real problem lay with the fact that most of the area's workers were independent-minded Americans whose ancestry went back many generations. Turning more common nativist arguments on their head, Just claimed in a private meeting with Verne Zimmer that the "principal difficulty is that this type of worker—unlike 'a foreign element'—will not take orders. . . . Because of their ignorance it is almost impossible to educate them in a sanitary way of living." Zimmer to Secretary Perkins, October 25, 1939, National Archives, Record Group 100, 7-0-6-13. Others from the area also placed the responsibility for poor living and working conditions on the independent "American" attitudes of the workers. See, for example, Reverend Titus, in Tri-State Conference, "Proceedings," April 23, 1940, 8–9: "We have a group of laboring men in our state which is all American. . . . They have quite a tradition behind them; they are pretty independent; they have pretty much done as they pleased. . . . Most of them own automobiles of some character. They could live, if they wanted to, in some town. . . . Most of them prefer to live down close to the mine, near the chat piles, because they would rather spend their money for something else. They are not so concerned about owning a home or renting a home that might furnish a lot of conveniences. Most of them live where they do because they want to live there."

cal, political, and social analyses. Labor saw silicosis and tuberculosis as inextricably related to management's control over the work process and community life. The Department of Labor's critique of Just's analysis was captured in the line-by-line comments made in the margins of the department's copy of his speech. One department safety engineer wrote that the document was "filled with half-truths and statements that rest on opinion rather than scientific analysis. It smells strongly of alibis it seems to me." He noted that "the view that I have gotten from a rather sketchy knowledge of this district is that the mining companies have done only what they felt they had to keep scandal down but have never whole heartedly gone after the job of eliminating silicosis."[77] The staff was particularly struck by Just's selective definition of silicosis itself. To Just's claim that only "excessive amounts of silica dust over a long period of time produces" silicosis, one member wrote that it "may not be so 'long' if excessive."[78] The staff was particularly sarcastic regarding Just's claim that in advanced cases of silicosis there was "shortness of breath while exercising." A staff member added in "or working!" The staff further noted that the clinic, which was organized by management, was of little value to the work force, since the workers undoubtedly distrusted it: "Is a clinic of much value in prevention? Doesn't it merely discover silicotics so that they may be fired?"[79]

To the Department of Labor, there was nothing "normal" or natural about dust in the workplace or silicosis among workers: "In plain English, silicosis is a disease of the lungs in which normal lung tissue is replaced by fibrous or scarred tissue due to breathing air containing silica dust. Silicosis is strictly an occupational disease." There was little to argue about concerning the appropriate response to the silicosis hazard. Silicosis was a disease that could be prevented and required relatively little new research or theoretical study: "Our job is one of applying [preventive] techniques and principles to every known silica dust hazard in American industry. We know the methods of control—let us put them into practice."[80]

Secretary Perkins arrived in Missouri well prepared and received tremendous local publicity as she made a whirlwind tour of the mines of the Tri-State region. In a photo display and article in the St. Louis *Post Dispatch*, she was

[77] Notes by R.P.B. [Blake], Senior Safety Engineer, on Just, "Dust Prevention."

[78] This is probably a reference to the development of acute silicosis among the workers killed at Gauley Bridge in the early 1930s. See Chapter III.

[79] Notations on Just, "Dust Prevention," in Just to Zimmer, December 6, 1939. For a further elaboration of management's views, see Evan Just, "Statement to the Honorable Frances Perkins, Secretary of Labor, Representing the Viewpoint of Mine Operators on Living and Working Conditions in the Tri-State District," April 23, 1940, National Archives, Record Group 174, Office of the Secretary, Joplin, Missouri; and Tri-State Conference, "Proceedings," April 23, 1940.

[80] "Silicosis (Some Pertinent Facts about This Occupational Disease for Use by the Secretary at Joplin, Missouri)," April 26, 1940, National Archives, Record Group 174, Office of the Secretary, Joplin, Missouri.

shown descending into a mine in miner's garb, speaking with local residents, and addressing an evening meeting of the International Mine, Mill and Smelters Workers' Union.[81] In her opening address to the conference, Perkins adopted a conciliatory tone.[82] She left to others in her department the task of analyzing the deficiencies in management's presentation on silicosis. But when it came to larger public health issues, and specifically the impact of tuberculosis on the Tri-State, she took a personal interest. As she listened to Just and others, Perkins revealed her frustration with the producers' protestations of helplessness in combating disease in the area. She objected to Just's attempt to focus attention on the life-style of employees as the cause of the high incidence of tuberculosis and Douglas's assertion that the area was "seeded" with the tuberculosis bacillus. Perkins found such explanations simplistic, noting that they served only to undermine effective public health measures and divert attention from the occupational and environmental implications of the community's health problems.

The Secretary of Labor especially objected to the eugenic idea that certain human "stock" carried a predisposition to tuberculosis. She recounted her own experience as a young public health worker on a street in New York's Lower East Side where tuberculosis rates were so high that it was called the "lung block": "It was our happy practice to console ourselves with the thought that the residents of that district were almost entirely of Irish extraction, and the Irish, we thought, were the 'seedbed' of tuberculosis. So we could safely ignore the fact that there was so much tuberculosis in that particular area." She described how Jacob Riis, Theodore Roosevelt, and other reformers initiated a very successful public health campaign that entailed rebuilding the block, sending in visiting nurses, setting up tuberculosis centers, and increasing medical and social work attention to the problems in the area. The tuberculosis rate declined substantially. "So we gave up the idea that it was the Irish who were the seedbed for tuberculosis and came to the conclusion that it was something in the environment that had made it a favorable environment for the growth of whatever seeds might be planted anywhere in the human body."

In contrast to the producers' and medical community of the Tri-State, she was optimistic regarding the ability of human action to control the environment. She laid out a very different model of disease causation and cure, which

[81] "Madam Perkins Comes to Missouri to Study Silicosis," *St. Louis Post Dispatch*, April 28, 1940. Perkins' address to the miners was a tremendous boost to their morale and was initiated by the miners themselves: "In a few days you will receive an invitation from a joint A.F. of L.–C.I.O. committee to address a large evening meeting at Joplin, composed entirely of workers. . . ." Zimmer to Secretary Perkins, "Tri-State Conference," April 8, 1940, National Archives, Record Group 100, 7-0-4(3).

[82] Frances Perkins, in Tri-State Conference, "Proceedings," April 23, 1940, National Archives, Record Group 100, 7-0-4(3), 5–7.

evolved from her experiences in public health work during the Progressive Era. Perkins believed that disease could not be prevented or cured by identifying particular germs and treating specific diseases. Rather it was attention to the overall environment—both occupational and social—that would ultimately address problems of human health:

> Undoubtedly all of us—the American stock and Irish and German and Scotch, and recently the Italian and recent Czech and Slovakian, the whole human race— are all pretty good seedbeds for tuberculosis if we get exposed to it. And probably it is very largely the environment in which we live that determines whether we are disabled and crushed by it or whether we manage to lift our heads above it and go on.

Perkins maintained that the miners' susceptibility to tuberculosis was due to the weakened state of their lungs caused by silica dust inhalation over a long period of time. The widespread presence of tuberculosis was a confirmation of, not an excuse for, the hazardous working conditions and terrible living conditions of the miners and their families.[83] The real problem was one of prevention:

> Aren't we aiming today at techniques of preventing that silica complication of tuberculosis? And silica is a complication if a person that is well but has the germ within him, is exposed to a silica hazard. That irritation probably aggravates the situation. And aren't we looking for a method of prevention, and shouldn't we discuss the techniques of prevention?[84]

The labor position closely paralleled Perkins's own analysis. Tony McTeer of the IUMMSW told the conference that the problems of the area were intertwined. The inhalation of silica dust caused silicosis, which in turn predisposed workers to tuberculosis. Despite the owners' claims that wet drilling had eliminated the problem for miners in the newer mines, McTeer told the audience, "I have never worked in mines except where water layner drills were used and I have silicosis or dust on my lungs." Nor, he asserted, was he unique: "We can produce hundreds of men who have never worked except under wet drilling conditions. We have buried a great many of these boys. . . . Since wet drilling alone does not solve the problem and the problem still

---

[83] Tri-State Conference, "Proceedings," April 23, 1940, 22–23.

[84] Tri-State Conference, "Proceedings," April 23, 1940, 23–24. Alice Hamilton supported Perkins's position in her own statement to the conference: "I noticed that one or two people said that this region is thoroughly 'seeded' with tuberculosis. Why should it be? One can understand why an old neglected tenement, a slum area that has been standing in the city for a couple of generations, why those houses should be seeded with tuberculosis, but off here in the country there must be some reason for it. If that is true, then your housing problem really does become quite serious." *Ibid.*, 40.

is dust control and we must get at the route [*sic*] of the problem."[85] McTeer told the audience that the problem went beyond the mines and affected every aspect of life in the region. "Our district has proportionately the greatest percentage of widowhood in the United States, a sad commentary," he remarked. "To reduce the high death rate among miners, requires better dust control and better working conditions in the mines. Stopping silicosis is one step in the direction of curbing the infection of tuberculosis." But addressing the silicosis problem was one part of a broader attack on the problems of the community. In addition to cleaning up the workplace, McTeer called for improvements in the medical care system, specifically hospitals and the provision of adequate housing for miners and their families. McTeer rejected the producers' free-market ideology, which held that workers "chose" to live in the hovels and shacks surrounding the mines.[86]

Alice Hamilton, the noted industrial physician, was also present at the conference and also dissented from the generally upbeat tone of industry's speakers. While most spokespeople paid lip service to the industry position that there had been tremendous improvements over the past decades in living and working conditions, Hamilton pointed out that she saw no such improvement. "I was here about 25 years ago," she began. "I am sorry to say that it seemed a very familiar landscape to me as I looked over it going through it today— the heaps of tailings (only they are bigger now), and the housing that I saw reminded me of 25 years ago." She agreed that her memory might be faulty, but "the area is singularly unchanged in its outward appearance from when I was here."[87]

In addition to affirming the similarity over a twenty-five-year period, Hamilton also made a very important point about the relationship between environmental and occupational conditions. She pointed out that the communities of the Tri-State region were surrounded by the refuse of the mining process. Mountains of tailings—the rocks, gravel, sand, and low-grade ore called "chat" by local residents—surrounded the shacks and towns of the region. On dry, windy days, these piles gave rise to tremendous dust, which permeated the atmosphere in the region. Hamilton and others suspected that these

[85] Tony McTeer, "Resume of Conditions in the Tri-State Mining Area," April 23, 1940, National Archives, Record Group 174, Office of the Secretary, Joplin, Missouri.

[86] Tony McTeer, "Resume of Conditions." For further information on labor's position, see Statement by Mr. Reed, in Tri-State Conference, "Proceedings," April 23, 1940, 35–36. Alice Hamilton, the noted industrial physician, concurred with labor's position that wet drilling was inadequate in preventing silicosis: "It was admitted [at the conference] that wet drilling and mucking are practiced in most of the mines . . . but since cases of miners' consumption [silicosis] are still appearing and the victims are not 'gougers' but those employed regularly, even in wet mines, it is clear that there is still silica dust in the air." Alice Hamilton, "A Mid-American Tragedy," *Survey-Graphic* 29 (August 1940): 435.

[87] Tri-State Conference, "Proceedings," April 23, 1940, 39–40.

piles of refuse were in and of themselves a possible source of silicosis or, at least, other lung diseases for the families of the miners.[88]

Others echoed Hamilton's observations but detailed how the new industrial processes employed in the seemingly "clean" Picher mines actually increased the environmental problem of dust exposure. In a piece entitled "The Menace of the Slime Pile," members of the Tri-State Health and Housing Committee pointed out that in addition to the "chat" piles of broken rock and refuse, the newer refining processes broke down the rock even more finely so that the newer " 'flotation process' for recovering mineral values from the [finds] that had been [formerly] lost in the waste water" could be employed. The process created a slime that ultimately was pumped out into the environment "that when dry became the source of these clouds of dust." "It is ironical that a mining company that has, at great expense, followed all modern practices for suppression of the dust in the mining operation should deliberately stack these death dealing [finds] in the open; there to remain a menace for years to come," the report observed.[89]

Although the conference produced few concrete results, labor spokespeople were euphoric over the support they felt Perkins and the Department of Labor showed on their behalf. Reid Robinson, president of the International in Denver, wrote to Zimmer saying it was "one of the greatest things that has happened in the Tri-State area for many years."[90] The publicity generated by the conference combined with the successful conclusion of the NLRB hearing to give new life to the union.[91]

The conference resulted in the establishment of a number of committees whose activities appeared to be limited. However, the Department of Labor continued to act on behalf of the miners in the area. True reform, it believed, would not be brought about by the voluntary initiatives of the mine owners. Rather, improvements in working and living conditions would occur only after the area's economy was sufficiently diversified to destroy the control that the producers exerted over the life of the community. "From my observation I have no hesitancy in venturing the thought that there are few districts in greater need of buttressing through the development of additional industrial operations," wrote Frances Perkins in November 1940.[92] Especially during the

[88] Tri-State Conference, "Proceedings," April 23, 1940, 40. Speaking for the producers, Evan Just claimed that the major source of dust was from the roads, not the chat piles. He went on to claim that "there are no cases in medical annals where surface dust conditions have produced silicosis." Evan Just, "Living and Working Conditions," *Mining Congress Journal* 25 (November 1939): 45.

[89] Tri-State Health and Housing Committee, "The Menace of the Slime Pile, Disposal of Mill Tailings in the Tri-State Zinc and Lead District," in Tri-State File, Tamiment Library.

[90] Reid Robinson to Zimmer, April 30, 1940, National Archives, Record Group 100, 7-0-4(3).

[91] Elwood B. Hain to Reid Robinson, June 5, 1941, Western Federation of Miners Mss. [International Union of Mine, Mill and Smelter Workers], Western Historical Collections, University of Colorado, Boulder, Box 37-17, Elwood Hain, 1942.

[92] V. A. Zimmer, "Committee on the Tri-State Area," in National Archives, Record Group

arms buildup before World War II, the Department of Labor attempted to promote economic diversification of the Tri-State region. In a memo from Zimmer to Secretary Perkins about "our pet problem district in the country," Zimmer noted that the Army had recently completed a nitrate plant eight miles from one of the towns in the region. Zimmer also reported that the "powder plant which we tried to get for the Tri-State area is being erected . . . 75 miles southwest of Baxter Springs in the heart of the Tri-State area." He optimistically concluded that "these operations will obviously furnish employment for all available labor in that general district, probably including some of the ex-miners who might be ruled out of the lead mines because of 'potential or incipient' silicosis." He also informed Perkins that the Eagle-Picher Mining and Smelting Company was "reinstating the miners who struck several years ago and have been kept out of employment ever since" probably because of the severe labor shortage occasioned by the war. The only negative occurrence to report was that "apparently no housing program has been evolved and probably all of the old shacks will continue to be used for some time."[93]

The union certainly agreed with Zimmer's assessment that the war and economic diversification improved the bargaining position of workers in the Tri-State area. In a memorandum prepared at the national office of the International Union of Mine, Mill and Smelter Workers in Denver, Colorado, organizers noted the effects of a growing labor shortage on labor conditions in the Tri-State. The memo began by pointing out that despite the need for lead and zinc production during the war, "production of lead and zinc concentrates has suffered a serious drop in the past two months due solely to lack of manpower." The International identified several reasons for the growing labor shortage. First, the able-bodied men were leaving the area to join the armed forces, leaving behind a large proportion of disabled or diseased workers, who, because of industry decisions, were excluded from employment in the larger companies. Second, those able-bodied men who remained in the area sought employment in the other industries that were then springing up. Especially important in this regard was the growing government support for war industries. Even those able-bodied men who sought furloughs from the army in order to stay in mining generally avoided mining jobs in the Tri-State. Rather than accepting the low pay and the poor working conditions in the

---

174, Frances Perkins Committees; Perkins to William S. Knudsen, November 9, 1940, National Archives, Record Group 174, Office of the Secretary, Committee on the Tri-State Area, Frances Perkins Committees.

[93] Zimmer to Secretary Perkins, February 3, 1942, National Archives, Record Group 174, Committee on the Tri-State Area, Frances Perkins Committees; see also William L. Connolly to William J. Cassidy, August 7, 1947, National Archives, Record Group 100, 7-0-6 for statement of the inactivity of the various standing committees associated with the Tri-State Conference. See also W. J. Cassidy, "The Tri-State Zinc-Lead Mining Region: Growth, Problems and Prospects" (Ph.D. diss., University of Pittsburgh, 1955), 181: "Some of the well-informed professional men in the area have confided to the present writer their opinion that the operators sabotaged the program by delay."

region, they sought jobs in the Western metal mining fields: "True, remedial measures removing some of the silicosis hazards have been effected by the Tri-State operators, but the remaining health hazards are not an incentive to new recruits." Even though the operators sought to mechanize their plants by introducing "power loading devices" to replace hand shovelers, they were not able to meet production goals.[94] In a meeting with the U.S. Employment Service in November 1942, the union was asked why it thought the companies were having such difficulty recruiting workers. A union representative responded that "the wages being paid in the industry in this area, with the background of working conditions, does not act as an inducement to even inexperienced workers to accept employment."[95]

The social and economic conditions in the area undercut management's hegemony over the lives of workers and their families. Also, the successful, if draining, conclusion of the NLRB hearings gave impetus to the local union's organizing efforts. "It seems to me that the time is now ripe for an organizational drive in the Tri-State," declared an organizer in June 1941.[96] An organizing drive was undertaken in October 1941, and the union made silicosis and health central issues once more. "During the past 20 or 30 years," one organizer declared, "thousands of miners, millmen and smeltermen have died from silicosis. . . . Many of these workers have been 'cliniced out' as soon as the company discovered the individual's health to be in a failing condition."[97] The organizing efforts went on throughout the war and reached fruition in 1946 with successful organizing of all the Eagle-Picher plants[98] and most of the other companies throughout the district. In mines throughout the area, joint

[94] "Statement of Manpower and Labor Supply in the Tri-State Lead and Zinc Mining Field— Oklahoma, Kansas and Missouri," [ca. November 19, 1942], Western Federation of Miners Manuscripts, Box 36-29, Gobel Cravens, Western Historical Collections, University of Colorado, Boulder.

[95] Gobel F. Cravens to Ben Riskin, November 13, 1942, Western Federation of Miners Manuscripts [International Union of Mine, Mill and Smelter Workers], Western Historical Collections, University of Colorado, Boulder, Box 36-29, Gobel-Cravens. See also A. Hadlock, Secretary, International Union of Mine, Mill and Smelter Workers Local 596, Joplin, August 9, 1943, in Western Federation of Miners Manuscripts, Box 132: "The production if [sic] metals in the tristate area is slowing down . . . for the reason that so many experienced miners have quit the mines to go to other defence jobs that pay them more money and is cleaner and more healthier work."

[96] Elwood B. Hain to Reid Robinson, June 5, 1941, Western Federation of Miners Manuscripts [International Union of Mine, Mill and Smelter Workers], Western Historical Collections, University of Colorado, Boulder, Box 37-17, Elwood Hain, 1942.

[97] "Address No. 3 by Elwood B. Hain," October 6, 1941, Western Federation of Miners Manuscripts [International Union of Mine, Mill and Smelter Workers], Western Historical Collections, University of Colorado, Boulder, Box 37-17, Elwood Hain, 1942.

[98] See "Eagle-Picher Contract, Labor School Signal a New Era in the Tri-States," *The Union*, December 16, 1946, 3; "3 New Contracts in Tri-State Bring Many First-Time Gains," *The Union*, November 18, 1946, 3; "Surface Victory at Eagle Picher Is Key to Greater Tri-State Gains," *The Union*, September 2, 1946, 3.

union-management safety committees were formed, and ventilating equipment was installed in a some of the worst.[99] While silicosis was not eliminated as a hazard for drillers, haulers, and shovelers, the union formalized a mechanism for addressing health problems.

The initial success of the union's efforts was aided by temporary changes in the area's economy brought on by the war. As many of the healthy, younger men entered the Armed Forces, management turned to diseased or partially disabled and formerly blacklisted workers. The federal government also played a role by building defense plants, which served to diversify the region's economy, thereby undermining the producers' control.[100]

The New Deal is often seen through the prism of federal legislation and presidential initiatives. We see Franklin Roosevelt, Frances Perkins, and other New Deal administrators as the inspiration and motor behind the fundamental changes that occurred during the 1930s. Yet the local context often provided the impetus for reform and sometimes shaped the programs to very local needs and circumstances. The New Deal unleashed a torrent of activity at the local level and gave people who were subject to horrendous local exploitation the sense that they could in fact effect change and assert control over their own lives. As the Tri-State struggle illustrates, the hope and expectation that administrators in Washington could come to their aid and provide both political and substantive support was important, but not sufficient to explain the enormous social and political turmoil that overtook the region during the Depression. We are comfortable with looking at the ways that the New Deal changed local communities. The Tri-State forces us to examine the ways that local struggles redefined the national agenda.

The Postwar Period

The union victories were short lived.[101] The return of soldiers from the war gave management a new source of labor, and alternative employment once

[99] See, for examples of the organizing efforts, Ben Riskin to Elwood B. Hain, October 23, 1942; Elwood B. Hain to Reid Robinson, October 10, 1942; Ben Riskin to Hain, October 20, 1942; and Hain to Riskin, July 27, 1942, all of which discuss different aspects of the organizing efforts. In Western Federation of Miners Manuscripts [International Union of Mine, Mill and Smelter Workers], Western Historical Collections, University of Colorado, Boulder, Box 166, Elwood Hain.

[100] V. A. Zimmer, "Committee on the Tri-State Area," in National Archives, Record Group 174, Frances Perkins Committees; Perkins to William S. Knudsen, November 9, 1940, National Archives, Record Group 174, Office of the Secretary, Committee on the Tri-State Area, Frances Perkins Committees.

[101] Hain to John Clark, September 16, 1947, Western Federation of Miners Manuscripts [International Union of Mine, Mill and Smelter Workers], Western Historical Collections, University of Colorado, Boulder, Box 79-55, Elwood Hain.

again became scarce. Furthermore, President Truman's veto of wartime subsidies for lead and zinc undercut the union by forcing nearly all the mines to shut down or scale back production.[102] Eagle-Picher closed twenty-four out of thirty-one mines immediately, and the smaller operations quickly followed suit, as they were unable to compete with the more efficient Western mines and less costly foreign operations.[103] But the crowning blow was the political attack on the left-wing International Mine, Mill and Smelter Workers Union. The passage of the Taft-Hartley Act of 1947 and, specifically, the anti-Communist affidavit that was required of unions seeking protection under the National Labor Relations Act was the death knell for the union in the Tri-State. More conservative unions began organizing in the area including the United Cement, Lime and Gypsum International Union, an American Federation of Labor union, and the Cherry Tri-State Association, a company union. In 1949, the NLRB authorized a new certification election that excluded the International Union of Mine, Mill and Smelter Workers from the ballot because its officers had refused to sign the anti-Communist affidavit.[104] In a last-ditch effort to remain the bargaining unit, the International emphasized safety and health, urging miners to "remember what it used to be like" before the union came and organized the region. They wrote, "Hey, Joe Remember? When you didn't know what wet drilling was and you had to eat the dirt and die like flies with the 'con'[sumption]? . . . When you had no say about the safety conditions?"[105]

In an agreement signed by the International and a smaller producer in the area shortly before the passage of the Taft-Hartley Act, it is apparent that the union paid close attention to protecting the rights of workers to a safe workplace. Article XI of the agreement between the IUMMSW and the Beck Mining Company in the Tri-State region laid out a plan for active union involvement in determining the safety and healthfulness of the mine. Most pointedly,

[102] As early as September, 1945, the union recognized the potential impact of the ending of wartime subsidies on the economy and union drives in the Tri-State region. Responding to a letter from a local in Treece, Kansas, asking for an organizer, Reid Robinson, the president of the International, wrote: "My great concern for the Tri-State area has been to establish the necessary government aid in order that all the mines can continue to produce, giving jobs to the workers. It will be little good to organize the area if it cannot operate. I am therefore carrying on an active campaign with Congress, trying to continue the premium price or subsidy program used during the war." Robinson to Harold Feagan, September 7, 1945, Western Federation of Miners Manuscripts [International Union of Mine, Mill and Smelter Workers], Western Historical Collections, University of Colorado, Boulder, Box 134, No. 489.

[103] Memorandum. Leary to Sanderson, October 10, 1947, Western Federation of Miners Manuscripts [International Union of Mine, Mill and Smelter Workers], Western Historical Collections, University of Colorado, Boulder, Box 238-10.

[104] "Miners and Employees of the Tri-State Mining District, Stop-Think-Vote!" [n.d.] Pamphlet, Tri-State Mining Collection, Tamiment.

[105] "Hey, Joe Remember?" Pamphlet, Tri-State Mining Collection, Tamiment.

the agreement acknowledged that the "employees may be at times in a position to observe dangerous conditions and practices," and had the obligation to bring this information to the union-appointed Safety Committee. Furthermore, the company and the Safety Committee had "to immediately investigate . . . all such reports and if hazards are found to take all reasonable steps necessary to eliminate them." The most important aspect of the agreement, however, was that management accepted the union's demand that "no employee shall be required to work in a place found by the [union] Safety Committee to be unsafe, until the condition is corrected."[106] The International urged miners to vote for "neither" of the other unions on the ballot in a futile attempt to remain the bargaining unit. This campaign was the last serious attempt by the International Union of Mine, Mill and Smelter Workers to maintain its position within the region.[107]

In the 1950s and early 1960s, the International continued to press the issue of silicosis on the national level, but in the Tri-State, with the union destroyed and the region in economic decline, the issue faded. Also, with the passing of the New Deal administration, the resignation of Secretary Perkins, and the death of the Division of Labor Standards head, Verne Zimmer, silicosis itself ceased to be a priority for an increasingly conservative labor department.

The IUMMSW's decline in the region paralleled that of the area. After World War II, the center of metal mining shifted away from the Tri-State region and, by the 1960s, mining had ceased entirely. Only the scars remained. The population of the region declined as healthy workers and their families

[106] "Agreement" [between IUMMSW and Beck Mining Company], April 18, 1947, Tri-State Mining Collection, Tamiment. See also "Proposed Agreement" [between the union and Eagle-Picher Company], 1945, Western Federation of Miners Manuscripts [International Union of Mine, Mill and Smelter Workers], Western Historical Collections, University of Colorado, Boulder, Box 172, Local 105, Joplin; and "Proposed Agreement" [between the union and Federal Mining and Smelting Company], Western Federation of Miners Manuscripts [International Union of Mine, Mill and Smelter Workers], Western Historical Collections, University of Colorado, Boulder, Box 34-21, Alex Cashin.

[107] For a portrait of the destruction of the union, see the Semi-Monthly Reports of Howard Mooney and Elwood Hain, International organizers in the Tri-State in 1949, in Western Federation of Miners Manuscripts [International Union of Mine, Mill and Smelter Workers], Western Historical Collections, University of Colorado, Boulder, Box 95, Hain, Mooney. Evidence points to the accuracy of the union's claim that it was very attentive to the health and safety issue. "Agreement" [between IUMMSW and Beck Mining Company], April 18, 1947, Tri-State Mining Collection, Tamiment. For other examples, see "Proposed Agreement" [between the union and Eagle-Picher Company], 1945, Western Federation of Miners Manuscripts [International Union of Mine, Mill and Smelter Workers], Western Historical Collections, University of Colorado, Boulder, Box 172, Local 105, Joplin; and "Proposed Agreement" [between the union and Federal Mining and Smelting Company], Western Federation of Miners Manuscripts [International Union of Mine, Mill and Smelter Workers], Western Historical Collections, University of Colorado, Boulder, Box 34-21, Alex Cashin.

left, creating a net decline in population during the 1950s. Alice Hamilton, the noted industrial physician,[108] summarized the terrible price that the region had paid for "industrial progress."

> Zinc and lead mining started in the Missouri area, around Webb City, then as those mines were exhausted, the producers moved on into Kansas and then into Oklahoma . . . . As the industry abandons an area, it leaves behind not only exhausted mines but a wasteland, of no value for any purpose. This cannot be farmed, the soil was never very good though usable, but now it is ruined. No factories will be built there, for now only the human refuse is left behind, most of the able-bodied have moved on. . . . And will Kansas and Oklahoma follow its example, giving a free hand to the mining companies as long as it is their pleasure to mine, and then taking up the burden of a ruined land and a derelict people after they have departed? Surely an industry should be made to clean up its own refuse, to care for its human wastage and restore its wastelands.[109]

In 1956, at federal hearings on the problem of silicosis among the nation's metal miners, a study was introduced that spoke to the continuing legacy of this exploitation. The population of Cherokee County, Kansas, was plagued by endemic tuberculosis more than five times the state average due to the continued presence of poor housing and a large silicotic population.[110] Even today, the legacy of disease and environmental destruction is still with us. In 1981, the Environmental Protection Agency issued a listing of the ten most polluted areas in the country. One of them was the area around Picher, Oklahoma, where contamination from the mines threatened the entire area's water supply.[111]

What can we learn from the experience of the Tri-State struggle? How do work and disease become a part of the working-class experience? How does this experience shape the awareness of the scientific and medical communities? What have the experiences of the zinc and lead miners taught us about how occupational disease comes to be defined and ultimately controlled? Together, these questions tell us why historians should pay attention to this episode. We suggest that to understand the history of this prolonged conflict demands attention to the complex and historically specific interrelationships among labor, business, political, and public health interests. As the process of

[108] Tri-State Conference, "Proceedings," April 23, 1940, 40. See also Tri-State Health and Housing Committee, "The Menace of the Slime Pile, Disposal of Mill Tailings in the Tri-State Zinc and Lead District," in Tri-State File, Tamiment Library.

[109] Alice Hamilton, "A Mid-American Tragedy," *Survey-Graphic* 29 (August 1940): 437.

[110] U.S. Congress, House, Subcommittee on Mine Safety of the Committee on Education and Labor, *Hearings on Inspection and Investigation in Metallic Mines*, 84th Cong., 2d sess., 1956, 409.

[111] "Technical Report Data," *Superfund Record of Decision: Tar Creek Site, OK*, June 6, 1984.

production changed with the introduction of new tools and the intensification of work, workers were exposed to new and potentially more hazardous conditions. In the Tri-State, they organized and struggled to resist these changes. As larger companies employed pneumatic tools and introduced piecework into the mines, the conditions for labor unrest developed and focused attention of public health officials on the area. After the defeat of the union in 1915, management gained hegemony over the region, and the issue of industrial disease was defined in purely medical and technical terms. It was not until the Great Depression, as the labor movement revitalized and thousands of workers were dismissed from their jobs, that the issue of health and disease became redefined as a social and labor issue rather than as a public health concern alone. Ultimately, the nature of the definition of occupational "disease" depended upon the social and economic context within which different groups vied for legitimacy and control. With the end of World War II, the issue was once again transformed into a medical and engineering problem. Without the pressures created by unemployment and labor strife, professionals were once again able to assert control over the issue.

It would not be until the 1960s, when coal miners, textile workers, asbestos workers, and others once again mobilized around the issues of industrial lung diseases that occupational health would be placed back on the national agenda. The reality of the changing social environment forced workers once again to struggle over the very definition of disease. This struggle involved public health workers, government, and industry in a public discourse over who was responsible for its creation and, ultimately, led to the passage of national legislation in the form of the Mine Safety and Health Act of 1969 and the Occupational Safety and Health Act of 1970.

1. Inside the Picher Clinic. The Clinic examined all workers in the Tri-State area for signs of silicosis or tuberculosis. (*Source: National Archives Still Picture Division.*)

2. Mechanization of Mining in the Tri-State. Mechanical cutting devices produced high levels of silica dust. (*Source: National Archives Still Picture Division.*)

3. Drilling Breast Hole with Water-Injection Drill. In the early 1900s it was hoped that ''wet'' drilling would eliminate the dust hazard. (*Source: National Archives Still Picture Division.*)

4. Miners' Housing in the Tri-State Region. Note the "chat" piles surrounding their dwellings. (*Source: National Archives Still Picture Division.*)

5. An early twentieth-century small mining operation. (*Source: National Archives Still Picture Division.*)

6. Panorama of a mining area in the Tri-State region. (*Source: National Archives Still Picture Division.*)

7. The Main Street of Treece, Kansas, was sometimes called the "Street of Walking Death" because of the prevalence of silicosis in the community. (*Source*: St. Louis Post-Dispatch.)

8. Secretary of Labor Frances Perkins inspects the Ballard Mine of the St. Louis Smelting and Refining Company near Baxter Springs, Kansas, while attending the Tri-State conference, April 23, 1940. The tub she rode in usually held five people. (*Source*: St. Louis Post-Dispatch.)

9. Blast-Hole Drillers at a Zinc Mine of the Eagle-Picher Company near Cardin, Oklahoma, January, 1943. (*Source: Library of Congress.*)

10. Exterior of the Picher Clinic where systematic screening of area miners took place. (*Source: National Archives Still Picture Collection.*)

11. Cartoon in International Union of Mine, Mill and Smelter Workers' newspaper *Mine-Mill Union* May 9, 1955, p. 8. (*Source: University of Colorado, Boulder, Western Historical Collections.*)

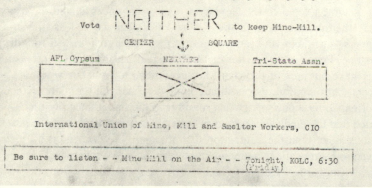

12. The International Union of Mine, Mill and Smelter Workers, barred from a 1949 certification election, urged miners not to vote for either of the eligible unions. (*Source: Tamiment Library, New York University.*)

VI

LAST GASPS: THE DEATH OF THE SILICOSIS ISSUE

> It is readily comprehended that if an industrial company desires a
> new substance to be tested for toxicity, premature publicity about
> biotoxic propensities of the product may involve the company in
> labor union trouble and decrease sales of the commodity. It is
> reasonable to require the investigating scientist to delay
> publication of his observations until the substance has either been
> eliminated or hazardous situations have been corrected.
> (*G.W.H. Schepers, Director, Saranac Laboratory, 1956*)

> I'll bet you, Frank, that were General Steel producing goods of
> such a type that the dust had a harmful effect on the quality of the
> product,—I'll bet you that, in such a case, dust at General Steel
> would be as scarce as flecks of gold in the air. But since the dust
> has a harmful effect *only* on the laborer, and since a laborer is
> born every second, and since there are millions of more laborers
> waiting to get into America from the rest of the world, why
> bother bearing down on safety infractions and taking
> precautionary measures which cost time and money and which
> subtract from profits.
> (*Joe Koloedey, 1949*)

O N OCTOBER 3, 1948, Joe Koloedey of Wilmington, Delaware,
wrote a letter to the New York *Times* that encapsulated the irony of
the silicosis issue in the 1940s. His father worked as one of four
"chippers," workers who removed sand from castings in a steel foundry, in
Eddystone, Pennsylvania. After eighteen years of steady, conscientious work
in the shake-out area of the plant, he succumbed to what the workers called
chippers' consumption, a condition common to many at the plant. Koloedey
was offended by a news story that minimized the importance of silicosis and
reported that the medical community believed it was a disease of the past. He
also took issue with the contention that silicosis could be cured by medical
intervention. Prevention, he maintained, was the only protection.[1]

Two years earlier, Koloedey had written to his father's union, the United
Steelworkers of America, about the horrid industrial conditions that had led to
his father's death. "The many deaths from silicosis at General Steel Corp.,

---

[1] Joe Koloedey, Letter to the Editor, *New York Times*, October 12, 1948, 24.

Eddystone, is so horrifyingly shocking that one can liken it to the bestial, Nazi system of slave labor.'' No corporation had the ''right to sentence a man to 17 years of hard labor, 15 months of excruciating torture, and a premature grave.'' He was particularly outraged that his father was never warned that he worked ''in the midst of a killing hazard.'' The union response appeared more concerned with maintaining good relations with management than with sympathizing with its own work force. The staff representative wrote to Koloedey that his father's death, while probably preventable, might well have been due to his own negligence. He suggested that ''a great deal of the hazard is created by the men'' rather than by the negligence of management. For example, chippers such as his father ''frequently blow the sand off their work with an airhose'' even though it is ''forbidden by the company.'' Ignoring the fact that the airhose and the supply of air was available to the workers in the chipping area because of planning decisions made by management, the union representative charged that ''both the company and the union have warned the men many times that breathing Silica sand is dangerous and that they should use every precaution against it.'' At the end of the letter, the union representative acknowledged that ''the company, too, is at fault.'' The union had been pressing for ventilation equipment to be installed in light of the silicosis hazard, but agreements were still pending on this issue.[2] Koloedey rejected the union's position, and wrote that it should not stand by and watch its members ''being dismissed empty-handed and being sent home as broken, gasping shadows to suffer and die in misery, worry and want.''[3]

Until World War II, labor, management, insurance, government, and professionals in public health and medicine all participated in the debate over silicosis. After the war, however, the views of labor and political reformers were no longer taken as seriously because the condition was now seen as the exclusive preserve of the scientific community. The language of science and medicine replaced the language of politics and negotiation in discussion of silicosis. Silicosis was now defined as a disease of the past that could be adequately addressed by medical researchers, and engineers working with an enlightened business community. Within medicine, specialties arose that made an understanding of the disease inaccessible even to the general practitioner. Even the history of silicosis was rewritten in biomedical and highly technical terms as the history of the laboratory. The very texts became inaccessible to the laypeople, workers and politicians, who had forced it onto the national agenda in the first place. This reliance on the scientist in defining silicosis

[2] Joseph Koloedey to Frank E. Ritter, Staff Representative, United Steelworkers of America, January 1, 1949, National Archives, Record Group 100, 7-1-1-8-1, Box 30; Ritter to Koloedey January 4, 1949, National Archives, Record Group 100, 7-1-1-8-1, Box 30.

[3] Koloedey to President, Congress of Industrial Organizations, February 13, 1949, National Archives, Record Group 100, 7-1-1-8-1, Box 30.

stripped away the legitimacy of nonprofessionals in shaping the discourse about chronic industrial disease.

Because of the economic and social crisis of the 1930s, silicosis and illness became a legitimate surrogate for problems created by dependency. During the postwar years, the absence of pervasive unemployment along with the introduction of a public social security system and widespread union-management welfare packages allowed the crisis over silicosis in particular and disease in general to recede. The absence of a public discourse had a dramatic effect on scientific agendas. During the 1930s, scientists and professionals wrote hundreds of articles about various aspects of the silicosis problem; in 1961, there were only sixteen articles published in American medical and public health journals. In the 1930s, books on the topic, such as the novel *The Citadel*, went through numerous printings and even made it to Hollywood. By the 1950s, there were no popular books, much less movies, that used as a symbol the silicosis issue. Even though government estimates suggested that roughly the same number of workers were at risk of contracting silicosis in the 1930s and the 1950s, the attention paid to it by physicians and even pulmonary specialists declined.

The social perception of what constitutes a "serious" health problem also had an important impact on our understanding of the silicosis issue. In a society traditionally racked by early death from infectious and epidemic diseases, the measure of significance was age-specific mortality rates. Chronic conditions that did not result in early death were seen as less serious problems for the medical community. Despite the fact that chronic diseases were disabling and killing more people than were acute illnesses, public and professional understanding of disease was rooted in this earlier experience.[4] Because silicosis predisposed workers to tuberculosis and silico-tuberculosis was life threatening, the continuing decline in tuberculosis death rates after the war affected public and professional perceptions of its severity. As tuberculosis was controlled through the aggressive use of antibiotics and as tuberculosis in general declined in prevalence, doctors and laypeople alike assumed that silicosis was at worst an inconvenience and only partially disabling condition of the elderly. Also, because ventilation and wet drilling in some of the newer worksites reduced the amount of silica dust in the air, for many workers there was probably a longer latency between exposure to silica and the onset of disease. It is reasonable to assume that the relationship between exposure to silica and labored breathing was obscured even more and, in the absence of widespread public and professional attention, was diagnosed as emphysema, asthma, and other cardiopulmonary conditions. It is ironic that silicosis—which had helped awaken the public health and medical communities to the problem of chronic industrial disease—was itself masked by the chronic dis-

---

[4] The Public Health Service focussed primarily on infectious diseases.

eases that became the focus of attention in the postwar era. As workers lived longer and as the period of time between exposure and disease lengthened, the relationship between work and illness receded from view. People were living longer and suffering, but their suffering became most evident in the years of retirement, after they left the workplace. It would not be until the 1970s that the public would once again link chronic disease to conditions at work.

Despite the consensus that the pneumoconioses were a relatively minor health problem in the America of the 1950s, there were isolated groups that rejected this view. Silicosis remained a concern for workers in metal mining, quarrying, and foundries. But the industries themselves were no longer playing a prominent role in America's postwar boom; their unions were small and shrinking and, in the case of the metal miners, politically isolated. For other, more powerful unions, the decline of silicosis meant that there was both the necessity and the space to press for new means of addressing the problem of dust and workers' health. In the 1960s, unions allied with a small cadre of doctors forced the medical and public health communities to acknowledge and ultimately define new dust diseases. Coal miners in particular pressed their own union to address pneumoconiosis, leading to legislation that defined coal workers' pneumoconiosis (black lung) as a disease. Silicosis was forced off the public health agenda and relegated once again to the "cabinet of curiosities." At the same time, diseases that had been kept in the shadow by all the public attention to silicosis emerged as new symbols of the sacrifices workers made for industrial "progress."

Declaring Silicosis a Dead Issue

There were many objective reasons for the decline in interest in silicosis in the postwar years. But in addition the business community and especially the Industrial Hygiene Foundation were active in shaping a postwar consensus among professionals in industrial hygiene and medicine that silicosis was a disease of the past. Koloedey's father was considered an anomaly, which at worst symbolized nothing more than an unfortunate legacy of an earlier era. Professionals were the new authorities in the field of industrial hygiene, and they all agreed with the leaders of the Air (now Industrial) Hygiene Foundation that "[t]he dangerous trades of our fathers has [sic] all but disappeared." Dust was now considered more of a danger to the inner workings of machinery than to the lungs of workers. "Not infrequently we find nuisance dust exposures to be more injurious to the mechanical equipment than to workmen," these experts declared.[5] In 1946, *Business Week* wrote that the only silica problem was

[5] "Silicosis Is Not Threat to Workers' Health," *Science News Letter* 50 (November 30, 1946): 345.

that some workers were hypersensitive to dust.[6] In this perspective's most absurd manifestations, silicosis was seen as a product of racial or ethnic characteristics that made certain workers susceptible. The *Business Week* article claimed that in one mill where there were some cases of silicosis still appearing, this was just proof that the company should have avoided hiring blond workers: "Brunettes, who generally have more hair on the body, naturally have more hair in the nostrils, which tends to keep silica dust from reaching the lungs." At the prestigious Saranac Laboratory symposium on silicosis, one state official echoed earlier management arguments of the 1920s and 1930s that technological innovation had eradicated the silicosis problem: "The most important accomplishment of these preventive measures is that silicosis is becoming a negligible factor, and that in the future it will largely be stamped out by preventive measures that have been instituted."[7] The Industrial Hygiene Foundation joined with researchers at Saranac to lend authority to this position.

The interlocking relationship between the industry and the very foundations involved in silicosis research raised few ethical qualms for scientists during the 1930s and 1940s. In fact, even the most prestigious independent research centers, such as the Saranac Laboratory (officially, part of the Trudeau Foundation) in Saranac Lake, New York, openly and sometimes aggressively pursued corporate funding because there were few other alternatives. Traditionally, Saranac had conducted studies of tuberculosis and in the 1920s had gradually involved itself in studies of the relationship between tuberculosis and industrial dust. When the silicosis crisis hit in the early 1930s, it sought to expand its involvement in this potentially rich arena. In 1932, for example, Saranac's director began an aggressive campaign to gain the support of the insurance industry and various mining companies. One such letter soliciting support held out the prospect of information that might translate into "direct financial value to the insurance companies writing industrial compensation policies."[8] By the late 1940s, Saranac had succeeded in establishing important contracts with a variety of mining interests and had come to depend upon these contracts for support. The relationship became so close that even when the laboratory's scientific experts, such as Leroy U. Gardner, sought to assert ostensible neutrality in labor-management disputes, few accepted his claims. The attorneys for one mining company scoffed at Gardner's reluctance to testify in a silicosis suit: "We did not agree with him that his refusal to testify would help maintain Saranac as an independent research organization because

[6] "Lung Lab Pays Off Quickly," *Business Week*, July 20, 1946, 54.

[7] Voyta Wrabitz, "Silicosis Legislation: Administration," in B. E. Kuechle, ed., *Fourth Saranac Laboratory Symposium on Silicosis* (Wassau, Wisc.: Employers Mutual Liability Insurance Company, 1939), 342.

[8] Director to Mr. E. O. Jones, Belle City Maleable Iron Company, June 4, 1932, Vorwald Collection, Box 3.

. . . all of the mining companies were associated with Saranac and certainly, in the eyes of everyone, excepting Dr. Gardner, Saranac was a 'mining company institution.' "[9]

Industry's victory was in gaining scientific authority for the idea that silicosis was a disease of the past. This could not easily be confirmed or denied. There were no systematic or comprehensive surveys of the dust conditions in the nation's foundries, metal mines, or granite sheds. Industry argued that engineering techniques, respirators, and ventilation equipment were available for the elimination of this disease and that this equipment was widely used. During World War II, however, the need to conserve and protect scarce labor led the federal government to conduct comprehensive surveys of war production plants, especially the industries associated with shipbuilding. These surveys give us an opportunity to evaluate the claims of industry that silicosis was a dead issue. The surveys indicate that while improvements had certainly been made in the foundries and shipyards of the nation, the impact was neither uniform nor complete. One major complaint was that "the dusty operations are frequently performed with other types of foundry work, [and] all foundry employees may be exposed to the dust hazard to some extent." Other federal inspectors[10] visiting the Bethlehem Steel shipyard observed that even in this national company, "of all the shops in the yard, the foundry exposes the men to the greatest health hazard." This was in part due to the fact that so many of the foundries were old and lax in their observation of safety and health precautions. Pressed by the demands of war for increased production, many plants pressed workers to work overtime, in very crowded and unsanitary conditions.[11] By the end of the war when business had declared silicosis to be of little significance, the Navy still listed foundry workers and sandblasters as

[9] Humphrey & Humphrey to Robert Downs, September 24, 1947, Vorwald Collection, Box 27.

[10] The U.S. Maritime Commission had responsibility as liaison between the Navy and contract shipyards and sent inspectors, often trained by the U.S. Department of Labor.

[11] "Official Report of Proceedings before the Children's Bureau of the Department of Labor in the Matter of Proposed Finding and Order Relating to the Employment of Miners between 16 and 18 Years of Age in Occupations in the Building and Repairing of Ships Under the Fair Labor Standards Act of 1938," Washington, D.C., April 15, 1942, National Archives, Record Group 155, Records of the Wage and Hour and Public Contract Division, "Hazardous Occupation Order—16-17"; U.S. Navy–U.S. Maritime Commission–War Shipping Administration–Industrial Health and Safety Program, "Industrial Health Re-Survey of the Bethlehem Steel Company Shipbuilding Division (Fore River Yard), Quincy, Massachusetts, May 23, 24 and 25, 1945," National Archives, Record Group 178 (Maritime Commission) Production Division–Administration, Shipyard and Labor Relations Health and Safety Surveys, 1943–1945, Bethlehem Steel, Box 450; U.S. Navy–U.S. Maritime Commission–War Shipping Administration–Industrial Health and Safety Program, "Industrial Health Re-Survey of Cramp Shipbuilding Company, Philadelphia, Pennsylvania, February 14, 15 and 16, 1945," National Archives, Record Group 178, (Maritime Commission) Production Division–Administration, Shipyard and Labor Relations Health and Safety Surveys, 1943–1945, Box 450, Folder: Cramp Shipbuilding Co.

being in "occupations considered to be hazardous." The Navy recommended to its contractors in the private sector that all such workers have a chest x-ray every six months to uncover the disease.[12]

The Industrial Hygiene Foundation chose to ignore this information and, instead, played a crucial role in the postwar years in the demise of silicosis as a serious public health problem.[13] The most frequent complaint of the foundation's leaders was that doctors, pressed by the demands of workers and their families trying to meet the rigid criteria of state compensation systems, were too quick to equate breathing difficulties after a lifetime of work in a dusty trade with a diagnosis of silicosis. It was time to write silicosis's obituary. In a 1945 symposium on "accurate diagnosis of silicosis," sponsored by the foundation, Leroy U. Gardner, The Trudeau Foundation's director, apologized for devoting a session "to such a trite and hackneyed subject." But attention was necessary, he warned, because far too many doctors and technicians were still diagnosing silicosis when, in fact, few such diagnoses were appropriate.[14] Dr. O. A. Sander of the Industrial Hygiene Foundation's medical committee went even further, maintaining that the term *pneumoconiosis* should be redefined because it was "widely misunderstood" to imply pathology. Sander held that *pneumoconiosis* should simply mean "dust added to the lungs without any implication of fibrosis or disability."[15] Sander suggested that there were really very few deleterious dusts. Cotton dust, for example, was too often suspected of causing pneumoconiosis. He suggested that byssi-

[12] Ross T. McIntire (Surgeon General, U.S. Navy) to J. M. Geer, Factory Personnel Manager, Sears, Roebuck and Company, November 25, 1946, National Archives, Record Group 52, Records of the Bureau of Medicine, P2-4, Box 140.

[13] At the beginning of World War II, the Air Hygiene Foundation signaled to the rest of the public health and medical world that one way to deal with silicosis was simply to ignore it. Between 1937 and 1939 the foundation expanded its purview into other areas of occupational health and disease. But in 1940 Roger A. Hitchens, then the chairman of the board of trustees, explained that the foundation had suffered unavoidably with the reputation of being just a "silicosis institute." And in 1941 the foundation changed its name to Industrial Hygiene Foundation of America. See Air Hygiene Foundation of America, *Fifth Annual Meeting of Members* (Pittsburgh, Pa., November 12–13, 1940), 1–5; Industrial Hygiene Foundation of America, *Sixth Annual Meeting of Members* (Pittsburgh, Pa., November 12–13, 1941). See also John F. McMahon, "Progress Report for Week Ended June 29, 1940," Mellon Institute of Industrial Research, Carnegie Mellon University Archives, Papers of the Mellon Institute, Industrial Fellowship 259-6, in which McMahon reports that Dr. Meller and Dr. Lanza met at Lake Chautauqua, New York, "to discuss changes in the Foundation's research program for next year. It was felt that in view of world affairs and emergency production for defense, the Foundation should emphasize work of immediate, practical plant benefit."

[14] Leroy U. Gardner, "Accurate Diagnosis of Silicosis—Possible Sources of Error," in Industrial Hygiene Foundation, *Transactions, Medical and Engineering Session, 10th Annual Meeting* (November 14–15, 1945; Pittsburgh, Pa., 1946), 10–12.

[15] O. A. Sander, "Discussion," in Industrial Hygiene Foundation, *Transactions, Medical and Engineering Session, 10th Annual Meeting* (November 14–15, 1945; Pittsburgh, Pa., 1946), 21–23.

nosis, due to cotton fiber exposure, was really nothing more than "an allergic response resulting in typical asthma, without any demonstrable lung pathology." He mentioned this "only to show how easy it is to be misled in the pneumoconiosis field."[16] Gardner noted that radiologists were still using x-ray evidence alone as a basis for diagnosing the disease and that doctors were using this evidence in conjunction with workers' statements about their work history to diagnose disease. For Gardner, neither was adequate to legitimate a diagnosis. It was essential to have, in addition, "the details of the occupational history that will indicate whether the dust contained significant quantities of free silica." There were too many other causes that could produce suspicious x-ray films and even labored breathing to lay the blame for the condition on silica dust produced in the plant.[17]

Theodore Hatch of the Industrial Hygiene Foundation was more explicit. In a paper for the Radiological Society of North America in 1947, Hatch took issue with the adequacy of the diagnostic tools used by physicians to define the condition, denouncing the crudeness of medical criteria for defining the disease. Hatch maintained that both x-rays and occupational histories generally exaggerated the true extent of silicosis in the United States. The x-ray was inadequate because "certain types of dusts, like iron oxide, produce x-ray shadows simulating silicosis." Furthermore, the dependence of clinicians on occupational histories was suspect. Hatch warned that the work history could be misleading without a plethora of information about exposure levels, which was generally unavailable. A worker in a foundry, for example, might have been employed in a shake-out where dust levels were extremely high or low. Without exact quantitative data on the levels of dust in any particular plant, a work history, according to Hatch, "provides very little meaningful information."[18] In the absence of tools sensitive enough to adequately measure the seriousness of dust exposures, the clinician could not diagnose the disease. A logical conclusion was that if the disease could not be diagnosed scientifically, it might not exist.[19] In the postwar period, the Industrial Hygiene Foundation

[16] O. A. Sander, "The Pneumoconioses," *Industrial Medicine* 15 (September 1946): 528.

[17] Leroy U. Gardner, "Accurate Diagnosis of Silicosis—Possible Sources of Error," in Industrial Hygiene Foundation, *Transactions, Medical and Engineering Session, 10th Annual Meeting* (November 14–15, 1945; Pittsburgh, Pa., 1946), 10–12.

[18] Theodore F. Hatch, "Significance of Occupational History in Diagnosis of Silicosis," *Radiology* 50 (June 1948): 747. See also L. E. Hamlin, "Some Thoughts on Silicosis," *Industrial Hygiene Newsletter* 8 (February 1948): 5, which says that "as more unrelated conditions whose x-ray appearances closely simulate silicosis, the unreliability of the roentgenogram alone as a diagnostic becomes obvious and accurate interpretation becomes difficult. A situation of this kind points out the necessity of accumulating factual data on exposure through industrial hygiene surveys."

[19] Representatives of Union Carbide reinforced these experts' suspicions, documenting inaccurate diagnoses of silicosis in their industry. A. G. Cranch, "Accurate Diagnosis of Silicosis—Some Examples of Error," and L. E. Hamlin, "Accurate Diagnosis of Silicosis—Atypical Nod-

and its scientific committees sought to forge a consensus that silicosis was a dead issue. By 1948, when Joe Koloedny wrote his letters, eminent researchers were apologizing "for bringing up such a shopworn, dusty topic."[20]

The Industrial Hygiene Foundation represented the interests of a small, elite group of engineering, public health, and medical personnel who were seeking to promote specialization in the fields of occupational medicine, pulmonary disease, and industrial hygiene. But these fields still depended upon the thousands of local practitioners who through their private practices served the hundreds of thousands of workers in the dusty trades. These physicians had formed their opinions regarding silicosis in the 1930s, when labor activists and public health and labor department officials as well as specialists were part of a public debate about the nature and cause of the disease and who therefore believed that silicosis represented a serious threat to workers, families, and communities. Therefore, the foundation's experts embarked on a campaign both to inform family doctors of the complexity of diagnosis and to warn them against attempting any diagnosis on their own. The foundation maintained that suspected silicosis cases should be referred to pulmonary specialists. Its spokespeople argued that local medical practitioners were incapable of employing the new technologies that could distinguish silicosis from "benign" pneumoconioses. Without the skills and training of these professionals, there was the continued danger that patients would be misdiagnosed, that workers' compensation boards would be overburdened, and that industries would be unjustly accused of negligence. O. A. Sander complained, for example, that "too many physicians still make a positive diagnosis when the x-ray reveals a nodular pattern and the history reveals past work in a foundry, at stone cutting, and other dusty trades." He concluded that "a doctor is not qualified to evaluate the nature and extent of the past dust exposure in all cases and must depend on industrial hygienists to give him this information."[21] Others reinforced this point. Citing a study of foundry workers, W.C.L. Hemeon, a ventilation engineer for the foundation, noted that measurements by an industrial hygienist were essential ingredients in discrediting the initial diagnosis of silicosis. Without air sampling, dust counts, and exact measurement data, medical diagnosis was of little value or, even worse, harmful to the reputation of

---

ulation in Foundry Grinders and Burners," both in Industrial Hygiene Foundation, *Transactions, Medical and Engineering Session, 10th Annual Meeting* (November 14–15, 1945; Pittsburgh, Pa., 1946), 13–18; See also, "Pneumoconiosis," *National Safety News* 51 (June 1945): 36–38, which quotes an AMA report and uses the term *benign pneumoconiosis*.

[20] L. E. Hamlin, "Some Thoughts on Silicosis," *Industrial Hygiene Newsletter*, 8 (February 1948): 5.

[21] O. A. Sander, "The Pneumoconioses," *Industrial Medicine* 15 (September 1946): 530. See also George F. Wright, "The Tasks and Responsibilities of the Medical Profession," Industrial Hygiene Foundation, *Joint Medical-Legal Conference, 16th Annual Meeting* (Pittsburgh, Pa.: 1951), 15.

industry. "How often does this situation occur in other industries with other dusts where there is a silicosis reputation?" he asked rhetorically.[22]

The drive to establish strict criteria for the diagnosis of silicosis was disingenuous at best. Even when silicosis was undeniably present, it was often impossible to reconstruct the victim's personal history. In the numerous case files of the Trudeau Foundation's records of victims of the pneumoconioses, there are relatively few that have other than the most cursory personal data. In one such case, a Finnish immigrant worked as a miner from 1908 until his death in 1947 at the age of sixty-one. As far as the pathologists at Saranac were concerned, this brief synopsis was all that was really necessary, and brevity appeared to be the rule rather than the exception: "It is impossible to furnish the exact nature and kind of dust these miners are exposed to other than ore, or rock. . . . Sorry the occupational histories are not so specific or complete, they are particularly sketchy in cases such as this, an old timer who speaks and understands little English." In this miner's case, however, Saranac had a series of x-rays going back to 1933 that confirmed a diagnosis of silicosis advancing from Stage 1 in 1933 to Stage 3 by 1936. The immediate cause of death was a cerebral hemorrhage, and the company escaped having to pay compensation. The head of the Trudeau field office at Ironwood, Michigan, wrote to the research director, "It looks as if they may win this one as death was apparently caused by cerebral hemorrhage. If successful, a good sum of money will be saved."[23] By 1949, silicosis had disappeared from public attention and workers and their families were robbed of their just compensation. While some former New Dealers argued that the locus of authority should reside with a better-educated group of community practitioners,[24] most who

---

[22] W.C.L. Hemeon, "Controlling Industrial Health Hazards," in Industrial Hygiene Foundation, *Transactions, Medical and Engineering Session, 10th Annual Meeting* (November 14–15, 1945; Pittsburgh, Pa., 1946), 29–30.

[23] Case Files, Vorwald Collection, P-48-428, Box 127.

[24] It is not that everyone immediately accepted the model that the foundation developed; in fact, some argued that local practitioners were *under*diagnosing silicosis. Some members of the old New Deal coalition suggested that the new emphasis on putting more power in the hands of specialists was misplaced. Mary Donlon, the chair of the New York State Workmen's Compensation Board, agreed that it *was* difficult to establish disability claims "short of obvious total disability." It was necessary to rely on two criteria: work history and the x-ray. She argued that the neighborhood physicians often lacked the "informed curiosity that would seek promptly the complete history of the patient's occupational exposures." But, rather than abandon community practitioners, she held that they should be educated in better methods of diagnosing occupational disease and should be provided with the tools to do so. It was the medical profession that was responsible for maintaining the integrity of the workers' compensation system; local practitioners, with their roots in communities and their daily experience with a large, diverse patient population, were the core of that profession. For Donlon, workers' compensation for disease, a direct outgrowth of the New Deal, was an essential element in establishing justice in labor-management relations. See Mary Donlon, "Compensation Aspects of the Pneumoconioses," *New York State Journal of Medicine* 49 (April 1, 1949): 833–35. She concluded her relatively technical article

spoke widely on the subject agreed that the local practitioners were unreliable because they were prone to see occupational disease even where it did not exist. In an article published in the *Journal of the American Medical Association* at the end of 1949, George W. Wright argued for a reevaluation of traditional medical methods for evaluating health and illness. Historically, he wrote, physicians sought to determine if a patient had suffered decreased capacity in their everyday life. Disease and disability were measured against the patient's earlier abilities, and the doctor's responsibility was to restore the patient as far as possible to full health.

By the 1940s, silicosis was incorporated into almost all the state workers' compensation systems. But, instead of resolution of the contention over the disease, new tensions arose, centered on the medical practitioners' diagnosis of the disease. The recent experience with silicosis and the workers' compensation system that had grown up around it had changed the physician's traditional responsibilities. The compensation system now defined disability "in terms of lack of ability to earn wages and not in terms of a diminution of capacity to breath or exercise." Wright pointed out that physicians should no longer think, "as one usually does in terms of loss of ability." Rather a new emphasis should be placed on the evaluation of a worker's ability to earn a living: "It would be helpful if the usual approach to problems of health could be changed by deemphasizing the question whether or not the man has suffered an injury, and directing attention to determining whether or not the claimant still possesses sufficient physical capacity to earn wages as stipulated under the compensation act."

There were two problems that the medical community faced. First, was there an impairment? Second, was the cause rooted in work? Wright argued that evaluation of an impairment was an extremely difficult and highly technical issue. "In evaluating the competency of a man to earn wages there is considerable danger of drawing unwarranted conclusions from laboratory data, physical signs and the history," Wright pointed out. In light of the fact that patients' own subjective evaluations of their condition were unreliable and motivated by "frank malingering," physicians had to rely on their own experience and interpretation of the data. Furthermore, the data itself were highly suspect. He complained that an x-ray showing "an anatomic alteration of the lungs or heart is still commonly used as evidence that these organs must of necessity be functioning abnormally . . . and the extent of the anatomic change is frequently considered an index of the degree of functional impairment." But, Wright argued, repeated experiments had shown that there was little correlation between the clinical evidence and measurements of the pa-

---

with a statement that put the workers' compensation system within the context of the cold war: "Political choice between free enterprise and state control is seldom made on a historical battlefield. It is made from day to day in the people's estimate of the effectiveness with which freedom functions."

tient's capacity to do work. Reversing the consensus developed in the late 1930s, which defined silicosis in terms of x-ray evidence and history, Wright argued that only functional impairment could be used in diagnosing silicosis: "The careful observer should always seek direct evidences of functional damage rather than rely on inferences which are obtained from evidences of anatomic alteration."[25]

The second issue—was the condition related to the individual's work?—was equally troubling. Wright pointed out that lung diseases were common throughout the general population and that employment in a dusty trade did not give the worker "an immunity to diseases of a nonindustrial origin." Workers may develop tuberculosis or emphysema, or even fibrosis of the lung for reasons totally unrelated to conditions on the job. Wright argued that local physicians were all too ready to diagnose the disabilities of workers in mining, foundries, quarries, and potteries as work related without sufficient evidence: "Several diseases of a nonindustrial origin are especially prone to mimic the symptomatology of industrial pulmonary disease and also to lead to physiologic alterations that cause an incompetency to earn wages." He decried the lack of data on the incidence of pulmonary disease generally and among the industrial work force in particular. Without such data it was impossible to reach a reasoned judgement regarding the severity of pneumoconiosis as a disease of industry.

For Wright, the problem was that local physicians all across the country had been alerted to the prevalence of silicosis as an occupational hazard. But there was "a grave danger," Wright warned, that these "physicians may be inclined to ascribe all the pulmonary ailments of men who have been exposed to dust or fumes to the inhalation of those foreign substances." These local physicians had tremendous power, he argued. They could declare "that a man is or is not physically competent to carry on a job." Wright pointed out that these doctors generally knew little or nothing about industrial plants, most never having stepped inside one. It was far better, Wright argued, to depend upon the testimony of "the experienced plant physician."[26] Unlike those who saw the private practitioner as the center of the new system for identifying and diagnosing industrial disease, Wright called for more control by industrial physicians and industrial hygienists.

Wright's arguments (and those of others in the Industrial Hygiene Foundation) regarding the need for greater and greater amounts of quantifiable, measurable, scientific information in making accurate diagnoses resonated with the beliefs of the medical community in the late 1940s and 1950s. The use of antibiotic therapy, antipsychotic drug therapy, and, most significantly, the

[25] George W. Wright, "Disability Evaluation in Industrial Pulmonary Disease," *JAMA* 141 (December 24, 1949): 1218–22.
[26] Wright, "Disability Evaluation," 1218–22.

Salk and Sabin polio vaccines had given tremendous legitimacy and power to the long-standing belief in the potential of a truly scientific medicine based upon the laboratory, technology, and objective criteria for evaluating illness.[27] Less and less emphasis was placed upon the clinician's apparently subjective evaluation of evidence provided by patients, whose own statements regarding their own health and history were seen as subjective and, ultimately, suspicious sources. The positions of significant portions of the medical community reinforced the opinion that the significance of silicosis, a disease that had appeared to threaten large portions of the American work force only ten years before, was grossly overestimated.

Technology and the Changing Picture of Disease

The shifting epidemiology of tuberculosis during the twentieth century and especially after World War II greatly affected the medical community's views on the seriousness of silicosis. Most significantly, the link between silicosis and the life-threatening nature of the opportunistic tuberculosis infection was fundamentally altered by the development of antibiotic treatments for tuberculosis in the 1930s and 1940s. Experiments with sulfanilamide and diamino-diphenyl-sulfone in the 1930s had shown that the tuberculosis bacilli was effectively controlled in guinea pigs. "Although these two drugs proved useless in the treatment of human tuberculosis," the experiments stimulated the long-standing search for other antimicrobial agents.[28] In the fall of 1944, studies of the efficacy of streptomycin in human tuberculosis were begun, with initial results confirming the ability of the antibiotic to suppress symptoms. But longer-term treatment with streptomycin revealed that the palliative impact was mitigated by the development of resistance in the patient. In 1947, it was concluded by the Committee on Chemotherapy of the American College of Chest Physicians that "streptomycin is *not* an overnight cure-all for the different types of tuberculosis in humans" but that it might very well have a "place in our armamentarium against this disease."[29] By the early 1950s, the use of streptomycin, para-amino-salicylic acid (PAS), and later isoniazid (INH),

[27] See Harry F. Dowling, *Fighting Infection* (Cambridge: Harvard University Press, 1977), ch. 11, and Rosemary Stevens, *American Medicine and the Public Interest* (New Haven: Yale University Press, 1971), for detailed discussions of medical research and government policy during the postwar era.

[28] Rene Dubos and Jean Dubos, *The White Plague, Tuberculosis, Man, and Society*, with introduction by Barbara Rosenkrantz (1952; reprint, New Brunswick: Rutgers University Press, 1987), 154.

[29] "Report on Streptomycin in Tuberculosis by The Committee on Chemotherapy," *Diseases of the Chest* 13 (March 1947): 169–70.

while still suffering serious drawbacks with regard to resistance, was becoming standard in the treatment of the disease.[30]

Throughout the twentieth century, death rates from tuberculosis had steadily declined, going from about 20 per 10,000 in 1900 to less than 3 per 10,000 in 1950. Until the end of World War II, the decline in mortality rates paralleled the decline in new cases of the disease. However, following the war, one study of New York City found that deaths from tuberculosis declined substantially although new cases of the disease remained relatively constant. Significantly, the decrease in relative mortality "coincided with the introduction of streptomycin" and other antimicrobial agents.[31] The introduction of the antibiotics was met with a rush of excitement on the part of the general public and the medical profession, as well with newspaper articles about "miracle" drugs for the treatment of tuberculosis. Although some were wary of the enthusiasm over the antibiotics, most clinicians and the public as well saw the long search for a "magic bullet" finally paying off. It appeared that while tuberculosis still remained an important disease in the 1950s, death resulting from it could be postponed and even avoided with medical intervention.[32] With the general decline in mortality from tuberculosis and the introduction of specific antibiotics for its treatment, the aspect of silicosis that had been of greatest concern to the medical community suddenly ceased to cause alarm. Silico-tuberculosis, while still severely disabling, was no longer viewed by physicians as a life-threatening disease.

The decline in tuberculosis rates among all Americans was paralleled within the industrial work force. Louis Dublin documented that the life expectancy of American workers insured by Metropolitan Life had risen 11.5 years between 1911 and 1949. He particularly noted that the reduction in mortality from respiratory diseases had played a major role in this improvement: "Spectacular has been the decline in the death rate from tuberculosis in this period— from 433.5 per 100,000 to 42.3, a drop of more than 90 percent." He acknowledged that improvements in plant hygiene and safety practices accounted for much of the gain. But he believed that other factors "may have been even more important." He based this assessment on the fact that the mortality rate for "the wives and sisters of the male policy holders, who have the same home environment but who are not exposed to serious industrial

[30] Dubos and Dubos, *White Plague*, 155.

[31] Harry F. Dowling, *Fighting Infection* (Cambridge: Harvard University Press, 1977), 236–37; and Abram S. Benenson, *Control of Communicable Diseases in Man*, 11th ed. (Washington, D.C.: American Public Health Association, 1970), 267–68.

[32] Dubos and Dubos, *White Plague*, 157. Dubos and Dubos were very skeptical about the efficacy of these antibiotics, writing that the " 'miracle' drug which made for such exciting headlines and photographs, in the press of mid-February 1952, will probably be regarded as just another treatment when re-evaluated in the light of experienced judgement."

hazards has declined faster than the rate for males."[33] This indicated that industrial conditions were still producing disease and that this disease was causing excessive mortality for the industrial work force.

Dublin's point was largely ignored. Even before the antibiotics were used to improve the prospects of tubercular patients, silicosis itself was thought to be yielding to another magic bullet. In 1936, investigators at Ontario's Mc-Intyre-Porcupine Gold Mines maintained that a small amount of aluminum powder could protect against the deleterious effects of silica dust. In 1937, the same doctors reported that inhalation of fine aluminum dust prevented the development of silicosis in guinea pigs. Follow-up studies in which silicotic miners in Ontario and then in Pennsylvania inhaled aluminum dust concluded that such daily treatments alleviated symptoms. In the United States, the Air Hygiene Foundation pounced on the Canadian reports. John McMahon, a head administrator, quickly contacted the Canadians suggesting that the foundation "serve as an instrument for building industrial goodwill," specifically by providing a forum for this work at the November meeting.[34] Two months later, in July 1939, McMahon traveled to New Kensington to discuss with officials of the Aluminum Company's research executive staff the possibility of the foundation's serving as the "United States representative for granting licenses to industrial concerns on the patent held by Canadian scientists covering their process for combatting silicosis with aluminum powder."[35]

Only a month earlier, an article appeared in *Collier's*, entitled "Dust Fights Dust," that hailed aluminum therapy as spelling the end of the silicosis hazard: "It looks as if before long there shouldn't be any more new cases of silicosis . . . no more at all. All that is needed is a good supply of aluminum dust and the proper equipment to disperse it."[36] Popular attention to the new treatment paralleled medical and scientific opinion that aluminum inhalation therapy was a potential magic bullet in the fight against this disease. Holding out the prospect of a relatively simple therapy, aluminum therapy reinforced clinicians' reductionist view of silicosis as a treatable, if not curable, condition. Anthony Lanza himself was greatly impressed by the possibilities of aluminum therapy, noting that upon his visit to the Porcupine clinic, he had observed that "there is no question but that a number of the silicotic employees who had undergone this treatment experienced considerable relief of their symptoms." Although

[33] Louis Dublin and Robert J. Vane, "Longevity of the Industrial Worker," *American Journal of Public Health* 41 (June 1951): 700–701.

[34] Air Hygiene Foundation, "Progress Report for the Week Ended May 27, 1939," Mellon Institute Archives, Carnegie-Mellon University.

[35] Air Hygiene Foundation, "Progress Report." See also Executive Committee of the Porcupine Clinic for Silicosis Research to H. K. Sherry, Vice-President, Canadian Johns-Manville Co. Limited, Sept. 7, 1943, Vorwald Collection, Box 2, for further discussion of the attempt to get institutional financial support for research and distribution of information.

[36] Hannah Lees, "Dust Fights Dust," *Collier's* 103 (June 3, 1939): 56; see also "Hope for Silicotics," *Time* 44 (July 10, 1944): 90.

he qualified his enthusiasm by pointing out that not everyone benefited from the treatment, he concluded that "only time will give us a final answer" as to the therapy's efficacy.[37]

Leroy U. Gardner was also an enthusiast of aluminum treatments, although he questioned whether it was effective as a true cure for the disease. He maintained that aluminum was an effective preventive measure but that its use as a cure was largely "psychological" in that it raised the morale of silicotic workers.[38] And other scientists associated with the Air Hygiene Foundation lined up in support of aluminum therapy. In 1940, the Ontario Mining Association asked the foundation to serve as the U.S. licensing agent. While the foundation hesitated in light of the absence of definitive proof of aluminum's efficacy, it continued to help publicize and popularize the notion that aluminum dust could prove an effective preventative.[39] By the end of the war, the foundation had sought to study the practicality of adding amorphous aluminum hydrate to mold-dusting compounds as an alternative to installing expensive exhaust ventilation equipment in foundries.[40] Despite continuing skepticism among researchers regarding the efficacy of such treatments, the reports of aluminum therapy reinforced prevalent medical opinion that silicosis was similar to other diseases for which specific treatment could be developed.[41]

[37] A. J. Lanza, "Recent Developments in Pneumoconiosis," *Journal of the Missouri State Medical Association* 42 (December 1945): 768–69.

[38] L. U. Gardner and George Wright, "Disability in Silicosis," Industrial Hygiene Foundation of America, *Eighth Annual Meeting of Members* (November 10–11, 1943), 49–50; "A New Treatment for Silicosis" *Science* 92 (October 18, 1940): 10. See also the posthumous quotation from Leroy U. Gardner that "against free silica, aluminum dust inhalation offers good prospects of prophylaxis," in Peter W. Edwards, "Aluminum Therapy and Prophylaxis for Silicosis," *Silicosis Pneumoconiosis and Dust Suppression in Mines* (London: Salisbury House, 1947), 99. Despite public affirmation of the importance of aluminum, the researchers at the Trudeau Foundation at Saranac Lake continued to be uncertain and confused about the effectiveness of aluminum in treating silicotic patients or preventing disease. See Arthur J. Vorwald, Director of Research, Trudeau Foundation, to Ernest W. Brown, December 2, 1948, Vorwald Collection, Box 2.

[39] Air Hygiene Foundation, "Progress Report."

[40] Air Hygiene Foundation, "Progress Report." "It is planned to study the use of aluminum in rendering mold dusting compounds innocuous. The control of this hazard by exhaust ventilation would require a very great expenditure."

[41] For more modern efforts to evaluate the efficacy of aluminum treatments, see Murray Finkelstein, "A Review of Aluminum Prophylaxis against Silicosis," *Occupational Health in Ontario*, 1 (April 1980): 22–26, who concludes that the treatment is not effective; and Howard L. Hartman, *Mine Ventilation and Air Conditioning*, 2d ed. (New York: John Wiley and Sons, 1982), 125–26, who states: "The AMA continues to follow a wait-and-see policy, withholding a final verdict until ample medical substantiation is furnished. There is still some question of the toxicity of the aluminum dust." See also E. J. King, S. C. Ray, and C. V. Harrison, "Inhibitory Action of Aluminum on Quartz in Experimental Silicosis," in International Labour Organization, *Third International Conference of Experts on Pneumoconiosis, Record of Proceedings*, vol. 2 (Sydney, February–March, 1950; Geneva: International Labour Office, 1953), 140–45.

The work force was not immune to the enormous growth in the prestige of medical science or to the propaganda that accompanied self-proclaimed "cures" for silicosis. Such faith in the ability of medicine to treat or even come up with a cure for silicosis was reflected in the pages of the *International Molders and Foundry Workers Journal*. For three years during and after the war, articles appeared in its pages hailing the discovery of aluminum therapy. In November 1944, a representative of an Ohio local wrote that "it is a great comfort and relief to know that a preventative for silicosis, the most dreaded disease of the foundry, has been discovered and is now available under certain conditions to our foundry industry." The *Journal* carried a report of the treatment from the experimental laboratory in Ontario and a firsthand account of the treatment from a union member who had traveled to Washington, Pennsylvania, to undergo it.[42] Many workers accepted the general medico-business consensus because they believed that science had achieved unanimity regarding the nature of the disease, its biochemistry, and its physiological mechanisms. If experts agreed that silicosis was a disease of the past, then surely it was understood by the experts.

The authority of experts was reinforced by the use of the x-ray, dust-sampling technologies, and highly technical statistical studies that were inaccessible to the general public and that had an aura of scientific accuracy and political neutrality. Historically, the x-ray symbolized the esoteric and almost magical powers of specialists in medicine to see into the body and diagnose disease, and enumeration and statistical analysis were part and parcel of scientific discourse. Science, expertise, professionalism, and technical sophistication legitimated the dominance of public health, medicine, and engineering. The establishment of standards for the amount of dust in the air constituted a concrete symbol of this power. The rising professions of occupational medicine and industrial hygiene gained authority because of the highly technical problem of measurement. This reinforced the growing dependence on experts to define objective criteria for judging physiological response to silica dust. By 1950, nearly everyone had fallen into line behind the common view that silicosis was a disease of the past—that by adhering to strict voluntary standards, industry had reduced dust levels to "safe" limits that posed a negligible risk to the work force.

A review of articles listed in *Index Medicus* for the period 1929–1964 con-

[42] See Eldred E. Crizer, "Preventative for Silicosis," *International Molders' and Foundry Workers' Journal* 80 (November 1944): 590; W. D. Robson, "Silicosis: What It Is and How It Can Be Prevented," *International Molders' and Foundry Workers' Journal* 81 (August 1945): 403–06; John F. Metcalf, "How Fight Silicosis?" *International Molders' and Foundry Workers' Journal* 81 (September 1945): 480–81; John A. Bolton, "Aluminum Dust Therapy Fights Silicosis in Canada," *International Molders' and Foundry Workers' Journal* 81 (October 1945): 538; John Metcalf, "Meeting the Silicosis Problem," *International Molders' and Foundry Workers' Journal* 83 (November 1947): 655.

firms that the American medical community accepted this view of industrial lung disease (see Table 2). The number of articles published worldwide on the pneumoconioses rose during the Depression, tapered off during World War II, and then rose dramatically during the late 1950s and early 1960s with the growing attention to coal workers' pneumoconiosis and asbestos-related disease. In the United States a similar pattern prevailed during the Depression but diverged dramatically after World War II. While the number of articles on the pneumoconioses published worldwide expanded, the percentage in American journals declined from 37.3 percent of all articles during 1933–1936 to only 13.2 percent by 1961–1964. The absolute number of articles on the pneumoconioses also steeply declined, from over 50 per year during 1933–1936 to only 31 per year by 1957–1960. Only growing attention to asbestos-related disease and coal workers' pneumoconiosis seems to have reversed this declining interest.

Similarly, the average number of American journal articles on silicosis specifically declined from a Depression-era high of 35.25 per year during 1937–1940 to a mere 9 per year during 1953–1956. Furthermore, the small number of articles on silicosis in the journals of the 1950s were in specialty journals, rather than regional and local medical journals commonly read by local

TABLE 2

Articles on Silicosis and Other Pneumoconioses Published in
Selected Years, 1929–1964

	Pneumo- coniosis Articles Worldwide	Pneumoconiosis Articles in U.S. Journals		Silicosis Articles in U.S. Journals		
	Average No. per Year	Average No. per Year	% of All Articles	Average No. per Year	% of All U.S. Pneumo- coniosis Articles	Average No. Published in Local Journals
1929–1932	80.5	19	23.6	7.25	38.2	3.75
1933–1936	135.5	50.5	37.3	31.5	62.4	11.25
1937–1940	136.25	48.25	35.4	35.25	73.1	7.5
1941–1944	81.75	25.25	30.9	16	63.4	8.0
1945–1948	113.5	26.25	23.1	14.75	56.2	4.5
1949–1952	128	21.25	16.6	9.75	45.9	4.75
1953–1956	159	28.75	18.3	9.00	31.3	1.75
1957–1960	262.3	31	11.8	9.66	31.2	1.0
1961–1964	341.25	45.75	13.2	16	34.8	0.75

Source: *Index Medicus*, 1929–1964.

Note: The numbers and percentages for 1957–1960 and 1961–1964 reflect the growing attention to asbestosis and coal workers' Pneumoconiosis.

practitioners. In 1933–1936, for example, over 11 percent of articles on silicosis were in local journals. By 1961–1964, less than 1 percent were in these local organs. One might conclude that local practitioners, who made up the bulk of the readership of local medical society journals, were no longer exposed to reports about silicosis in their regions and that the condition became the preserve of a specialty group. This movement away from the generalists and toward specialization is reflected in the subject matter of the articles as well. During the 1930s, the articles were descriptive and therefore accessible to the generalists. By the 1950s, the articles were more technical, appealing to specialists in the emerging fields of pulmonary and thoracic medicine.

But a little-noted Bureau of Mines review of the scientific literature in 1950 questioned every basic assumption that lent legitimacy to this benign view of silicosis and the other pneumoconioses. The review concluded that the optimistic dismissal of the condition was unwarranted. Although the exact number of workers suffering from silicosis could not be known, silicosis was still "a widespread industrial hazard which probably is increasing and affects appreciably the death rate among industrial workers exposed." The Bureau of Mines investigators took particular umbrage at the idea that a "standard" could or had been established that guaranteed safety for workers.

While the Industrial Hygiene Foundation, industrial hygienists, workers' compensation boards, and others had readily accepted that a maximal allowable limit on dust particles in the air would protect the work force, the Bureau of Mines investigators pointed out that the standards were arbitrary at best, and terribly misleading. While there was no national law that codified a particular standard, states, localities, industry hygienists, and workers' compensation statutes had by and large adopted a simple formula: Air that contained less than 5–10 million particles per cubic foot of air of dust that measured more than 10 microns was assumed to be "safe." Larger dust particles, of more than 10 microns, were generally assumed to be "safe" since it was believed that the nasal passages, mucous membranes, and other protective mechanisms of the nose, throat, and lungs captured and removed them. This assumption was based upon autopsy evidence that showed that silicotic lungs rarely contained larger particles. The Bureau of Mines investigators suggested that even this apparently empirically valid observation was based upon half-truths and ignorance rather than fact and knowledge. They pointed out that if the protective mechanisms of the nose, throat, and lungs were clogged by overexposure to large particles, this would permit "virtually free, unobstructed entrance of the so-called harmful dusts (say, .2 to 10 micron sizes) into the lungs to perform maximum injury."

These authors further questioned the validity of the air samples taken, pointing out that even the most careful technicians rarely could duplicate their own results: "The technique of determining quantity of dust particles in air is by no means definite, accurate, fair, or dependable, not only as regards conditions between different plants but between different time periods in the same place in any one plant." As a result of these problems, the Bureau of Mines authors concluded that "the attempt to embody in laws and regulations having the force of law rigid standards as to air dustiness would seem to be a travesty of justice."

For these investigators, the assumptions of standard setting were bad, the theory was inadequate, and even the technology upon which measurement was based was greatly flawed. But even more was wrong with the entire thrust of standard setting as it had evolved in the 1930s and 1940s. There was little place for taking into account the wide range of variables that affected the health of individual workers. They agreed that the longer a worker was exposed to dangerous dusts, the greater the risk. But they objected to the corollary that short exposures were safe. Further, they also questioned the assumption that the percentage of pure silica in the air determined toxicity:

> No one knows whether a dust of 1 percent silica is or is not more harmful than a dust of 2 or 3 percent or even of 30 percent. Moreover, air with a certain number of dust particles per cubic foot with a silica content of 1 percent (or any other percentage) probably would be far more harmful to a person working on a contract basis than to one on a day-pay basis, or more harmful to a person working in an atmosphere of 85 [degrees] or 90 [degrees] F., relative humidity 90 or 95 percent, than to one working in an atmosphere of 60 degree F., relative humidity 60 percent.

The innumerable variables that determined danger were not translatable into a simple numerical formula. Such a formula was merely a cover for the inability of the tools of science and technology to answer complex questions regarding the cause, nature, and treatment of chronic industrial diseases. The new "science" of standard setting did little to clarify but did a great deal to obscure:

> So numerous and far reaching are these uncertainties that almost the only definite fact is that dust is a menace and that all kinds of it likely to come in contact with human beings should be reduced to a minimum or at least be held under positive control until much well-planned, well-correlated research and investigation (field and laboratory) have been conducted on almost every phase of the subject.

The study recognized the importance of x-ray evidence in diagnosing the disease, but cautioned that "the x-ray in itself appears to be anything but reliable in the definite determination of the disease."[43] The Bureau of Mines study echoed long-standing questions concerning the x-ray's use in distinguishing

---

[43] J. J. Forbes, Sara J. Davenport, and Genevieve G. Morgis, *Review of Literature on Dusts*, U.S. Department of Interior, Bureau of Mines, *Bulletin No. 478* (Washington, D.C.: Government Printing Office, 1950), 1–15.

silicosis and tuberculosis. At best, all the x-ray did was show a mass on the lung, and the lack of adequate standards in the manufacture of x-ray equipment, clinical use of that equipment, and development of films brought into question its efficacy. Different manufacturers developed machines with differing capacities, and "slight changes in temperature, in chemical composition of developing and fusing fluids" could "alter the character of shadows." Furthermore, variations in the size, shape, and musculature of the individual made any standard x-ray criteria for the diagnosis even "more confused." An even more significant problem lay with the training of diagnosticians and their own working conditions: light intensity, length of the workday, and attention to detail could also confound the meaning of any x-ray interpretation. There was no "standard" for use of the machinery and, therefore, no standard for the diagnosis of the disease.[44] While the experts' views were trumpeted in popular magazines, business periodicals, and labor journals, this troubling document from the Bureau of Mines, the most comprehensive review of the literature compiled to that point, received virtually no attention and no publicity.

While the medical and scientific communities continued to ignore the health hazards posed by silica exposure, one union, the International Union of Mine, Mill and Smelter Workers, conducted a successful campaign to bring the silicosis problem to national attention again. Despite the fact that the union was under political attack for its officers' refusal to sign the anti-Communist affidavit of the Taft-Hartley Act of 1947, it was able to mount a legislative campaign in Congress and a number of Western mining states. Whereas in the 1930s, labor could force the New Deal administration in Washington and a variety of industrial states to place the silicosis issue on the national agenda, by the 1950s, this politically isolated union found itself fighting alone.[45] In 1949, despite industry and professional assurances that engineering innovations had solved the dust problem, the union noted that regulations regarding silica dust "were criminally lax in most states." The technology might exist, but the union doubted that the widely scattered mines in the highly competitive industry were initiating reforms. In an article illustrated with a drawing of a miner doubled over and coughing into his hands, the union pointed out, "Silicosis, or 'miners' con,' is The Great Killer in the hard rock mining industry. It comes near to being 'the root of all evil' for those exposed to silica dust, because other maladies flow from it."[46]

[44] Dr. Jones to Starr, "Preparation of a Standard Set of X-Ray Films," October 5, 1936, National Archives, Record Group 100, Department of Labor, Division of Labor Standards General Files.

[45] See, for example, "Statement of Policy and Program," *Mine-Mill Union*, August 12, 1946, 2; "Ask Public Health Aid for Tri-State," *Mine-Mill Union*, November 10, 1947, 9; "Pointers on Tuberculosis," *Mine-Mill Union*, January 31, 1949, 11.

[46] Eugene Hartman, "Silicosis," *Mine-Mill Union*, March 14, 1949, 9.

Even though tuberculosis was on the decline, the union maintained that silicosis was an even greater hazard because of its role in promoting new chronic degenerative diseases. Specifically, it held that the recent rise in heart disease among miners was due to silica's role in damaging the circulatory system. The union took issue with the narrow interpretation of the silicosis problem promulgated by the medical community: "In evaluating how serious a silica dust hazard is in a place, one must not only look at the silicosis records alone, but also the excessive TB rate, deaths from heart disease, etc." The medical model had obscured, rather than illuminated, the role of dust in creating many of the more modern scourges then emerging as issues of general medical and popular interest.[47]

From the union's perspective, industry had also undermined medical and engineering advances in controlling the problem by establishing standards that were too lax. The union took specific issue with the development of minimal exposure levels for miners. It noted that even the director of the Industrial Hygiene Foundation had admitted that "we find silicosis where, according to present standards, it should be impossible to develop." The union was also aghast at the manner by which standards were developed. It pointed out that in a context involving human life, standards were often established that reflected industry needs rather than the needs of the work force. Rather than establishing exposure levels that would guarantee protection for all workers irrespective of age, years on the job, or previous health record, management had pushed for standards that protected only those workers least likely to be affected by dusty air. The union contrasted the establishment of standards for human exposure to known disease producing agents with standards established for constructing bridges or buildings. In the former, the highest allowable limits would protect the portion of the work force at lowest risk. In the latter, "the engineers do not use the maximum strength of steel and other building materials in their calculations . . . they design a bridge to bear a maximum load of only 1/3 or 1/5 of what they know it should hold." Underlying the lax standards was the greed of the corporations. In addition to urging the end of the speed-up and increased mechanization, the union called for a five-day, seven-hour workweek with no reduction in pay to lessen exposure to silica: "Such precautions may cut down on production somewhat, but it will mean much less silicosis. And surely human lives are worth much more than corporation profits."[48] During the New Deal, the union's efforts in the Tri-State had an impact on the scientific and medical discussion regarding industrial chronic disease. But in the new postwar era, the union recognized that it could have only a negligible impact on the professional debate and shifted its focus to the legislative arena.

[47] Hartman, "Silicosis," 9.
[48] "Silicosis," *Mine-Mill Union*, March 28, 1949, 11.

The union's legislative program emphasized the need for stricter standards, better regulation, a national program to enforce standards in the nation's mines, and the establishment of health insurance and care for its victims.[49] The International Union of Mine, Mill and Smelter Workers became very active in promoting reform at both the local and national levels. In 1949, after a prolonged fight in Idaho, a union-backed compensation bill was passed that included silicosis as a compensable disease. After Governor C. A. Robbins vetoed the bill, the union quickly pointed out that the governor had long been "in bed" with mine owners of the state since he had once been a company doctor.[50]

Less than a year after this defeat, the union began a concerted drive to enact federal legislation to control the silica hazard. Bernard W. Stern,[51] the research director of the International Union of Mine, Mill and Smelter Workers, went to Washington to consult with sympathetic senators and congresspeople about the importance of beginning a campaign about silicosis and introducing legislation to deal with the problem. In a letter to Senator James E. Murray of Montana, the longtime supporter of progressive health and labor legislation, the union noted that there had not been "a comprehensive survey of the silicosis problem" since Frances Perkins had invited labor representatives to the National Silicosis Conference of 1936. He urged that the senator hold hearings on the need for federal legislation because of the "inability of most state governments to establish and enforce proper control and preventive regulations or to make adequate provision for the care of victims of silicosis and their families."[52]

By 1953, despite the union's political difficulties during the McCarthy period, it succeeded in pressing its case to the point where congresspeople were speaking on the House floor and introducing legislation to address the silicosis hazard. In July 1953, Lee Metcalf, representative from Montana, introduced House Resolution 286, addressing "a growing national health problem," silicosis. In a speech delivered in support of that resolution, Metcalf asserted that the disease was "not commonly diagnosed" and was not reportable or noted on death certificates.[53] In the next session of Congress, Metcalf introduced a

---

[49] "Silicosis," *Mine-Mill Union*, April 11, 1949, 11. See also "Silicosis," *Mine-Mill Union*, September 12, 1949, 17.

[50] "Idaho Silicosis Bill Killed by Veto," *Mine-Mill Union*, April 11, 1949, 12.

[51] Not to be confused with Bernhard J. Stern, the noted medical sociologist, who also wrote on silicosis in his book, *Medicine in Industry* (New York: The Commonwealth Fund, 1946), 61–62.

[52] Jack Clark, President, and Orville Larson, Vice President, International Union of Mine, Mill and Smelter Workers, to James E. Murray, June 1, 1950, Western Federation of Miners Manuscripts [International Union of Mine, Mill and Smelter Workers], Western Historical Collections, University of Colorado, Boulder, Box 199, F 21.

[53] "Speech by Congressman Lee Metcalf on the Floor of the House," Press Release, July 27, 1953, Western Federation of Miners Manuscripts [International Union of Mine, Mill and Smelter Workers], Western Historical Collections, University of Colorado, Boulder, Box 219-1.

stronger bill, patterned on the older Murray bill of 1939, that sought to provide funds for state labor departments to develop and enforce standards for the control of silicosis.

The union was vigorous in its support of the bill. In one article, Orville Larson, the International's vice president, pointed out that there was a "tragedy in the mines . . . you never read about in the papers." Most people thought about mine tragedies as being explosions, fires, and other disasters but, Larson warned, "there is another kind of tragedy we do have—a disease that kills more workers than these 'big catastrophes' do. I am talking about silicosis." He noted the discordance between medical and industry avoidance of the issue and workers' own recognition that they were slowly dying of disease: "It's a grim joke in mining camps that miners never die of silicosis. That's because silicosis brings on tuberculosis or heart failure, or some kind of infection. You will find these other diseases on the records but without the silicosis they wouldn't have occurred." He said that the Metcalf bill would not solve all the health problems for the miners but it was "a small but necessary step in the right direction. It deserves our fullest support."[54]

This was the beginning of a major national campaign to gain legislative relief for the health problems of hard rock miners, particularly those affected by silica dust. At the union's fiftieth annual convention in March 1955, a panel devoted to the problem of silicosis was attended by over 200 union representatives and some younger, progressive medical and public health experts. The major point of the panelists was that the union should begin an active, national campaign on behalf of the Metcalf bill in light of the fact that the industry, medical personnel, and government appeared to be engaged in a "conspiracy of silence" regarding "the true facts as to the extent and seriousness of the disease."[55] In an internal memorandum that evaluated the success of the panel, Herman Clott, the union's Washington representative, identified its real significance. First, the physician on the panel, Dr. Leon Lewis of San Francisco, was a needed antidote to the "confusion [regarding the disease] created by company doctors" who downplayed "the seriousness which this disease continues to be in our mining camps." "For the first time," Clott pointed out, "we finally had a medical man who could speak objectively and with deep knowledge in the field." Second, the success of the panel illustrated the importance of the issue to the rank and file of the union. But most important, the panel illustrated the need to take the issue beyond the talking stage and to

[54] Orville Larson, "Metcalf Bill Provides for Prevention, Compensation," *Mine-Mill Union*, February 28, 1955, 2. See also U.S. Congress, House, H.R. 2622, 84th cong., 1st sess., 1955, in Western Federation of Miners Manuscripts [International Union of Mine, Mill and Smelter Workers], Western Historical Collections, University of Colorado, Boulder, Box 324-18.

[55] "Silicosis Prevention Is a Problem in Engineering, Expert Tells Convention," *Mine-Mill Union*, April 11, 1955, 8. See also "Silicosis Panel Will Be Held during Convention," *Mine-Mill Union*, February 28, 1955, 3.

organize legislative efforts for federal intervention. The union decided that it was important to seek support for its movement from the United Mine Workers since this union had "a similar interest in silicosis in the anthracite field."[56]

The union carried on its campaign over the airwaves as well as through its newspaper. In a radio address produced by Local 18 of the union in Kellogg, Idaho, a union representative joined a nationally known safety expert to discuss the methods and politics of silicosis. Lewis, the San Francisco physician, rejected the idea that silicosis was a disease of the past and also attacked the x-ray as an adequate tool for its diagnosis. Taking issue with the predominant medical model that sought to develop objective, technical criteria for establishing the presence and extent of the disease, Lewis argued that the actual disease process was more complex and required functional tests and workers' input. The union representatives maintained that there were two principles that guided the union in its effort to eliminate "the dread disease." First, they reiterated labor's long-standing view that engineering, rather than medical control, was essential. Second, they objected to the still-prevalent system of state and local regulation of the worksite and called for "federal responsibility for handling the problem."[57] After the convention, the union intensified its lobbying efforts by pressing for congressional hearings to dramatize and publicize the need for national legislation and sought broader labor support for its activities. "What's next?" the Washington representative asked rhetorically. "The job we now face is to translate concretely and actively our International program into reality. We have to, in other words, get our program off the drawing boards."[58]

There were three aspects of the campaign against silicosis. First, the leadership intensified its organizational efforts within the union. Second, "and of equal importance," the union sought to "secure the aid of our allies in other unions." The final aspect of the program was to secure public support and to "counteract the propaganda of the companies" that would undoubtedly seek to head off any federal effort.[59]

The union's efforts to publicize the continuing problem of silicosis among

[56] Herman Clott, "Mine-Mill Campaign for Silicosis Legislation," *Mine-Mill Staff Bulletin*, April 8, 1955, 2, in Western Federation of Miners Manuscripts [International Union of Mine, Mill and Smelter Workers], Western Historical Collections, University of Colorado, Boulder, Box 324-18.

[57] "Silicosis—There Is No Known Cure . . . Our Fight Must Be for Prevention," *Mine-Mill Union*, May 9, 1955, 8; "Silicosis-Federal Legislation Needed to Force Dust Control by Companies," *Mine-Mill Union*, May 23, 1955, 8.

[58] Clott, "Mine-Mill Campaign," 2.

[59] *Ibid.*, 2–3. See also, for letters to Congress and efforts to build support for legislation, Western Federation of Miners Manuscripts [International Union of Mine, Mill and Smelter Workers], Western Historical Collections, University of Colorado, Boulder, Box 359-13; and Herman Clott to The National Officers, April 1, 1955, Western Federation of Miners Manuscripts, Box 324-18.

its workers was felt at the Public Health Service, where investigators began to reevaluate their long-held belief that silicosis was no longer a problem. Henry Doyle, the chief of the Occupational Health Program of the Public Health Service's Division of Public Health Services, told Representative Metcalf's Subcommittee on Mine Health and Safety in Washington in December 1956 that after 1935 there was "a diminishing emphasis by the Public Health Service on the epidemiology of silicosis" because it was assumed "that the fundamental research on silicosis had been largely completed and that prevention was simply a matter of applying the developed environmental and medical controls." But Doyle acknowledged that such an assumption was not valid and that, as the union and Congress already understood, silicosis was still a problem. In a retrospective study of workers' compensation records from 1950 to 1954, the Public Health Service found that silicosis remained a significant health problem even "among younger men with recent and short exposure to dust."[60] In this preliminary research conducted in the midst of the growing union campaign and congressional activity, the Public Health Service investigators decided that "silicosis continues to be an occupational disease of considerable importance."[61]

The distinct positions of mine owners and the union were presented at these hearings. After a year's preparation, the International Union of Mine, Mill and Smelter Workers came to the hearings with the idea that such a forum would give national attention to the silicosis problem. Union representatives presented a detailed picture of the silicosis hazard in the metal mines, noting that workers afflicted with the disease were suffering "a kind of living death." Orville Larson, the vice president of the union, suggested that if any member of the committee had "not yet seen a silicotic in the final stages of the disease, I would strongly urge a visit to some hospital or sanitarium." He decried the "popular impression," which he said was "shared by some public health officials," that "silicosis is no longer a serious health problem."[62] He argued, in fact, that the situation had grown worse with the introduction of new mechanical devices in the recent past: "In underground mining, for example, we now have greater use of block-caving, faster drilling machines, automatic conveyor belts, and much faster handling of ore and materials." For the producers, this meant more production and more profits. But for the miners, the

[60] U.S. Congress, House, Subcommittee on Mine Safety of the Committee on Education and Labor, *Hearings on Inspection and Investigation in Metallic Mines*, 84th Cong., 2d sess., 1956, 297, 316.

[61] See Victoria M. Trasko, "Some Facts on the Prevalence of Silicosis in the United States," *AMA Archives of Industrial Health*, 14 (October 1956): 379–86, for the complete statement of the position of the Public Health Service in 1955–1956.

[62] U.S. Congress, House, Subcommittee on Mine Safety of the Committee on Education and Labor, *Hearings on Inspection and Investigation in Metallic Mines*, 84th Cong., 2d sess., 1956, 400.

union maintained, it meant "more dust and more and greater hazards, as machines and instruments take over control tasks previously performed by men."[63] In testimony before the committee, Ernie Sjomen, a miner from Butte, Montana, described how mechanization had undermined the limited protective measures that had been introduced into metal mining in the 1940s. In the past, "There seemed to be a habit when we were shovelling this rock in the drifts by hand that we wet that pile extremely through." But now, "with more improved machinery and production per man gone up we think, by God, I don't know what's the trouble; but there seems to be no time for wetting down these places and they are extremely dusty."[64]

In contrast to the manufacturers, who continued to maintain that silicosis was a disease of the past that was rooted in earlier and more primitive mining procedures, the union argued that newer technologies were actually increasing the risk: "The most serious hazard still facing workers in hard rock mining and milling is silicosis."[65] The secretary-treasurer of the International, Albert Pezzati, pushed even more strongly for a federal effort on behalf of miners and other workers. In an attempt to link the interests of the metal miners and the broader labor movement, Pezzati called for the establishment of a "National Industrial Health Institute that would be responsible for the promotion, coordination, and support of continuous medical and engineering research in the field of industrial health."[66] Fourteen years later, two landmark pieces of legislation would be enacted that incorporated the ideas set forth by the International Union of Mine, Mill and Smelter Workers in 1956.

It was not surprising that the mine owners rejected every major tenet of the union. They continued to maintain that silicosis was not a serious hazard and that the states provided "close and effective supervision of safety and health conditions." For the federal government to interfere in mining was, from the perspective of the American Mining Congress, an infringement on states' rights and an unnecessary duplication of function. Further, the employers ar-

[63] "Links Accidents, Diseases to Output," *Mine-Mill Union*, special supplement, December 1956, 3.

[64] U.S. Congress, House, Subcommittee on Mine Safety of the Committee on Education and Labor, *Hearings on Inspection and Investigation in Metallic Mines*, 84th Cong., 2d sess., 1956, 232–33.

[65] "Links Accidents, Diseases to Output," *Mine-Mill Union*, special supplement, December 1956, 3.

[66] "Tells Mine-Mill Health Safety Plan at Capital," *Mine-Mill Union*, special supplement, December 1956, 4. See also Bernard W. Stern to President John Clark et al., November 21, 1956, Western Federation of Miners Manuscripts [International Union of Mine, Mill and Smelter Workers], Western Historical Collections, University of Colorado, Boulder, Box 219-3, in which is described a meeting on health legislation attended by a number of unions, which concluded that "one of the most needed and most attainable immediate goal should be the establishment of an Occupational Health Institute." Stern suggested that the union's two federal legislative objectives should be the establishment of such an institute and the enactment of the mine safety and health bill.

gued that they were committed to protecting the health and safety of their work force: "Our mines and plants are small enough that we know our employees individually. They are our friends and neighbors." While acknowledging that the tuberculosis rates of states such as Arizona were abnormally high, they suggested that this was due to the influx of tubercular patients attracted by a dry and sunny climate. In fact, "the lack of rain has increased the dust problem all over the state and those who were tubercular are especially subject to damaging dust in their lungs." Reverting to the earlier notion that the population of the state had been "seeded" with tuberculosis, the representatives of the mine owners argued that the disease was a natural product of the state's climate and population characteristics.[67]

In a report to the union's membership, Vice President Orville Larson described the mixed results of the hearings. First, he believed that many of the subcommittee members were impressed by the seriousness of the silicosis problem in light of the evidence provided by the union. This augured well for future efforts at reform. But he also noted that the power of the mine owners' trade association had limited public exposure to the hearings. Only a few newspapers gave any coverage to the three days of hearings. Thus, "We built a record on the need for federal action in this field—a lot more work will be required to get that action."[68] The union concluded that it should push for a comprehensive federal survey of health and safety in metal mining with the right of federal inspection. In January 1957, Representative Metcalf introduced a bill, H.R. 3639, that embodied the union's program.[69] While the bill never passed, its introduction was seen by the union as the first salvo in an ongoing effort to involve the federal government in the struggle against silicosis once again. Even though professionals had lost interest in silicosis, the union was able to apply enough pressure on Western congresspeople. They, in turn, pressed the Public Health Service to do yet another study of the prevalence of silicosis in the metal mining industry.

The efforts to enlist the federal government in inspection efforts reached fruition in the middle of 1958, when the Bureau of Mines and the Public

[67] "Statement of Orr Woodburn," Western Federation of Miners Manuscripts [International Union of Mine, Mill and Smelter Workers], Western Historical Collections, University of Colorado, Boulder, Box 219-4.

[68] "Larson Says Safety Hearings Point Way," *Mine-Mill Union*, January 1957, 7. See also John B. Stone, editor, "On the Washington Record," December 5, 1956, 1: "The hearings were almost entirely boycotted by the daily newspapers, a testimonial to the power of the American Mining Congress and its members." Western Federation of Miners Manuscripts [International Union of Mine, Mill and Smelter Workers], Western Historical Collections, University of Colorado, Boulder, Box 219-4, reprinted in *Gazette and Daily*, York, Pa., December 10, 1956.

[69] John Clark to Marling J. Ankeny, Director, Bureau of Mines, December 19, 1956, Western Federation of Miners Manuscripts [International Union of Mine, Mill and Smelter Workers], Western Historical Collections, University of Colorado, Boulder, Box 219-4. A copy of the bill can be found *ibid.*, Box 219-7B.

Health Service initiated a study of silicosis among metal miners. "Mine-Mill's long fight against silicosis won a major objective last month with the disclosure that the most comprehensive investigation of the dread disease . . . ever launched by the government is now underway," declared the *Mine-Mill Union*, the union newspaper. "Trained field teams of the U.S. Bureau of Mines and the Public Health Service are already at work," it continued. "In breadth and scope, this is actually the first investigation of its kind ever undertaken by any federal agency and represents an essential step," the union concluded.[70] The union also noted that "another direct result of Mine-Mill activity in Washington . . . was the inclusion of a special appropriation to step up and increase the scope of the silicosis investigation. . . ."[71] Carl Hayden, senator from Arizona, and Lister Hill, senator from Alabama, included a $128,000 special appropriation for the study of silicosis in the appropriation bill for the Department of Health, Education and Welfare.[72]

Despite the union's enthusiasm regarding the Public Health Service–Bureau of Mines study, the union recognized that the inspectors lacked the right of entry and had to depend upon the goodwill of the operators for much of their data. Thus, while supporting the efforts of the investigators, the union continued to push for legislation that would guarantee federal investigators the right of entry. In 1961, Congressperson James O'Hara, Democrat from Michigan, introduced a bill "authorizing annual or necessary federal inspections in metallic and non-metallic mines and quarries (excluding coal and lignite mines) with the right of entry for the purpose of inspection or investigation, and for reporting by the operating companies of accidents and bodily injuries or loss of life."[73] After hearings in which mine operators reiterated their long-standing objections to federal inspection of mines[74] and Bureau of Mines officials asked for postponement of the bill until its ongoing study was completed, a new bill was substituted by O'Hara and Arizona Congressperson Stewart Udall. The new bill differed in one important way from the previous one in

[70] "Federal Investigation Started on Silicosis in Metal Mines," *Mine-Mill Union*, July 1958, 1, 12.

[71] "Silicosis," *Mine-Mill Union*, January 1959, 3.

[72] "Bulletin," *Mine-Mill Union*, July 1958, 1.

[73] "Statement of the Director, Bureau of Mines on H.R. 5435," presented before the House Select Subcommittee on Labor of the Committee on Education and Labor, July 11, 1961, 1, Western Federation of Miners Manuscripts [International Union of Mine, Mill and Smelter Workers], Western Historical Collections, University of Colorado, Boulder, Box 219-7a.

[74] "National Safety Program Launched by Mining Group," *Pay Dirt*, August 14, 1964, 6, in which this industry journal states: "The Mine Safety resolution in the Declaration of Policy adopted by the American Mining Congress . . . clearly stated the industry's position that the retention of mine safety responsibility at the local and state levels is essential to continually improve safety programs. . . . Despite industry's position, there has been a concerted movement to extend the enforcement authority of the U.S. Bureau of Mines to include metal and non-metal mines. . . ."

that it eliminated the annual inspections and substituted a one-time study of mining conditions and government regulation. Although disappointed by the limited scope of the bill,[75] the union supported it because for the first time it "empowers the Bureau of Mines to inspect mines in the course of this investigation and to require reports from mine operators." They hailed it as "the first mine safety bill covering non-ferrous metals industry workers ever."[76]

The union's faith that the Public Health Service studies would confirm the significance of silicosis was only partly borne out. While the Service did find that silicosis was a continuing problem, it generally maintained that the extent of disease was largely due to exposures to dust prior to 1935, when ventilation technologies had been introduced into many mines. Furthermore, the Public Health Service issued no call for federal intervention in the regulation of mines. In its conclusions, the Public Health Service maintained that "considerable progress has been made in the metal mining industry in the prevention of silicosis" and that the industry's efforts to monitor and control dust in the atmosphere had "resulted in marked reductions in dust exposures." The fact that over 125 miners who had entered the mines after the introduction of dust control technologies had been found to have silicosis was evidence "that effective dust control has not been universally practiced." The report advised that the "data obtained in the study do not permit judgement of the adequacy of present standards," thereby avoiding the politically charged issue of the need for federal regulation.[77]

The International Union of Mine, Mill and Smelter Workers, initially reacted negatively to the report claiming that the report implied "that silicosis

[75] "Mine-Mill's Fight for Mine Safety," Leaflet, Mine-Mill Research Department, October 1, 1963, Western Federation of Miners Manuscripts [International Union of Mine, Mill and Smelter Workers], Western Historical Collections, University of Colorado, Boulder, Box 220-6.

[76] "Mine Safety Bill Passed by House," *Mine-Mill Union*, September 1961, 1, 3. See U.S. Congress, House, *Metal and Non-Metallic Mine Study Act*, 87th Cong., 1st sess., H. Rep. 997. For statements by industry, labor, and government, see Western Federation of Miners Manuscripts [International Union of Mine, Mill and Smelter Workers], Western Historical Collections, University of Colorado, Boulder, Box 219-7a, particularly Mine-Mill Research Department, "Mine-Mill's Fight for Mine Safety," October 1, 1963: "Mine-Mill has carried on a 15-year fight for a federal mine safety program in metal and non-metallic mines ever since the first metal mine safety bill was introduced. This bill was modeled on the Federal Coal Mine Safety Act of 1941 and was introduced year after year, first by Senator Murray of Montana and then by his successor, Senator Lee Metcalf. . . . Mine-Mill mobilized rank and file support for this bill all over the country, and it was finally passed over the bitter, last-ditch opposition of the companies." See also "Mine Safety Bill Now Law!" Leaflet, Western Federation of Miners Manuscripts [International Union of Mine, Mill and Smelter Workers], Western Historical Collections, University of Colorado, Boulder, Box 219-7B.

[77] U.S. Department of Health, Education and Welfare, Public Health Service, Robert H. Flinn, Hugh P. Brinton, Henry N. Doyle, Lewis J. Cralley, and Robert L. Harris, Jr., *Silicosis in the Metal Mining Industry, A Revaluation—1958–1961* (Washington, D.C.: Government Printing Office), 1963, 19–20.

no longer constituted a major health problem in the mining industry.'' More specifically, the union criticized the report's methodology, which excluded miners who were no longer employed in mining or who had been employed in other dusty trades for five years or more. In a stinging resolution at their national convention in 1964, the union condemned this approach because it excluded a group ''which presumably would include a higher proportion of silicotics than employed miners.''[78] A month later, the union shifted its emphasis. Rather than focusing on the shortcomings of the methodology and conclusions, it emphasized the findings, which the union argued showed that silicosis was still ''a serious health hazard in the U.S. metal mining industry.'' The union contrasted the Public Health Service report with the report to Congress issued by Stewart Udall, the secretary of the interior. Udall's presentation, according to the union, ''flatly endorsed the extension of federal safety legislation'' to metal mines, while the Public Health Service took no position.[79]

The International's campaign was important because it kept industrial lung disease on the public agenda. The campaign achieved a significant result in providing the political muscle necessary for the enactment of legislation providing for the inspection of metal mines. The attention generated fostered ongoing agitation among union leaders and their rank and file members for the recognition of industrially caused lung disease. This activity would culminate in the late 1960s in the political movements around black lung, byssinosis, and asbestos-related disease. Yet, in contrast to earlier decades when Public Health Service reports generated intense interest and activity among medical and public health professionals, the new generation of specialist studies fell on deaf ears in the professional community. With a few notable exceptions, such as Lorin Kerr and Irving Selikoff, physicians long involved with working men and women, professionals responsible for the nation's health, had long ago lost interest in silicosis.

Silicosis in the Foundry and Granite Cutting Industries

In the two other industries where there had been major studies, foundries and granite cutting, the controversy over silicosis also refused to go away. However, in the absence of a strong labor program to publicize and organize around the issue, the attention paid to the issue was of a decidedly different nature. In 1949, the Industrial Hygiene Foundation did its last study of silicosis in the foundries, concluding that ''dust concentrations were found to be extremely low and were, indeed, comparable to levels found in many industrial estab-

[78] ''Government Releases Silicosis Study Covering 67 U.S. Mines,'' *Mine-Mill Union*, July–August, 1964, 13.

[79] ''Report Calls Silicosis Continuing Hazard,'' *Mine-Mill Union*, September 1964, 8.

lishments classified as non-dusty." As a result, the foundation made "no recommendations for specific improvement."[80] The problem was seen as of decidedly less significance than in the past by scientists and politicians alike in
these two industries, although controversy regarding the existence of the disease continued. In these industries, little was done legislatively at the state or
federal levels. Unlike metal mining, where a weak but politically active union
had lobbied at all levels of government to gain a mine safety bill and force
Public Health Service studies of the problem, foundry workers were studied
over the years by investigators from government and academe, with ambiguous conclusions regarding the extent of the silicosis hazard and its seriousness.

In 1949, following complaints from health officials in three Midwestern
states, the Public Health Service reevaluated their earlier assumption that the
silicosis hazard had been solved in that industry: "Mounting evidence has
pointed to the foundry industry as a remaining source of exposure to silica
dust, but at the same time it has been felt by some that the cases still coming
to light in this industry are the result of preexisting rather than present improved conditions."[81] In their detailed study of eighteen "representative"
foundries in Illinois, all of which were generally clean, employing dust control
equipment, the investigators found signs of silicosis in 9.2 percent of the
workers. The study concluded that the problem of silicosis should be addressed by maintaining and improving the exhaust systems and dust collection
equipment, making sure that new foundry construction incorporated up-to-
date designs.[82] In the early 1960s, the Michigan Department of Health found
that little had changed over the preceding decade. Foundries in that state continued to produce diseased workers even though many foundry owners still
believed "that silicosis is no longer a problem in the foundries."[83]

The International Molders and Allied Workers' Union for the most part represented workers in smaller jobbing shops, not in the large "captive" foundries integral to the steel and automobile industries. In the late 1930s, in part
because of the breakdown of craft control over the work process, it had be-

[80] Theodore F. Hatch, "Highlights of Foundation Staff Activities in 1949," in Industrial Hygiene Foundation, *Transactions of 14th Annual Meeting* (Pittsburgh, Pa., 1949), 75.

[81] U.S. Federal Security Agency, Public Health Service and Illinois Department of Health,
Health of Ferrous Foundrymen in Illinois (Washington, D.C.: Government Printing Office,
1950), 1.

[82] PHS and Illinois, *Ferrous Foundrymen*, 4–5.

[83] "Silicosis—A Continuing Problem in Foundries," *Michigan's Occupational Health* 9 (Fall
1963): 1. See follow-up studies *ibid.* through Summer 1966. For other studies of the foundry
industry, see Norbert Enzer, Ernst Simonson, and A. M. Evans, "Clinical Physiological Observations on Welders with Pulmonary Siderosis and Foundrymen with Nodular Uncomplicated Silicosis," *Journal of Industrial Hygiene and Toxicology* 27 (June 1945): 147–58; "New York's
Foundry Industry," *New York State Industrial Bulletin* 35 (August-September 1956): 8–11;
Richard J. Wolf, "Foundry Safety and Hygiene," *American Foundryman* 13 (March 1948): 25–
33.

come an industrial union, representing common laborers in addition to molders and core makers. Since it was among the former workers, who performed
the shake-out, mixing, and cleaning operations, that silicosis was most prevalent, it is not surprising that in the 1940s the union newspaper began to pay
attention to the problem. At the end of the war, the molders' union journal
presented statistics that documented the rising prevalence of silicosis within
the union. In 1936, only eleven union members were receiving sick benefits
as a result of silicosis. By 1943 and 1944, over a hundred members received
such benefits each year. The journal noted that "silicosis is becoming more
and more serious each year."[84] Throughout the next few years, the seriousness
of the issue was reflected in the continuing series of articles that appeared in
the union journal's pages.[85] But despite this attention in its paper, the union
did relatively little, as its interest in health shifted to new and totally uncharted
terrain. In the 1950s and 1960s, as new chemical binders were introduced into
the mixing and molding process, the union began to pay greater attention to
the possible carcinogenic effects of chemical fumes and skin contact, abandoning its longer-standing concern over silica dust.

Studies of the granite sheds of Vermont during the 1950s and 1960s generally concluded that silicosis was no longer a problem. In follow-up studies in
the 1950s and 1960s by the Public Health Service and the Vermont Department of Health, researchers concluded that the installation of ventilating
equipment in the granite sheds in 1937 had eliminated silicosis as a threat. In
1964, researchers concluded, "there have been no cases of silicosis found in
any person whose exposure was limited to the 26 years since dust control was
started in 1937."[86]

[84] Fred L. Baumgartner, "Silicosis in Our Membership," *International Molders' and Foundry Workers Journal* 81 (June 1945): 297.

[85] See "Foundry Conditions Held 'Intolerable,'" *International Molders and Foundry Workers Journal* 81 (March, 1945): 126: "The labor advisory committee [of the War Production Board] was unanimous in declaring that the chief stumbling block to increased production is 'intolerable' working conditions, which cause a high rate of pneumonia, tuberculosis, silicosis and industrial accidents"; Neil V. Pardo, "Silicosis: Where Silica Dust Comes From," *International Molders and Foundry Workers Journal* 83 (December 1947): 720; Neil V. Pardo, "Foundry Workers and Silicosis," *International Molders and Foundry Workers Journal* 83 (August 1947): 470; Neil V. Pardo, "Silicosis: What Is It?" *International Molders and Foundry Workers Journal* 83 (September 1947): 519; Neil V. Pardo, "Silicosis: How to Tell If a Person Has It," *International Molders and Foundry Workers Journal* 83 (October 1947): 585; Neil V. Pardo, "Silicosis, and What You and I Must Do about It," *International Molders and Foundry Workers Journal* 84 (January 1948): 12; John F. Metcalf, "History of Silicosis," *International Molders and Foundry Workers Journal* 84 (February 1948): 58; John Metcalf, "State Laws on Silicosis," *International Molders and Foundry Workers Journal* 84 (June 1948): 262; Carl Eberhart, "Dust Suppression and Control in the Foundry," *International Molders and Foundry Workers Journal* 87 (April 1951): 11–14.

[86] Harry B. Ashe and Donald E. Bergstrom, "Twenty-Six Years' Experience with Dust Control in the Vermont Granite Industry," *Industrial Medicine and Surgery*, February, 1964, 73–78. See also Andrew D. Hosey, Victoria M. Trasko, and Harry B. Ashe, *Control of Silicosis in Vermont*

How can we explain the differing experiences in these three industries? How can we understand the activities or lack of activity of the unions that represented workers? During the postwar period, one union, a small, politically radical union, under severe political attack during the cold war by both government and the American Federation of Labor–Congress of Industrial Organizations alike, initiated a program that led to federal action in the hard rock mining industries. Another industrial union, the International Molders and Allied Crafts Union, recognized the problem of silicosis but appeared to move on to other issues. A major industrial union, the United Steelworkers, did not make silicosis a major priority, and a fourth group, the Granite Cutters, accepted researchers' findings that their industry was free of the disease.

While each union had its own internal frictions and conflicts, an important element in the story concerns the history of the general labor movement in the postwar period. Immediately after the war, labor militancy reached an all-time high, with more strikes involving more workers than at any other time in U.S. history. The labor-management tensions during the war had built as workers were subjected to speed-ups, wage freezes, and long hours. Because of the unions' commitment to the war effort, the labor movement's "no-strike" pledge, and the Smith-Connally Act of 1943, which gave the National War Labor Board authority to impose labor-management settlements for the duration of the war, after the war union members sought redress for numerous issues, from pay to workplace conditions. While the strikes were successful in gaining large wage increases in 1946, many of the gains were eroded by the inflationary spiral that accompanied the end of price controls. Moreover, as Nelson Lichtenstein has illustrated, the strikes fed the growing antilabor and antileft sentiments that resulted in the passage of the Taft-Hartley Act of 1947 and other antilabor legislation.[87] The effect on the labor movement was profound. As David Montgomery has pointed out, trade union militancy was hampered because "both actions of class solidarity and rank-and-file activity outside of the contractual framework were placed beyond the pale of the law."[88] In addition, left-wing leadership, which had come to prominence in the unions in the 1930s and 1940s, was forced out under the provisions of the Taft-Hartley Act.

In this atmosphere, struggles over safety and health were profoundly unsettling for U.S. labor. The conflict over such issues as dust in the workplace and the need to reorganize the work process was highly politically charged. The

---

Granite Industry, Progress Report, U.S. Department of Health, Education and Welfare, Public Health Service (Washington, D.C.: Government Printing Office, 1958); Harry B. Ashe, "Silicosis in Dust Control," *Public Health Reports* 70 (October 1955): 983–85.

[87] Nelson Lichtenstein, *Labor's War at Home, The CIO in World War II* (Cambridge: Cambridge University Press, 1982), 230.

[88] David Montgomery, *Workers' Control in America: Studies in the History of Work, Technology and Labor Struggle* (London: Cambridge University Press, 1982), 166.

issue of safety and health brought management and labor into conflict over control of the work process and the organization of the plant. In the conservative political climate of the cold war and McCarthy period, nearly all unions sought to win wage and benefit packages for their membership and to leave issues of workplace control to management. The 1950s were the period when the issue of work and health became synonymous with health insurance packages and third-party coverage for the American work force. Unions bargained for financial support of welfare funds and Blue Cross or private health insurance coverage rather than for prevention of disease at the workplace. In 1946, the United Steelworkers settled its strike for significant pay raises and benefit packages, and the American Federation of Labor was moving in the direction of supporting national health insurance legislation.[89] By 1949, major unions were developing welfare and pension packages, and in 1951, the United Steelworkers became the first national union to gain Blue Cross health coverage for its members.[90] Management gave labor significant increases in wages and benefits in exchange for control over the workplace. Management had reached an accord with union leadership to limit disruptive and unsettling unrest on the shop floor.[91] Negotiations over health insurance, welfare, and retirement plans replaced conflict over workplace health and safety for organized labor.

It is significant that the one union that maintained an active involvement in the politics of silicosis was a left-wing union outside of this postwar labor-management accord. During the 1950s, the International Union of Mine, Mill and Smelter Workers had been hounded by government and labor alike. In fact, the union was kicked out of the Congress of Industrial Organizations. With little to gain from avoidance of issues related to workplace control and organization, the union was able actively to pursue safety and health issues that affected its membership.

The irony of the history of silicosis is that the myopic attention to it in the 1920s and 1930s as the sole threat to workers in the dusty trades served to obscure the importance of other dust-related conditions. When, in the postwar era, professionals declared an end to the silicosis crisis, they were, in fact declaring an end to the problem of dust diseases in industry. In the 1960s and 1970s, other dust diseases—coal workers' pneumoconiosis, byssinosis, and asbestos-related disease—would become the focus of national attention. But this was not the result of medical research or the logic of scientific discovery. Rather, it was the work force itself that forced attention to these health risks in the 1960s. Today, coal dust, cotton dust, and asbestos dust are acknowl-

[89] See Nelson H. Cruickshank, "What Labor Expects from Medicine," *New York Medicine* 11 (May 20, 1946): 21–24, for a discussion of labor's interest in insurance.

[90] See Gerald Markowitz and David Rosner, "Blue Cross and the Unions" (unpublished paper, 1989).

[91] See Lichtenstein, *Labor's War*, 242.

edged as causes of life-threatening industrial lung diseases. Just as silicosis achieved notoriety in the 1930s, these conditions have today entered into the popular lexicon as black lung, brown lung, and white lung, symbols of the heartlessness of American industry.

Today, it is virtually impossible to find anyone outside of the specialties in occupational medicine and workers in selected industries who has heard of silicosis. Yet some researchers estimate that as many people are threatened with the disease now as during the 1930s, when it was the "king of occupational diseases." In the postwar era, professionals, industry, government, and a conservative labor movement tried to bury silicosis as an issue. The irony is that for decades silicosis masked the threat of other dusts to American workers, while today it is itself masked by the attention to other dusts.

In coal mining, the events of the postwar years were crucial to the emergence of coal workers' pneumoconiosis as a disease distinct from silicosis. Until that time, lung diseases of miners in the bituminous and anthracite coal regions of Pennsylvania, West Virginia, and the Southern states were understood to be of two variants: anthracosis and anthraco-silicosis. The first term, *anthracosis*, had been coined in the nineteenth century to describe the dangerous effects on the lungs of coal miners caused by breathing coal dust. Early in the twentieth century, anthracosis was discounted as a serious health threat to miners primarily, and it was even assumed that coal dust protected miners from the more terrible scourge of tuberculosis. While it was recognized that coal miners were dying, it was suggested that the true danger was not the coal dust itself but the silica that was present in that dust. Investigators in both the United States and England proposed to substitute the terms *anthraco-silicosis* and *silico-anthracosis* for the generic term *anthracosis*. It was suggested that anthracosis be reserved to describe non-life-threatening conditions or for describing the blackened color of miners' lungs on autopsy.

The most widely studied condition was anthraco-silicosis, which was often endemic among hard coal miners who lived in the small mining towns, particularly in eastern Pennsylvania. In one study conducted by the U.S. Public Health Service in 1935, "the prevalence of anthraco-silicosis among the entire group of employees was found to be about 23 percent."[92] Although the researchers recognized that the disease was somewhat different from simple silicosis because of the presence of large quantities of coal dust in the workers' lungs, they believed that the pathogenic agent was the silica dust. Even in studies of soft coal miners, where the silica content of the rock from which the ore was extracted was negligible, scientists maintained that any signs of disease among these workers were also a form of silicosis. In a study of three

---

[92] R. R. Sayers et al., "Anthraco-silicosis among Hard Coal Miners," in *Public Health Bulletin No. 221* (December 1935; Washington, D.C.: Government Printing Office, 1936), 5.

bituminous coal mines in Utah, the Public Health Service concluded in 1941 that "anthraco-silicosis, a modified form of silicosis due to silica mixed with large amounts of carbon dust, was the principal occupational disease found on medical examination" of the workers. Even when evidence suggested that coal dust itself was the source of pneumoconiosis, researchers rejected the claim. Emery Hayhurst opposed British research conclusions that anthracosis was a distinct "pathological entity." He observed that the Pennsylvania legislature was moving to modify its compensation system in order to include pneumoconiosis among anthracite coal miners in the schedule of disease. "But," he maintained, "I am sure that . . . in all probability, at bottom, [their disease] is true silicosis."[93] For many, miners' conditions were largely silicosis and "[t]his disease may occur during the mining or processing of either anthracite or bituminous coal."[94]

Because of all the attention that had been given to silicosis during the Depression and earlier, researchers generally understood all occupational lung diseases through the prism of their experience with silicosis. Lorin Kerr, the longtime director of occupational health and safety for the United Mine Workers as well as president of the American Public Health Association, pointed out the inhibiting nature of the silicosis debate on professional acceptance of coal workers' pneumoconiosis: "This lack of concern with coal miners pneumoconiosis has been due in part . . . to the conviction that only silica and dust containing silica are injurious."[95] It was widely accepted that silica posed the serious threat to workers' health, while coal dust and other organic and inorganic dusts were of far less importance: "So great is the difference in the toxic properties between silica and some others of this group [of mineral dusts] that if silica is represented by 100, the relative danger from coal, silica-free marble, iron, etc., is about 5."[96] "Anthracosis is primarily a silicosis and . . . it occurs not only in hard coal miners but also in workers in soft coals," was a common, almost universal assumption of public health officialdom during the 1930s.[97] If silicosis could be controlled, then there was little worry that coal or other dusts would prove to be a problem.

In the 1940s and 1950s, the medical community believed that silicosis was being brought under control by engineering and medical advances. Hence, it

[93] Emery R. Hayhurst, "Discussion of Dr. A. J. Lanza's Paper on Etiology of Silicosis," June 14, 1933, Vorwald Collection, Box 63.

[94] Robert H. Flinn et al., "Soft Coal Miners—Health and Working Environment," in *Public Health Service Bulletin No. 270* (Washington, D.C.: Government Printing Office, 1941), 5.

[95] Lorin Kerr, *Black Lung* (pamphlet, United Mine Workers of America, 1968), 8.

[96] Carey P. McCord, "Silicosis in the Foundry" (National Founders Association, 1933), quoted in Commonwealth of Massachusetts, *Report to the General Court of the Special Industrial Disease Commission*, February 1934 (Boston: Wright and Potter Printing Co., 1984), 10.

[97] "Silico-Anthracosis," *American Journal of Public Health* 23 (April 1933): 369–70, which quotes an article by W. E. Cooke in *Journal of State Medicine* 40 (December 1932): 702–08.

was similarly assumed that coal workers' pneumoconiosis would soon be a disease of the past. However, this was not to be the case. In fact, as Barbara Ellen Smith and Dan Fox and Judith Stone describe in their work, coal workers' pneumoconiosis actually began to increase rather than decline.[98] As new, power-driven tools were introduced into coal mining, huge numbers of workers were continuously exposed to high concentrations of coal dust. Further, as automation hit the coal mining industry, large numbers of miners were displaced and forced to turn to the union's health and welfare programs, thereby transforming the medical dialogue into a political and social crisis. By the 1960s, the definition of coal workers' pneumoconiosis as a condition separate and distinct from silicosis had emerged.[99]

The history of asbestos-related lung disease has remarkable parallels with that of coal workers' pneumoconiosis in that the dangers of asbestos were also masked by the silicosis crisis. As others have documented in enormous detail, the asbestos industry was aware of the high mortality rates from asbestos throughout the 1930s, and there were numerous articles in professional journals that documented early deaths and disabilities among asbestos workers. Yet because asbestos was often listed as another silica-related disease, it, too, was perceived as being of secondary importance to silicosis. It would not be until the 1960s, when the unions representing asbestos workers allowed Irving Selikoff to follow the health of their workers, that asbestosis, mesothelioma, and asbestos-related lung cancers would be perceived as monumental problems for workers and the general public alike. The growing demand for and use of asbestos in buildings and insulating materials in the postwar period allowed this occupational disease to emerge as a general threat to everyone. Again, the public attention to asbestos could emerge only after silicosis was submerged as an issue.

Throughout the decades before the Depression, chronic industrial disease was "discovered." Yet the postwar generation of professionals believed that they had learned how to control, if not eliminate, the threat. Professional expertise in the form of good medical care and engineering methods could effectively end any crisis. In the conservative, antilabor environment of the 1950s, the voices that had challenged industry and professionalism were muted. But the changing social environment of the 1960s and early 1970s would transform the issue one more time. Silicosis remained on the periphery of the struggles around chronic industrial disease. But an emboldened labor movement and an aging but politically active constituency of industrial workers and retirees

---

[98] See Barbara Ellen Smith, *Digging Our Own Graves, Coal Miners and the Struggle over Black Lung Disease* (Philadelphia: Temple University Press, 1987); Dan Fox and Judith Stone, "Black Lung: Miner's Militancy and Medical Uncertainty, 1968–1972," *Bulletin of the History of Medicine* 54 (Spring 1980): 54–64.

[99] Smith, *Digging*; Fox and Stone, "Black Lung."

would force professionals, government, and the public at large to return to the issue again. By the 1970s, chronic disease was understood to be the major health problem of an aging and an increasingly long-lived population. The links to our changing work environments would again be made, and new constituencies would raise again questions that had been asked for the first time in the early years of the Depression.[100]

[100] NIOSH estimated in 1983 that approximately 3.2 million workers in 238,000 plants were potentially exposed to silica. In one study, at least 5 percent of airborne samples contained more than twice the minimum standard of silica. In studies done between 1974 and 1981, in mines and other silica industries, between 2.2 and 40.9 percent of the air samples had levels above the standard. Workers in these industries had elevated rates of silicosis. See U.S. Department of Health and Human Services, National Institute for Occupational Safety and Health, *Health Hazard Evaluation Report*, HETA 82-302-1461, East Penn Foundry, Macungie, Pennsylvania, 1984; U.S. Department of Health and Human Services, National Institute for Occupational Safety and Health, *Recommendations for Control of Occupational Safety and Health Hazards . . . Foundries* (Washington, D.C.: Government Printing Office, 1985); Marcus M. Key and Howard E. Ayer, ''Silicosis in Hard-Rock Mining,'' *Journal of Occupational Medicine* 14 (November 1972): 863–65.

VII

CONCLUSION

W E READILY accept that the social and political activities of each generation build on the traditions of earlier generations: the New Frontier and Great Society programs of the 1960s were part of a long tradition that incorporated elements of both Progressive Era and New Deal programs; Medicaid and Medicare are linked directly to the struggles for social and health insurance during World War I and the Depression. But it is more difficult to understand the ways that disease reflects this process of historical reformulation and redefinition. We tend to think of disease as an objective reality whose existence transcends the boundaries of time and subjectivity.

We suggest that the case of silicosis raises questions regarding the exceptional nature of disease. The case of silicosis shows how the social and political environment shapes the variety of questions traditionally seen as the province of science and the laboratory. In a recent text on pulmonary medicine, Alfred Fishman wrote, ''Succeeding generations of physicians and industrial hygienists have had to 'rediscover' silicosis; and each new circumstance of occupational exposure seems to go unscrutinized until the health costs become obvious.''[1] In the course of the twentieth century, scientists, engineers, and medical researchers have done precisely that: Issues such as symptomatology, what constitutes disability, what is normal and what constitutes pathology in the human lung, what is an environmental danger, and what is an occupational risk were all questions that every generation in the silicosis debate redefined, reevaluated, and answered anew. This book illustrates that it is a complex of historically determined social and economic factors that allow for this process of rediscovery.

The history of silicosis raises for us a fundamental irony. In the agricultural communities of mid-nineteenth-century America, phthisis was understood to be a disease rooted in the personal and social environment of the victim. Yet this approach died out at the very time that it might have proven useful in understanding industrial sources of lung disease. As the country emerged as the world's major industrial producer and as new diseases were created in a radically changed environment, the medical and public health communities turned inward, toward the laboratory, microscope, and germ. Merging the highly personal understanding of disease with what they considered a new

---

[1] Alfred P. Fishman, *Pulmonary Diseases and Disorders*, 2d ed., vol. 1 (New York: McGraw-Hill, 1988), 829.

scientific orientation, the professions effectively removed themselves from the discourse over industrial disease. Turmoil in the laboring communities over work conditions and the attention to workers' deaths and disabilities by actuaries and statisticians in the insurance industry once again forced silicosis onto the agendas of the medical and public health communities. Professionals interested in understanding the social origins of silicosis would have to turn to a British and continental literature for guidance. There, the tradition of an organized and class-conscious laboring population helped shape the views of physicians familiar with the traditions of social medicine and population statistics. Physicians such as Thomas Oliver and others accepted the germ theory but did not let it blind them to the industrial sources of illness.

The history of silicosis reflects a broad discourse about the nature of and responsibility for risks in an advanced industrial society. Throughout the twentieth century, the programmatic questions revolved around the relative degree of responsibility for the dangers at work of individual or organized workers, managers, and government officials. Silicosis arose in the cauldron of the American industrial revolution, and its history reflected the dramatic growth and decline of America's industrial might. Through the first three decades of the century, laborers recognized that working conditions were related to their dependence, disease, and disability, and many believed that it was the responsibility of owners to change those conditions. Management, however, rejected the idea that long-term disease was the result of conditions at work. Rather, they understood disease to be the result of poor living conditions, inadequate diet, and poor personal hygiene.

The crisis of the 1930s forced a reformulation of the issue. The conflict over disease was conflated with a more general crisis in labor-management relations. Just as the New Deal sought to defuse the crisis between labor and capital by establishing federal boards and mechanisms to aid in negotiating resolution in strikes, so, too, did the government seek to find the means by which to promote compromise in the arena of industrial disease. On both the state and federal levels, government acted to finesse the question of responsibility by incorporating silicosis and later certain other chronic conditions into the workers' compensation system and by moving the discourse over disease into the arena of expert panels and professional organizations. Implicit in this solution lay the assumption that chronic disease was not the responsibility of management, labor, or government per se but was simply an inherent risk in the new industrial society. Despite the fact that individuals in the Department of Labor saw their role as empowering workers, this solution served management-sponsored organizations, such as the Industrial Hygiene Foundation in their goal of moving the discourse over disease out of the public arena and into the more controlled settings of professional organizations and journals.

In the case of the pneumoconioses, the very boundaries between diseased and healthy lungs became blurred as many argued that to live in an urban, industrial society changed the very standards that had previously been used. The presence of chemicals or dusts in the tissue of human lungs was no longer enough to define pathology. In the 1950s, some medical experts even asked whether it was appropriate to consider the pneumoconioses diseases since so many people throughout the society showed some evidence of lung damage. Meanwhile, some unions and some labor officials argued that the presence of any foreign substance in the human body was reason for concern. Implicit in the various historical debates about silicosis was an evolving argument about the boundaries delineating the personal, occupational, and environmental sources of disease.

Despite the immediate advantage gained by business in the years following World War II, the silicosis issue had sparked an increased awareness of the importance of chronic disease in American society. This awareness developed at the very time that antibiotics, vaccines, and other therapies seemed to auger the decline of the threat from infectious disease. In some sense, the solutions devised to cope with the immediate crisis over silicosis would prove to be the seeds of our generation's problem. Silicosis was hidden from public view in professional journals. But the very conception of disease had changed for professionals as well as the larger public. By the 1960s, some professionals had acknowledged labor's longtime contention that chronic diseases were often rooted in the workplace, and the wider population began to see a connection between disease and the chemicals, pollutants, and waste that came from the factory. By the 1970s, the postwar consensus that industrialization carried with it implicit trade-offs with regard to human health was no longer acceptable to a generation as concerned with protecting health and the environment as with producing more consumer goods. Public health reformers, consumer advocates, environmentalists, and others raised broad questions regarding the relationship between the arising recognition of epidemics of cancer, heart disease, and other long-term conditions and industrial society.

Throughout the twentieth century, we in the United States have tried to draw distinctions between environmental and occupational causes of disease. At the turn of the century, miners, foundry workers, granite cutters, and others in the silica trades who suffered from silico-tuberculosis were buffeted between those who saw this as an industrial condition and others who alternatively defined it as a peculiar case of tuberculosis—a disease of the home, poor sanitation, and poor nutrition. In the 1930s, those formulating workers' compensation policy argued over which diseases were specifically caused by particular industries and which were of broader environmental origin. In the 1950s, the pneumoconioses were reevaluated as some in industry argued that dust in the lungs was a normal, nonpathological event. Silicosis was specifically a workers' disease, which could be contained by reforming the workers' compensation system. It was never perceived as an environmental threat or a threat to the broader population. Unlike asbestos, which menaces children in schools, white-collar workers in offices, and middle-class homeowners with asbestos insulation, silica remained a problem for a discrete and economically peripheral group of workers. Unfortunately, the public attention to disease varies inversely to its distance from the problem.

Today, the relative importance of the workplace and the wider environment are hotly contested as policymakers, research scientists, and others try to develop criteria for distinguishing environmental and occupational sources of cancer. In 1970, for example, one government study estimated that between 85 and 90 percent of all cancers were environmental, but there was little agreement as to the distinctions between environmental and occupational factors.[2] The major source of contention has not been over medical researchers' competing claims, but rather over social policies about who should bear the cost of treating those who become ill. In the absence of a comprehensive social and health insurance system, the distinction between occupational and environmental origins of illness becomes more than an abstraction: Once again, the legal and labor communities seek redress for disease through the courts. Today, we are still grappling with questions of long-standing historical significance: What proportion of the new chronic diseases arising in the modern industrial community could be properly ascribed to industry itself? What part of the new epidemics of cancer, heart disease, and stroke should be understood as part of a broader social cost?

Since there were no established mechanisms for separating out environmental from occupational diseases, management argued that individuals had to assume the burden for the vast majority of poorly understood conditions that appeared to be endemic in the community. Some in the labor community argued that in the absence of a comprehensive social and health insurance system, it was essential that management assume the financial responsibility for workers who became ill. They maintained that in the absence of a clear distinction between environmental and industrial sources of chronic disease, the burden of proof should be on management to show that disease was not job related: If the labor force is made to work with toxic materials and years later workers become ill, the assumption should be that their suffering is rooted in their work experience.

The crisis over silicosis emerged during the Great Depression as millions of Americans were forced to contend with months and years of unemployment, dependence and disease. It was in this cauldron of discontent that silicosis lawsuits emerged as a legitimate alternative to charity for those workers seeking to provide for themselves and their families. It is probably no accident that the great upsurge of liability suits occurred in the early part of the decade

---

[2] "Man's Health and the Environment—Some Research Needs," in *Report of the Task Force on Research Planning in Environmental Health Science* (National Institute of Environmental Health Sciences, March 1970), 147, cited in Peter S. Barth and H. Allan Hunt, *Workers' Compensation and Work-Related Illnesses and Diseases* (Cambridge: MIT Press, 1980), 19.

before the passage of the Social Security Act, which provided for the elderly and disabled. Also, it is probably true that the growing involvement of the state and federal governments in providing unemployment insurance served to improve the prospects of the unemployed, thereby relieving the liability system of a role it had unintentionally assumed. In this sense, the "epidemic" that the public health and medical professionals of the decade documented in hundreds of articles about the disease was itself a social creation. In the decades after the Depression, social and epidemiological changes altered the context of the silicosis debate: The war absorbed even diseased workers; social insurance gave greater protection to the elderly and unemployed; postwar accords between management and organized labor provided insurance for medical and hospital bills to the unionized work force; granite cutting and hard rock mining declined; workers in other industries began to press for greater attention to other pneumoconioses; and antibiotic therapy lowered the danger of death from silico-tuberculosis. In these new social circumstances, public and professional attention to the condition waned.

Yet this acknowledgement that silicosis came out of special social and economic circumstances does not imply that workers did not suffer or that the disease was not real. It may be that the apologists of the 1930s were partially right in saying that the estimates of the disease's prevalence were inflated by "ambulance-chasing" lawyers. It may also be true that the attention to silicosis obscured other pneumonoconioses, such as black lung and asbestos-related disease. But it is undoubtedly equally valid to say that the lack of awareness of the silicosis issue in the postwar decades has led to an understatement of its prevalence. Philip Landrigan, the chair of the Department of Community Medicine at Mount Sinai Medical School, recently remarked that New York State's workers' compensation statistics are insensitive to the true extent of silicosis among the state's work force. Tragically for those whose lives have been destroyed, the legacy of the political history of silicosis is that the system cannot even document their suffering.

In the Hope Cemetery in Barre, Vermont, a large monument depicting a woman holding a dying worker in her arms stands at the grave of the granite cutter who carved it. The sculpture is evocative of the *Pieta*, of the martyrdom of Christ and Mary's suffering. Yet the religious symbolism only reinforces what we know of this worker's life: that this worker—like others before and after him—was a martyr to the industrially created environment in which he toiled.[3] And that both he and his family suffered because of it.

[3] Brusa monument, Hope Cemetery, Barre, Vermont.

INDEX